WOMAN'S WAY TO GOD

ANNE FREMANTLE

St. Martin's Press, New York

Library of Congress Cataloging in Publication Data

Freemantle, Anne Jackson, 1909-
    Woman's way to God.

    1. Women—Religious life.   I. Title.
BL624.F74   248'.843   76-10553
ISBN 0-312-88690-X

TABLE OF CONTENTS

WOMAN'S WAY TO GOD
INTRODUCTION

"Male and female," the book of Genesis asserts (Chapter 1,v.27), "created He them." So in the tradition of Jews and Christians there is one relationship for every person in which biology is not history. Relationship with the Creator is initially the same for every human being, regardless of sex. Even if the Creator's absence rather than His presence is affirmed (or inferred, since "no" is also an answer), the relationship remains unique, with "ultimate reality" or with whatever is beyond the categories or with whatever obfuscating term is used.

At the beginning are two women: Eve, the mother of us all, who disobeyed her maker; and Antigone, the Greek girl who defied the state. Whether they existed doesn't matter; what does is the reality of their situation and the longevity of their myth. They freely chose to be disobedient, the first to the spiritual, the second to the secular power. Thereby each demonstrated their absolute freedom to choose.

Eve's choice was wholly deliberate: "So when the woman saw that the tree was good for food and that it was a delight to the eyes, and that the tree was to be desired to make one wise, she took of its fruit and ate, and she also gave some to her husband and he ate." Then God, scared because "the man has become like one of us, knowing good and evil" and lest "now he put forth his hand and take also of the tree of life, and eat and live for ever therefore, the Lord God sent him forth from the garden of Eden . . . He drove out the man." Woman's first choice was wisdom.

V

What that choice entailed is described by Charles Peguy
(1873–1914)[1]:

O mother, buried outside the first garden
You have no longer known the climate of that grace
And the spring and the fountain and the high terrace,
And the first sun on the first morning's face.

And I salute you, O first of women,
The most unhappy, the most delusive,
Mother of Our Lady, long-tressed forebear,
The most unmoved, most to pity conducive.

O you who pursue to the cracks of the corners
Dirt and disgrace and dung and dust,
Chase all the impure, the dishonest, unsuitable,
Mistress of duties, of vigils, of trust.

God himself you would tidy, O woman, I tell you,
If ever he dared show his face
Near your house, and the crime and the power almighty
You would put right back in their place.

And you know also what each man costs,
That the very blood of the Godhead cost he.
And thus you know by what terrible road
A condemned man climbs to the last high tree.

For Jesus is the fruit of a mother's womb,
Fructus ventris tui, in the husk and the bran,
In the straw the young nursling sleeps with his knees
Bent under his body, the body of a man.

Sophocles (495?–406? B.C.), whose *Antigone* was called
by W. Somerset Maugham the "perfect play," upheld a
women's right to defy the most potent male authority, the
state.

The play involves a family quarrel. Polyneices, supported
by an Argive (Athenian) army, marched against Thebes, to
wrest the city from his brother Eteocles. The invaders were
beaten back: at six of the city's seven gates, the Theban defender had slain the Argive contestant. At the seventh gate,
the two brothers killed each other. The Argive army fled.
Creon, uncle to the dead brothers and to their sisters, An-

VI

tigone and Ismene, ordered Eteocles buried with full honors, but Polyneices to be left unburied. Anyone disobeying this order was to be killed. The play opens with Antigone trying to persuade Ismene to help her bury Polyneices: "Will you help this hand to bury the dead?" Antigone asks. "You'd bury him when it is forbidden?" asks Ismene, and Antigone replies: "I will do my part, and yours, if you won't, to a brother." "When Creon has forbidden?" Ismene asks, and Antigone replies: "He has no right to keep me from my own." Ismene tells Antigone: "Go then, if you must—and of this be sure, that though your errand is foolish, to your dear ones you are truly dear."[2]

Creon has set guards to see his edict is obeyed: they tell him how they have "swept away all the dust that covered the corpse and bared the dank body well; then sat down on the brow of the hill to windward, so the smell from him should not strike us." Then "the maid was seen . . . When she saw the corpse bare, she lifted up a voice of wailing, and called down curses on the doers of that deed. And then she brought thirsty dust in her hands, and from a ewer of bronze held high, with thrice-poured drink she crowned the dead." And when the guard rushed forward, she declared, "I avow it, I make no denial."

Brought before Creon, she reiterates her admission: "I deny nothing." Creon asks her, "has she not heard his proclamation touching this matter?" and Antigone replies by declaring that it was public, how could she help not hearing it? Creon: "And yet you dared defy the law?" Then Antigone makes her supreme statement: "I dared. For it was not Zeus that had published that edict; not such are the laws given by the Justice that rules the gods below. Nor did I deem your edicts strong enough, that you, a mortal man, should overpass the unwritten laws of God that know not change. They are not of today nor yesterday, but live for ever, nor can man assign when first they sprang to being."

The dialogue continues: Creon twits Antigone with differing from all the other Thebans in her views. She retorts that they share her views but "curb their tongues for you."

Creon asks her, "And are you not ashamed to act apart from them?", to which she replies "there is nothing shameful in piety to a brother." Creon asks: "Was it not a brother that died in the opposite cause?" And Antigone replies, "brother by the same mother and the same sire." "Why then," asks Creon, "does Antigone render a grace that is impious to one brother?"

ANTIGONE: The dead man will not say that he so deems it.

CREON: He will, if you make him equal in honor with the wicked.

ANTIGONE: It was his brother, not his slave, that perished.

CREON: Wasting this land, while he fell as its champion.

ANTIGONE: Nevertheless, Hades desires these rites.

CREON: But the good desires not a like portion with the evil.

ANTIGONE: Who knows but this seems blameless in the world below?

CREON: A foe is never a friend, not even in death.

ANTIGONE: I was made for fellowship in love, not fellowship in hate.

CREON: Pass then to the world of the dead, and if you must need love, love them. While I live, no woman shall rule me.

Ismene now reappears and wants to share her sister's fate.

ISMENE: I did the deed, if she did, go with her, yes share her guilt and bear an equal blame.

But Antigone rejects her: "You didn't agree, nor did I let you join me."

ISMENE: Nay, in your troubles I am not ashamed to share, I want to be in the same boat with you to share your fate.

ANTIGONE: Who did it, Hades knows, and those below: I do not love a friend who loves in words.

ISMENE: Do not, my sister, put me to such shame, as not to let me join in death with you . . .

. *Antigone rejects her once more:* "You made your choice to live and I to die."

So Antigone is led off to her death, while her betrothed, Creon's son Haemon, furiously spurns his father who has condemned Antigone. Haemon then kills himself, as does his mother on learning of her son's death.

Antigone's great statement that there are "unwritten laws of God that know not change. They are not of today, not yesterday, but live forever" is as valid today as 2400 years ago. During the German occupation of France, Anouilh's French version of the *Antigone*, played in Paris, gave moral strength and comfort to the French Resistance.

But the very first time this tremendous statement, made often since by men, (as by St. Paul: "It is better to obey God rather than man" or by St. Thomas More: "I am the king's good servant, but God's first") was made, it was made by a young girl.

By disobedience to God's law the first woman, Eve, chose wisdom; by disobedience to man's law, Antigone, the greatest Greek heroine, chose the eternal laws of God.

Such were two women's ways to the gods they served.

The Historical Beginnings:
Goddessess and Priestesses

As Ortega y Gasset has pointed out, the twenty-one known civilizations proceed from seven originals, but they do not proceed from each other. These seven are: Sumerian, Egyptian, Aegean, Mayan, Incan, Chinese and proto-Indian (Mohenjo Daro). These "pose vigorously the problem of their origin": why, after more than 300,000 years of static life, did civilization suddenly emerge around 6,000 years ago? Whatever the answer, the first cultural objects were female figures.

In the Siberian Taiga in Late Paleolithic times, female figurines were used in ritual. In unbroken continuity from then until our own day, Yakuta and Ostaks worship such figures carved from reindeer bones. Figures similar to those found around Lake Baikal have been found in Austria, for example, the Venus of Willendorf. Dating from the seventh millenium B.C. is a statue found in Anatolia at Catal Huyuk of the "Great Goddess," who is shown as ruler of the dead who have returned to her womb. In Knossos, Crete, the "female figure with a child" of G.K. Chesterton's ballad appears, and in early Sumerian mythology the goddess Nammus is "the mother who gave birth to heaven and earth, eternal, uncreated." She was later called Ninhursag, and the Sumerian rulers described themselves as "nourished by the trustworthy milk of Ninhursag." "Her shrine, uncovered at Obeid in Southern Mesopotamia, had an oval shape designed to symbolize female genitalia."[3] Throughout the Bronze Age, the "original Mother without a spouse" ruled from Minoan Crete to Mohenjodaro and Harappa, including, of course, Egypt. Her worship reached even to China during the Shang era.

In Egypt, circa 2850 B.C., the goddess Hathor is shown in the Narmer palette as "straddling the earth, her legs the pillars of the four quarters, her belly the sky. The sun-god Horus entered her mouth every evening at dusk, and emerged the next morning from her loins: Hathor was thus both his consort and his mother."[4] In the *Divine Comedy*, Dante begins the thirty-third canto of the *Paradiso* with the words: "O Virgin Mother, daughter of your son," showing the continuity over some three thousand years of the idea of this dual relationship between male and female.

In the Babylonian Code of Hammurabi, woman is treated as the equal of man, and Ishtar, the great goddess, was, like Isis and Osiris in Egypt, consort and equal of Tammuz. Greatest of all, and oldest in Egypt, was Neit at Sais, on whose veiled statue was written: "I am everything which has been, which is and which will be, and no mortal has yet lifted my veil." One night each year all Egypt blazed with lamps in her honor, and from her feast derived the Christian Feast of the Purification of the Virgin (Candlemas, February 2nd). On that day, in every Catholic church the world over, the faithful still hold tiny lighted blessed candles in their hands during Mass.

As late as Aeschylus (525–456 B.C.), mother right prevailed in the Greek pantheon. In the *Orestia Trilogy* of Aeschylus the Eumenides, the Furies, themselves female, do not recognize the right of the father and husband. Clytemnestra, who killed her husband Agamemnon because he had sacrificed their daughter, Iphegenia, in order to get a fair wind with which to sail for home at the end of the Trojan war, is excused by the Furies: "she was no blood relation to the man she killed" and they demand the death of her son, Orestes, for killing his mother. Apollo, the God of light, who represented the male principle, says procreation gives the superior right, but the argument is only finally solved by a female deity, by Pallas Athena, the goddess of wisdom, who casts her vote for Orestes, but only because she herself is without a mother: she sprang fully grown from the mind of Zeus.

At the greatest flowering of Greek civilization, during the age of Pericles, a group of polished Ionian courtesans exerted great political and cultural influence. The greatest of these, Aspasia, the Milesian, was Pericles' concubine, famous for the lowness of her morals and the highness of her mind. She was also close to Socrates, and is said to have taught him rhetoric; her son by Pericles, also called Pericles, was one of the generals who, though they won the sea battle of the Arginusae Islands, were killed for allowing so many of the wounded to perish. Aspasia was impeached for irreligion, charged with blasphemy, and prosecuted, but was acquitted. Aeshines wrote a Socratic dialogue about her, called *Aspasia*.

The Greeks seem to have had both temple virgins and temple prostitutes; in the temple of Herakles and Thespiae, for example, the priestess was a virgin, and the Thesmophoriae (fertility festivals of the corn) were conducted exclusively by women.

In India, in the Vedas, one of the earliest hymns, that to Agni, God of fire, is ascribed to the poetess Visvavara, and Sarasvati, the wife of Brahma, credited with the invention Sanskrit, is the goddess of speech, and is addressed as "mother of the Vedas." Yet the Vedic religion was not "open to the lower classes or to women."[5] It is only in the Bhagavad-Gita (*The Lord's Song*), to which no firm date can be assigned, but which is almost certainly post-Buddhistic, that Krishna, God Almighty incarnate, as Arjuna's charioteer, instructs him in the way of *bhakti* (selfless devotion). "None who worships me," he tells Arjuna, "with love and loyalty is lost to me. For whoever makes me his haven, baseborn though he may be, yes, women too and artisans, even serfs, theirs it is to tread the highest way."

Buddha (563?–483? B.C.) was asked by his beloved disciple Ananda: "How do conduct ourselves with women?" Buddha replied: "Don't see them." Ananda asked: "But if we should see them, what are we to do?" Buddha: "Keep awake." Petitioned to allow nuns or rather, to allow women to enter the Sangha, the Buddhist monastic order, Buddha had declared that as a consequence of admitting women to it, the law would be forgotten in 500 years. Actually, the prophecy was not fulfilled, though Buddhism as a dominant religion only lasted 500 years in India. Women, according to Buddhism, *can* attain Buddhahood.

In the Buddhist (Pali) apologetic, *King Milinda's Questions*[6], King Milinda, a Bactrian Greek who probably reigned in North India around the first years of the Christian era (from roughly 44 B.C. to 38 A.D.), asks questions of the Buddhist monk Nagasena, and is converted to Buddhism at the end of the book. An extra-canonical lay-women follower, Cula-Subhadda, is mentioned as a disciple of Gautama Buddha, and she extols her own recluses:

> If I, angry in mind, were to hack one person with an axe
> If I, rejoicing, were to anoint another with scent
> There is no repugnance for that one; no attachment to this
>   one exists
> These thoughts are like the earth—such are my recluses."

She occurs again, with a couplet:

> "The world is uplifted by gain, depressed by loss
> Indifferent to gain and loss, such are my recluses."

Cula-Subhadda was married to Ugga, who patronized unclothed ascetics, but she managed to convince her mother-in-law of Buddha's superiority and invited him and his monks to a meal. They came, Buddha preached the Dhamma, and Ugga was converted to Buddhism.

Nuns are mentioned in *Milinda's Questions* as living in a dwelling-place. There "they can have a rendezvous with experienced monks, as it is easy for those who want to see them to do so; but if they have no home this would be difficult." They were not allowed to live alone or outside of a village, because of the various dangers which might beset them.

In the pagan cults of the far north, in England, there were Druidesses of three classes. Some were not separated from their families. They assisted the Druids, but had husbands. Others lived in a sisterhood, and the third class kept the holy fire always burning. In Kildare, in Ireland, at about the same date, there was a community of women consecrated to Brighit, the goddess of poverty, medicine, and iron.

In Rome, the Vestal Virgins kept the fire of Vesta always burning, and if they ceased to be virgins, the punishment was death. They were bound by vows for thirty years. During the first ten years they studied; during the second decade they officiated as priestesses; during the third they instructed the novices. Vesta herself had no statue; her only representation was a round temple. Another Roman goddess, the *Bona Dea*, had only priestesses and had a special May-Day celebration.

In Orthodox Judaism, the official attitude to women is more ambivalent even than in Buddhism. Every devout orthodox Jewish male prays, every day of his life: "Blessed art thou, O lord our God, king of the Universe, who has not made me a heathen, who has not made me a slave, who has not made me a woman." On the other hand, in the early days there arose prophetesses, such as Deborah, who judged Israel, and such heroines as Jael and Esther, Ruth and Hannah, who, at least after their deaths, were held in high honor. In the early thirteenth century A.D., one Dulcie, daughter to Eliazar of Worms, gave a sermon on the Sabbath; she was later martyred by the Knights of the Cross. Today there is, in Reform Judaism, a Woman's Liberation Movement, pressing for the ordination of women rabbis. It is not known how such

Reform advocates propose to deal with Leviticus 12: "If a woman conceives, and bears a male child, then she shall be unclean seven days, as at the time of her menstruation she shall be unclean . . . she shall not touch any hallowed thing nor come into the sanctuary until the days of her purifying are complete. For a female child the time she shall be unclean is two weeks, as in her menstruation, and sixty-six days." So every woman between twelve and, say, fifty, is unclean two weeks out of every four, even if unmarried. These Biblical strictures of course affect Christians also, since Jesus Christ declared He had not come to "destroy the Law."

Yet it is a Jewish woman who, of all women since recorded history began, has been, in her own words, most magnified, and who has most exulted in God her Saviour. Mary, the espoused wife of the carpenter Joseph and the mother of Jesus of Nazareth, claimed for herself, and has had claimed for her ever since, a closer relationship with the Almighty than any one else has dared to claim, except her only son. For all Christians, Orthodox, Catholic, or Protestant, she is the mother of God, and the Feast of the Annunciation, March 25, which celebrates her "*fiat*," her answer to the Angel Gabriel's salutation, is above all the feast of our freedom. For that four-letter word *fiat*, by which Mary gave us back the liberty lost by Eve, is the only reason for our existence. Mary and her Father-Lover-Son used the same word: *fiat*. He said, *fiat*, *be*, when He created; *fiat mihi*, said she, *be it to me*. And so even in Protestant England, March 25 is still "quarter day," on which rents are paid, and from which leases run; in Rome, it is the day on which the Vatican year begins, and all documents are dated. When Mary had said her word of total obedience, it cancelled out forever Eve's disobedience: Eve and her spouse became saints Adam and Eve, whose feast is the vigil of Christmas, December 24.

When Mary said her *fiat* she went into the hill country, to visit her cousin Elizabeth. " . . . and she greeted Elizabeth. And when Elizabeth heard the greeting of Mary, the baby leaped in her womb, and Elizabeth was filled with the Holy Spirit, and she exclaimed with a loud cry 'Blessed are you among women, and blessed is the fruit of your womb.

And why is this granted me, that the mother of my Lord shou'. come to me? For behold, when the voice of your greeting came to my ears the babe in my womb leaped for joy. And blessed is she who believed that would be a fulfillment of what was spoken to her from the Lord.' "

And Mary said:

"My soul doth magnify the Lord
And my spirit has rejoiced in God my Savior
For He has regarded the lowliness of His handmaiden
For behold, from henceforth, all generations shall call me
    blessed
For He who is mighty has magnified me
And holy is His name
And His mercy is on them that fear Him
Throughout all generations
He has shown strength with his arm
He has scattered the proud in the imagination of their
    hearts
He has put down the mighty from their seat and exalted the
    humble and meek
He has filled the hungry with good things and the rich He
    has sent empty away
He, remembering his mercy, has helped His servant Israel
As He promised to our forefathers
Abraham and his seed for ever."[7]

Unfortunately, having thus started at the top, woman in Christianity had nowhere to go but down.

St. Paul's view of women was about as low as anyone could get: "it is better," he declared, "to marry than to burn." And he said women should cover their heads in church "because of the angels"—did he think they would be seduced, as in Genesis: "the sons of God saw the daughters of men that they were fair," or did he just think they would catch their wings in women's hair? In any case, things slowly improved after Paul. By the time of the Shepherd of Hermas in the first century A.D. (in spite of Paul's strictures on women preachers), there were women teachers, and by the time of the "high middle ages" William of Ockham (d. 1349) could write in his *Dialogues* that the Pope was responsible to a General Council, and that this *must* contain women.

With Protestantism women's role changed again: Martin Luther (1483–1546) wrote:

"If a woman becomes weary or at last die from childbearing, that matters not, let her only die from bearing, she is there to do it" (Tabletalk) After many years of marriage to an ex-nun Luther said to his wife: "We do not pray as we used to before we married."

By mid-nineteenth century, Pope Pius XII (1939–1958) declared: "In their personal dignity as children of God, men and women are absolutely equal as they are in relation to the last end of human life which is everlasting union with God in the happiness of heaven."

NOTES INTRODUCTION

1   Holy Bible: Genesis III:6,22. Revised Standard Version. Thomas Nelson & Sons, 1952.

2   All quotations from *The Tragedies of Sophocles*, translated by Sir R.C. Jebb (Cambridge University Press, 1904).

3   Joseph Campbell, *Oriental Mythology*, p. 37.

4   Amaury de Riencourt, *Sex and Power in History* (New York: McKay, 1975), p. 36.

5   Bhagavadgita, 9.32, from *The Bhagavad-Gita, translated with a Commentary on the Original Sources*, by R.C. Zaehner (Oxford University Press, 1973), p. 2866.

6   *Milinda's Questions*, translated from the Pali by I.B. Horner (London, Luzac & Co., 1963).

7   *Book of Common Prayer* (SPC'K. 1930), p. 61.

THE CHRISTIAN IDEAL

Thomas Merton, a Trappist, has described a monk as a person who "gives up everything in order to get everything." Asceticism, the discipline voluntarily undertaken by an individual wishing to advance his spiritual life, is common to almost all religions. Either overflowing and capricious or canalized and directed, it expresses the attempts of the soul in love with perfection to reach its goal. At all times, and in all places, among all civilized peoples, some men and some women have deliberately turned aside from worldly pleasures and entanglements in order to devote themselves, in solitude, to contemplation and to the pursuit of another, invisible, good.

Among the pagans in Egypt, Serapis, Mithra and Isis all had ascetical votaries, but the belief that ascetical training and discipline are the means to a clearer perception of ultimate reality was not widely held. The ascetic ideal, a common element in all faiths, became historically rooted in Christianity. Jesus Christ Himself not only practiced chastity, poverty and obedience, but preached them to His disciples. God had bidden Abraham be perfect (Genesis XVII, 7). Christ explained to His disciples how they should become so; "Be ye perfect as your Father in heaven is perfect," and added, "If thou wilt be perfect, go, sell what thou hast and give to the poor and thou shalt have treasure in heaven, and come, follow Me" (Matthew XIX. 21.)

And He further explained that "to those that are accounted worthy to attain to that life there is no marriage nor giving in marriage." Man, Christ taught, was to seek first the Kingdom of God and His righteousness, and only after might he attend to other things. The first commandment is to love God, and how does man love God? By doing His will, and His will, in human history, is man's sanctification. Man was created by God, Christians believe, to love and serve Him here. Man was redeemed by the Incarnation of God, who gave Himself wholly to and for man. Man's response, through the Christian ages, to this total gift has been reciprocal: the gift of himself. Man's love has sought to match God's in kind, however ridiculous the scale. This total response is what Christians call the "religious" life. For religion means the thing that binds (*res*, thing, *ligo*, I bind), and in the technical sense a "religious" is, for a Christian, a person who replies to God's total love with the total gift of his entire being.

> Sic nos amantem
> Quis non redamaret?

(Who will not return his love which loved us so?) asks the Christmas hymn, and St. John, too, tells us we love God because He first loved us. In all religions men and women have dedicated themselves wholly to their search for God out of love for Him, or out of distaste for themselves, but only in Christianity is that gift a *reply* to God's gratuitous redemption of mankind here, now, in history, a response to the moment when "the Word was made flesh, and dwelt among us." So that for the Christian, the religious life is always lived by persons, for the sake of a Person—a *human* person, albeit divine.

From its very beginning, the Christian religious life was marked by a fundamentally different character from life "in the world." It assumes an orientation of the whole of life toward the single goal of union with God. The giving up of other things, of possesssions, of marriage, of one's own will, crystalized by the three vows of poverty, chastity and obedience, is a natural consequence, not a determining cause, of the Christian's love of God. Just as marriage to the girl or to the boy of one's choice, having children with him or her, and

2

raising of them by sweat or sin, are consequences of falling in love in the first place, so, too, giving up such immediate neighbors as extant fathers and mothers and siblings, and possible future husbands, wives and children, is a means to arrive at a more perfect love of God. If it's anything less than this, there is no religious life. If any man or woman, for example, refrain from marriage out of contempt for that sacrament, or out of distaste for the sexual act, he or she is guilty of contempt for a part of God's creation, and is travelling away from God, not toward Him. Let such a one be an anathema, insisted the Council of Chalcedon, in 451.

The religious life is not merely a natural life supernaturalized by the intention behind it. It is a quite other kind of life "hid with Christ in God." Whoever becomes a religious renounces the world, because God, such a person believes, has called them to establish their soul on a plane that is not human. "Those who do not understand its supernatural source, imagine that it is inhuman. And, indeed, this abandoning of human values would be inhuman, if it did not find its justification in God. It is necessary that God should be a personal, active Being, that love which both invades and absorbs, and which alone can explain the vocation."[1]

To belong to God means, for the religious, to belong to no human being. Of course, every human being belongs to God as Creator, and every baptized person is committed to live in awareness of that belonging, but the religious goes further, and carries the Christian vocation to "the furthest limits of its irresistible demands." The religious want God alone, God only. Thus, although monastic life is a contemplative life, a life of penance, and a life devoted to the celebration of the liturgy, it exists for none of these reasons. *Ad quid venisti?* For what did you come? the religious is asked, and St. Benedict insists that one thing must diligently be discovered about the aspirant to the monastic life, *si vere Deum quaerit?* Does he truly seek God? The contemplative life, the life of penance, the liturgy (that is called the *opus Dei*, the work of God), all these are taken for granted as means, important means, obvious means, but only means, to the one end.

"The search, the true search, in which the whole of one's

3

being is engaged, is not for some thing but for some one: the search for God—that is the beginning and end of monasticism."[2] And the conditions have been set by the object of that search, by God Himself, who plays—and pays!—the piper and calls the tune. Yet, as St. Thomas Aquinas pointed out, perfection does not lie in giving up of what we possess, but in the following of Christ.[3] Relinquishing possessions has no positive value unless what you get is worth more than what you give. As St. Augustine put it (*De Trinitate*, Chap. XII), "the less a man loves his private possessions, the more closely will he cleave to God." But possessions are still external. Christ said further, "If any man come to me and *hate* not his father, and mother, and wife and children, and brethren and sisters, yes, and his own life also, he cannot be my disciple" (Luke XII:26). Elsewhere He observed that "there are some who have made themselves eunuchs for the Kingdom of Heaven. Let him that can take, take it." So the monk has no wife and no family. But closer even than a man's wife, or a wife's husband, is a man's own will, and that must go too, be "offered up." "If any many will come after Me, let him deny himself and take up his cross and follow Me," said Jesus. So the vow, which of all the three religious vows, belongs most peculiarly to the religious life, is that of obedience.

" . . . First, because, by obedience man sacrifices to God his own will; by chastity, on the other hand, he offers his body; and by poverty, his external possessions. Now, since the body is worth more than material goods, the vow of chastity if superior in merit to that of poverty, but the vow of obedience is of more value than either of the other two. Secondly, because it is by his own will that a man makes use either of his body or his goods: therefore, he who sacrifices his own will, sacrifices everything else that he has."[4] St. Bernard (like Aquinas, a monk) had pointed out earlier, it is by the will that a man is a man. We possess, St. Bernard declared, "life in common with the plants, and, on the other hand, as well as life, sense perception and appetite in common with the beasts, while that which distinguishes us from both is what is called will . . . Therefore, save only the will, all that belongs

4

to man, seeing that it is incapable of self-determination, is a matter neither for the award of merit nor for judgment. Life, sense perception, appetite, memory, thought and anything else there is, are subject to necessity except in so far as they are subject to the will . . . The will can no more be deprived of its freedom than it can be deprived of itself . . . were a man able to will anything unwillingly, then and only then would the will be deprived of its freedom."[5] So the offering must be free: no one can be compelled to enter the cloister (though alas! many often were, by kings and powerful nobles, and even by bored or parsimonious parents, but one so forced was not considered a religious) nor compelled to remain there. The glory of God is a living man, *gloria Dei vivens homo*, and it is a free man's worship that he asks.

The world which the religious renounces is not itself evil, although evil exists in that world. It is the world which Christ loved enough to die for it. Indeed, all the things the religious renounces are in themselves good: possessions, marriage, his will. The world, the flesh and the devil, that old triad of evils, renounced in baptism by every Christian, are very different: their renunciation is elementary, a beginning. But perfection lies not in the denying of evil but in the exchanging of many goods for only one good, that pearl of great price, the Supreme Goodness itself.

Nothing the religious renounces is forbidden or sinful: power and freedom, riches and security, family and marriage are all in themselves good . . . But their use can be evil. As Walter Dirks notes, " . . .power, riches and sex. All three are not regulatable rights which are questionable only when they degenerate into superabundance of insufficiency or when they clash with other rights, but powers which endanger man in his humanity . . . . The powers which are supposed to develop man from solitary creatures to fullness, and which are the powers of generation, are able not only to perfect, to build, to awaken life, but also to destroy, to undermine, to annihilate." And Dirks goes on to compare riches with sand, which every hour, every day, restrains and hinders, is seldom recognized and usually overlooked. In fact, the spirit of acquisitiveness.

of, or of satisfaction with, money, makes people more inhuman and unholy than the furious pleasure of unbridled sexuality. Enterprise, endurance, ambition, the rich call it; the poor dub it envy and ruthless greed. "The love of money is the root of all evil" and, as St. Thomas Aquinas pointed out, money has a kind of infinity. Gold is the arch substitute for love; this is a truth to which all the saints as well as Freud and Marx, testify.

Power—the power a man has over his own will, and through the exercise of his will, over others—presents the greatest danger of all. For "all power corrupts, and absolute power corrupts absolutely," as one of the greatest of Catholic historians, Lord Acton, declared. The temptation offered mankind to misuse his power is as old as the myth of Prometheus, or the story of Adam and Eve: "ye shall be as gods," promised the serpent, and theirs was the exact same crime —of taking that for which they should have waited to be given, as was the sin of the Greek hero, *hubris*. As in Adam and Eve, our first parents, so in Prometheus, we all sinned, and as disobedience is the sin by which angels and men both fell, so obedience is the only virtue by which man can rise to angelic heights. Christ Himself practiced obedience to His Father perfectly, even unto death, the death of the Cross. So every religious person offers his or her obedience in unison with Christ's obedience, to Christ's Father who is ours too.

Yet no religious imagines that by turning aside from the world, and binding himself by the three vows, they can escape temptation. The devil, says an old proverb, rides outside and around every monastery. The temptations against poverty, chastity and obedience never end. Attachment to personal possessions can only too easily revive, camouflaged as "the zeal of Thy house" and the religious, male or female, can cling anew to all they gave up and more, not for themselves, but for their beloved order and its advancement. Likewise, the sex urge, sacrificed, can easily surface as any one of the several inordinate attachments. And the will to power has been expressed by many monks. Brother Elias and Savonarola are among many examples of monks shelled in selfwill.

From the beginning of Christianity, women were permitted, indeed encouraged, equally with men to dedicate themselves wholly to God. There were at that time only two ways to God: by martyrdom and by asceticism. Only by leaving this world, one way or another, could the other world be won. Martyrdom was the result of free choice, for women as for men. SS. Perpetua and Felicitas, and all the other women martyrs, were offered the chance to deny their God and live, and, just as their male fellow-martyrs did, they refused to deny their Lord. Asceticism implied a very different type of choice, though here again, the alternatives were much the same for women as for men.

Only one of Christ's twelve apostles is known to have been married, St. Peter. But St. Philip, according to the Acts, had four daughters, all of whom were dedicated virgins.

The discovery in 1947 of the Dead Sea Scrolls in the caves above Qumran in Israel has substantiated what was already known about the Jewish Essene monastic community from the writings of Josephus and of Philo the Jew. As Cardinal Danielou has put it: "As a matter of geographical fact, the Essenian community did live in Palestine and, more specifically, in a region visited by Christ. Historically, the final phase of its history encompasses a period of time that coincided exactly with the life of Christ and the first developments of the Church."[6] Cardinal Danielou goes on to prove categorically that early Christianity had very definite contacts with this community. The discovery of the Dead Sea Scrolls has, Cardinal Danielou declared, confirmed in an undeniable way John the Baptist's contacts with the monks of Qumran. Today, the Baptist must, indeed, be viewed against a specifically Essene background, instead of appearing suddenly out of nowhere. The Essenes were descended from priestly families, and referred to themselves in the scrolls as "sons of Zadok." Zadok was a high priest under Solomon. John the Baptist was raised by the Essenes, as is indicated by Luke 1:80: ". . . the child grew, and was strengthened in spirit; and was in the desert until the day of his manifestation in Israel." This "desert" is that of Qumran. Cardinal Danielou, commenting on

7

the fact that the Qumran monks boarded children, notes that the Baptist's later food, locusts and wild honey, was Essene fare. The Essene Damascus Document even explains that the locusts must be roasted. Celibacy and the total abstention from fermented liquors, too, were part of the requirements of the Essenes. John's disciples, who followed him personally rather than remain with the Essene community, form a link between the Essenes and Christ.

It is quite possible that St. Joseph took Mary and Jesus to Essene friends in Egypt, for no explanation is offered as to why the Holy Family went to Egypt rather than, say, to Syria, and through St. John and his parents they would have been in touch, closely and constantly, with Essenes. In Egypt, the Essenes may have found—or even have originated?—the *therapeutae*, those pre-Christian communities. Some Fathers insisted that these *therapeutae* were off-shoots from Jewish ascetics who had anticipated Christianity and were later grouped into a church around St. Mark. Since the Dead Sea Scroll discoveries some scholars are coming to agree with the early Fathers. The Greek word, *therapeutae*, means "the doctors" (in the medical sense), and the word *essenes* has the same connotation.

Justin Martyr (circa 100–165) writes of Samaria that there were to be found "Many, both men and women, who have been Christ's disciples from childhood, and who remain pure at the age of 60 and 70 years, and I boast that I would produce such from every race of men." Very early, in Syria, were to be found a Christian group known as the B'nai Q'yama, the Sons of the Covenant, who "gave themselves up to celibacy, poverty, vigils and fasting." This group refused baptism to candidates unless they were prepared to live celibate lives. Galen, the pagen philosopher, wrote around 150 A.D. of the Christians that "their contempt of death is patent to us all, as is their abstinence from the use of their sexual organs by a certain impluse of modesty. For they include men and women who refrain from cohabiting all their lives, and they also number individuals who, in ruling and controlling themselves and in their keen pursuit of virtue, have attained a state not inferior to that of real philosophers."

In the Syrian Christian community (circa 109) at the moment of baptism each candidate was asked to choose between marriage and celibacy, and those who chose celibacy were baptized first and occupied a higher rank. The organization of the Ebionites also presented two degress, and the higher degree was characterized by a higher level of asceticism which entailed virginity, and which corresponds to that which we learn from the Qumran documents: in the Essene community there was a higher degree of monks and a lower degree of married persons (Cardinal Danielou).[7]

This proof of a "double standard," of the simultaneous existence of a spiritual, alongside an institutional hierarchy, shows that in early Christianity the "religious" were not "out of this world," not marginal to the community as they later became, and are today, but represented rather within the community a spiritual aristocracy. Probably priests and bishops were recruited from among the monks (as is still the practice in the Orthodox Church) so that the two hierarchies actually overlapped. "It is because of this slant that the monasticism of Qumran can be considered as the source of Christian monasticism, not in that it was continued in a particular group, but in so far as it concerned the very structure of the ecclesiastical community," concludes Cardinal Danielou.[8]

It is indeed possible that the practice of celibacy among the Christian clergy came to them from the laity. It was practiced in Egypt among the monks and copied from them by the clergy. From Carthage at the end of the second century Tertullian wrote: "We as much as we can refuse meat and sex. How many voluntary eunuchs! How many virgins consecrated to Christ!"

St. Ignatius of Antioch (third bishop of Antioch, 50–109) in his letter to the Smyrnans salutes the virgins of both sexes, but warns them that ascetics must submit to the bishop. He also warns that anyone who boasted when abiding in chastity to the honor of the flesh of the Lord was lost. Christian virginity "a state of passionless waiting to put on the divine image," as St. Clement called it, was highly commended as a state of life in Egypt by the time of Bishop Demetrius (188–231), although his bishopric of Alexandria seems to have been the only one extant there then.

Although many Christians fled into the Egyptian desert to escape the Roman persecutions (Tertullian says the Carthaginian Jews set off the persecution there against the Christians), monasticism did not begin, except as an individual, isolated phenomenon, until the persecutions were on the wane. And the great rush to the desert was after 320, that is, after the conversion of Constantine had brought about the "peace of the Church." Father Bouyer, the French Oratorian, considers that "monasticism in the Church is nothing else than martyrdom reappearing under a new form required by altered circumstances."[9]

"If Christianity drew its world-shaking strength from its martyrs during the first three centuries, martyrdom itself found its highest and best strength among the Christian ascetics."[10]

Neither in the Jewish nor in the Christian faith can "flesh and blood inherit the kingdom of heaven (Col. 3.3)," for "no man can see God and live." The death necessary as a preamble to the vision of God is the consequence of sin, for death itself "was never of God's fashioning" (Wisdom 1.13), but "came owing to guilt." (Rom. 5.12) That guilt Christ expiated, and the martyr for Christ did so in His tracks by joining his testimony to that of his Lord. The religious male or female, sought, in and by his life, to achieve what the martyr did in and by his death: "You know well enough," warns St. Paul, "that we who were taken up into Christ by baptism have been taken up, all of us, into his death . . . if one man died on behalf of all, then all thereby became dead men." (Rom. 6.3,2; Cor. 5. 14-15)

It is doubtful whether any ascetics took vows at this time. Origen calls the ascetical the "apostolic" life, but Tertullian says that virgins "carnem suam sactificare *proposuit*," which looks as though they professed some sort of a vow. The second Clementine epistle (certainly not by St. Clement and probably late second century) refers to the "blessed virgin brothers who conserve their virginity for the king of heaven" and to the "consecrated virgin sisters," which again looks as if the women, anyway, made public promises.

St. Anthony the Great, or the Hermit, was born c. 251. His parents were Christians. He could not be persuaded to go to school, owing to his great aversion to the rough behaviour of the boys. Some authorities say he never could understand Greek, nor read even Coptic. His parents died when he was about eighteen, and he inherited much good land and slaves also. And one little sister, of whom he had to take care. After about six months, he was in church one day, and heard the Gospel: "If thou wishest to be perfect, go and sell everything which thou hast, and give to the poor, and take thy cross and come after Me, and there shall be unto thee treasure in heaven." (Matthew, 19-21) When he came home from church he set in order his house and the possessions he had inherited from his parents. Now he had three hundred fields, a great estate which produced abundant crops, and these he handed over to the people of his village. But the remainder of his other possessions he sold and gave the money to the poor . . . but he laid by a little which was sufficient for his sister's wants." So St. Athanasius (298?–373) tells, in his *Life of St. Anthony*.[11] Athanasius knew Anthony well, had stayed with him often (he wrote his *Life* when hiding in the Thebaid during the Arian persecution of 356–7). Anthony converted his sister with "words of love, and of truth, and of the fear of God, and he made her mind to be like his own, and he delivered her over to certain chaste nuns who were living there at that time."

St. Nilus preferred the desert to his wife and children. "An ardent desire to live in the desert of Sinai and to possess peace took possession of my heart," he wrote. "The love of solitude finally made my departure necessary. I no longer had strength to resist. Taking my children, still very young, I set them in front of their mother. I gave her one and took one. It was then I told her my mind. My face and my tone of voice gave her to understand that my resolution was irrevocable. When she saw it was impossible to prevent my departure, she gave me, not without difficulty, her assent. Sorrow choked her; tears coursed down her cheeks. You know how painful is a separation of those whom a legitimate marriage unites. Such suffering is not less than that of a sword plunged in the chest. . . ."

For what reason did so many men, and women, go forth into the desert? Cassain (360?–436) gives a conference of the Abbot Isaac which may suggest what they found.

"The end of all perfection is that the mind, purged from all carnal desires, may daily be lifted towards spiritual things until the whole life and all the thoughts of the heart become one continuous prayer. Sometimes a kind of prayer is arrived at, known and tried by but very few, which in truth is ineffable, and which transcends all human thoughts and is distinguished I will not say by any sound of the voice, by no movement of the tongue nor utterance of words, but when the mind, enlightened by the infusion of that heavenly light described in no human nor confined language, pours forth richly as from a copious fountain in an accumulation of thoughts, and ineffable utters to God, expressing in the shortest possible space of time, such great things that the mind when it returns to its usual condition cannot easily utter or relate."

And what good did all this asceticism do? As there has to be a literary climate—hundreds trying to write, scribbling indifferent verse, publishing second-rate novels—before a real flowering of literature, such as the Elizabethan age, can take place; or as a country has to be crowded with would-be painters, with Sunday painters, with daubers of every kind, before the Renaissance or the French Impressionists can occur—so the Egyptian deserts had to be full of good, bad and indifferent hermits, the Mediterranean islands crowded with monks, before the great body of Christian literature could be produced, and before the revoltingly corrupt, decadent and decaying Roman Empire could be truly converted and transformed into Christendom. From 310 to 451, during the golden age of the hermits, the human spirit reached unprecedented heights. The Roman aristocracy, deprived of all political power, were living in idleness and luxury, hiring barbarians to do their fighting, brutalizing slaves to do their living (a slave slow in bringing hot water could be given 300 stripes); they were without art, science or true civility. Only very gradually did Christianity permeate this world. It was the Christian *women* who first aroused themselves, freed their slaves, gave away their wealth, and followed men like St. Jerome in Bethlehem. Meanwhile, in Egypt, the monks were attracting more and more followers, and also visitors. "How do you live?" St. Melania asked one recluse, and he replied, "From the morning until 3 p.m. I pray, then I spin linen, read the lives of the Fathers and the Gospels; Come evening, I praise the Lord my God, eat a bit of bread, and spend several of the night hours in prayer." Many of the ascetics deliberately chose holes in the ground where they could neither lie down nor stand up: "I fear that widening of my earthly home would mean a narrowing of my heavenly one."[12]

"The true philosophers, Simias, are always occupied in the practice of dying, wherefore to them least of all men is death terrible," Plato had written, and by their *ars moriendi*, their art of dying, the Christian ascetics were seeking, by means of solitude, fasting and prayer, to pass from death to life. And that life was not hereafter: it was life here—for it was their own humanity "long obscured and ravished by idolatry, immorality and worldliness" that they sought now to reform. The vision Constantine had in 312 of the shining cross, in whose sign he would conquer, had to become the reality of every life; only in, and with, and on, the cross—not against it—could men conquer themselves.

Between 312 and 381 the Empire became Christian and Christianity became official. In the first centuries salvation had meant enduring the exile of this world, and remaining detached from, and uncontaminated by, the pagan society which flourished in forum and marketplace. Death by martyrdom had been the best, easiest and quickest passport to the eternal kingdom where a Christian could possess his true humanity. But now the daily humdrum life of forum and barrack and marketplace became the arena in which one began to perfect and cultivate salvation. In brief, Christianity had assumed something new and strange in its experience: a commonplace, tedious, earthly existence; it had inherited the hardest of responsibilities. It had to win the peace.

The thousands who sought the desert, found in mortification of the flesh, in prayer without ceasing, in reading, psalm singing and loneliness, the way to the Way. They learned that the whole man, body and soul and mind, must participate in the experimental discipline. Not unnaturally, there were many who couldn't take it, just as there were many false steps on the way to the first moon landing! Comparatively few of the human missiles that hurled themselves at eternal life made—or make!—it. The wonder is, that so many made it the desert way, and were given the final accolade —being raised to her altars—by the church. And those who made it were the wonder and admiration of ordinary folk. For quite soon the living Christians in the desert became objects of pilgrimage, and a visit to Egypt was a necessary corollary of a visit to the shrines in Palestine.

The desert saints were living models of the Christ Whose traces Jerome's friend Paula found in Jerusalem. St. Jerome describes how Paula: "prostrate before the Cross, adored it as though she saw the Saviour hanging upon the sacred wood. In the sepulchre she kissed the resurrection stone: ardently she pressed her lips against the rock upon which the body of Christ had lain. The whole city of Jerusalem witnessed the tears she shed, the groans she uttered, the outpouring of her grief in this holy place." Jerome then describes how Paula went on to the "second Holy Land" of Egypt, penetrating the Nitrian desert to venerate the ascetics there: "Whose cell did she not visit? At whose feet did she not kneel? She believed she saw Christ in each one of those saints, and rejoiced to render the Lord the honors she rendered them."[13] St. Paula died in 404; her spiritual father St. Jerome in 420.

St. Jerome was a great promoter of pilgrimages, and wrote: "Just as one understands Greek history better when one has seen Athens, or the third book of Virgil better when one has sailed to Sicily, so we understand Scripture better when we have seen Judea with our own eyes." (Letter 46) Pilgrimages have always been a specially Semitic pastime though a pilgrimage is any journey to a shrine or sanctuary for a religious motive. Men and women have been "going on pilgrimages," the English poet Chaucer put it, to hill or spring or tree, for all recorded time. There are many mentioned in the Bible: many open air heathen shrines were converted to the worship of Yahweh, and may reconverted back again, to the fury of the minor Prophets. Pilgrimages formed part of the Jewish festivals of Passover, Pentecost and Tabernacles, and the place where Abraham entertained the Trinity, under the trees at Mamre, has been a place of pilgrimage ever since.

From 160 on Christians went on pilgrimages to Jerusalem; Melito of Sardes went that year. The Emperor Constantine and Helena his mother encouraged pilgrimages to the Holy Land, but many Christian pilgrimages were to sites that had earlier been holy to pagans, as Fourvière (Lyon), one the site of a shrine to Mercury, then to the Virgin; and Chartres. In the New World, too, the preferred places of pilgrimage were already places of pilgrimage in pre-Christian days: Chalma and Guadalupe in Mexico, for examples.

Islam makes pilgrimage as one of the five pillars of the Muslim faith. Every Muslim is supposed to make the pilgrimage to Mecca once in his lifetime, and as early as in the third surah in the Holy Qu'ran (The family of Imran) it is stated in Verse 96: "Lo! The first Sanctuary appointed for mankind was that at Mecca, a blessed place, a guidance to the peoples." In Verse 97: "Wherein are plain memorial of Allah's guidance, the place where Abraham stood up to pray; and whosoever entereth it is safe. And pilgrimage to the House is a duty unto Allah for mankind, for him who can find a way thither." And in Surah XXII, verse 27, called *The Pilgrimage* the Prophet is bidden: "Proclaim unto Mankind the pilgrimage."[14]

In India, the temple of Kali at the Kalighat in Calcutta still has daily blood sacrifices, and during the annual autumn festiveal of Kal Durga over 800 goats are slaughtered in three days. Only the heads are left in the temple: "in the mud before the statue of the goddess, the animal's heads are heaped, while her pilgrims return home with the goats bodies and eat them."

Modern Christian pilgrimages include Lourdes (8 million visited it in 1958, the centernary of the Virgin's first appearance there). Lisieux, the shrine of St. Teresa of the Child Jesus is still visited by more than 1 million people annually.

NOTES CHAPTER I

1   Canon Jacques Leclerq, *The Religious Vocation* (Dublin: Clonmore and Reynolds, 1955), p. 26.

2   Louis Bouyer, *The Meaning of the Monastic Life* (New York: 1950), p. 8.

3   St. Thomas Aquinas, *The Religious State* (Maryland: Newman Press, 1950), p. 22.

4   *Ibid.*, p. 52.

5   St. Bernard, *Treatise Concerning Grace and Free Will* (Watkin Williams SPCK, 1920).

6   Jean Danielou, *The Dead Sea Scrolls* (Baltimore: Helicon Press, Inc., 1958), p. 14.

7   *Ibid.*, p. 12.

8   *Ibid.*, p. 122.

9   *The Meaning of the Monastic Life*, p. 54.

10   Julius Mayer, *Die Christliche Ascese*, p. 8.

11 See: Palladius, *Paradise of the Fathers*, trans. Sir Ernest Budge (London: Chatto Windus, 1907).

12 Theodoret, *Historia Religiosa*, Chap. II, in J.P. Migne, *Patrologiae Graecae* (Paris, 1849), LXXXII, p. 1310.

13 *St. Jerome*, letter 108.

14 Marmaduke Pickthall, *The Meaning of the Glorious Koran: An Explanatory Translation* (New York: New American Library, 1953).

ETHERIA'S PILGRIMAGE

To enter a religious order was one way to God; to go on pilgrimages was another, which both religious and lay women did from earliest times. In one of his great *Odes*, describing Helen of Troy, who brought this great city and civilization "to dust," to total ruin, Horace calls Helen *"Mulier peregrina,"* the "pilgrim" (or strange, or foreign) woman.[1]

One woman who travelled a very long way indeed—from Spain to Jerusalem—and kept a journal of her journey, was Etheria.

In 1884 a Latin text was discovered in a convent in Arezzo by an Italian scholar named Gamurrini. This text, which originally came from Monte-Cassino, was the account, by a pious lady of the nobility, written for her "sisters," of a pilgrimage she had made in Egypt and Palestine, and also described the magnificent ceremonies she had witnessed in Jerusalem.

Who was this "pious and noble" lady? She was probably the daughter of a Spanish official, a friend, possibly even a relative, of the Emperor Theodosius (379–395), who came from Galicia and brought his Spanish family to Constantinople after he became emperor. Some think she was a daughter or niece of Eucherius, the emperor's uncle. The manuscript must have been written after 363, since Etheria said that Romans could no longer visit Nisibis,[2] which had by then fallen to the Persians in that year, and before 540, when Antioch was destroyed, since Etheria mentions staying at Antioch. The most likely date is sometime between 393 and 396, since St. Jerome (342–420), in a letter to Furia (letter 54, paragraph 13), mentions a lady "related to the sovereign" as having visited Bethlehem.

At the time she undertook her pilgrimage, Etheria must have been over 40, because in 380 the Council of Saragossa had insisted that "consecrated virgins" must have arrived at that age. She may indeed have been abbess of her convent. In any case, it is probable that she had a *diploma*, a sort of passport, which enabled her to use the *cursus publicus*, the imperial post, organized throughout the Empire. She could then stop at the *mutationes*, where the horses were changed, and at the *mansiones*, post-inns, which also had shops and stables, where individual horses could be hired and provisions purchased. In general Etheria had enough of her own servants for her protection, but when going through dangerous places (*loca suspecta*) she traveled with an escort of Roman soldiers who, commanded by their officers, took her from one fort to another. Etheria also stayed with bishops, priests and monks, upon whom the duty of receiving travelers was incumbent as Christians: "the guest is God," St. Benedict was to write later.

Etheria's language is rather tarnished silver Latin, far removed from the classical. She makes "barbarian" faults of declension and conjugation and mistakes in the use of cases and even of genders, and above all she has not the faintest interest in art or literature and no interest in antiquity. On the other hand, she was what Germans called *"Bibelfest"*: she has an accurate and exact knowledge of both the Old and New Testaments, and she repeats her quotations from these without embarrassment.

The manuscript begins suddenly, describing her arrival at Mount Sinai.

"We were shown everything, just as related in the Scriptures. On the way, we came to a place (the plain of er Rahah) where one can see between the mountains to a far distance, and there appeared the holy mountain of God, Sinai. Near here are buried "those who coveted" [the Israelites struck dead by God, for having eaten quails (Numbers 11, 34)]. Our holy companions (the monks who were guiding her party) said 'It is the custom to say a prayer here at the first sight of the mountain of God.' So we also prayed. We were about four miles away from Sinai. It was this valley we now had to cross. It was in this immense and flat valley that the Israelites waited for forty days and forty nights while Moses went up the mountain of God; it was in this valley that the golden calf was made, and a great stone has been set up at the place. At the opposite end of this valley is where, while Moses was minding his father-in-law's flocks, God spoke to him twice from the burning bush.

"On the Saturday evening, we started up the mountain, and we arrived at one of the hermitages inhabited by the monks who live there, and who fulfilled towards us all the duties of hospitality. There is a church there, with a priest. We spent the night there, then, next morning, Sunday, with the priest and the local monks, we began the ascent. It is very hard to climb these mountains, for one does not go up them turning around gently, like a snail, but one goes straight up as though following a wall, and one has to go down them also vertically . . . And so I walked with great difficulty, as there was no possibility of going up on horseback, but I didn't feel my fatigue, such was my longing to realize my desire. At the fourth hour [10 A.M.] we arrived at the top of the holy mountain of God, where the law was given, on the day when the mountain was all smoking. At this place there is a church, not very big, because the summit of the mountain itself is not very big, but very beautiful [it was destroyed in the 6th century]. Coming to meet us, leaving his hermitage, was the priest of the church, a venerable old man, monk since his youth, and one whom they call here *ascetic*. Other priests and all the monks who lived thereabouts also, came out to meet us. But on the very summit no one lives, there is no one there but the church, and a cave where Moses was. The relevant passages from Moses were read, oblation was made and we all took communion and as soon as we came out of church the priests gave us fruits from the mountain itself. Although the holy mountain is so stony that there is not even a bush, yet around there is some earth. The holy monks take the greatest pains to plant fruit trees, and gardens next to their hermitages; they appear to produce these fruits from the mountain soil, but it is above all from their labors. . . .

"I want you to know, venerable ladies, my dear sisters, that from where we stood, that is to say just outside the church, on top and in the middle of the mountain, we could see above all the mountains we have previously ascended with such difficulty; compared with the one whereon we stood they looked like small hills, yet they are so immense that I do not think I have ever seen higher ones, except the one on which we stood which was so much higher than they. At our feet we saw Egypt, Palestine, the Red Sea, the sea between Pelusa and Alexandria, and the country of the Saracens which stretches further than eye can see; we had difficulty believing all this, but these holy men showed us all these places.

"Having thus realized all the desires that had made us climb up so fast, we came down from the mountain of God on to another mountain next to it which is called 'en Horeb': there is a church there. This is the mountain to which fled the holy prophet Elijah from king Ahab, and where God asked him 'what are you doing here, Elijah?' and here is the cave where St. Elijah hid, still shown today, outside the church door; and the stone altar is shown built by St. Elijah himself upon which to offer sacrifice to God. We made a fervent prayer there and made oblation and read the relevant passage from the book of Kings. After the oblation, we went to another place which was not far from there, shown us by the priests and the monks, it was the place where St. Aaron waited with the 70 elders while St. Moses was receiving from the Lord the law for the children of Israel. Though there is no building there, there is a huge stone, having on it a circular platform on which, it is said, all the elders stood. We read the passage in the book of Moses, and said an appropriate psalm, and, after having said a prayer, we came down. It was now about the 8th hour [2 P.M.] and we still had three miles to go to get out of the mountains . . . But we could not come back the way we came, because we had had to visit all the holy places I spoke of. About the 10th hour [4 P.M.] we got down to where is the bush out of which the Lord spoke to Moses in the fire; there are many hermitages here and a church. In front of the church, there is a very pretty garden, and excellent and abundant spring water. In this garden is the bush. We were shown just beside it the place where St. Moses stood when the Lord said to him 'unlatch the thong of thy shoe' etc. It was too late for us to make the oblation. But we said a prayer in the church and also in the garden, near the bush. As it was now evening, we ate there, in the garden, in front of the bush, with the holy men, and we camped there. Next day, awaking early, we asked the priests to make the oblation there, which was done . . . they also showed us an enormous stone, against which Moses, in his anger, broke the tables he had brought down from the mountain . . . that same day, we also went to see other very holy monks, who, because of their age or infirmities, had not been able to go up to the mountain of God for the oblation; they deigned, when we arrived in their hermitages, to give us most hospitable welcome. Thus we saw all the holy places we had wished to see, and having also seen all the holy men who dwelt there, we returned to Pharan. I know that I must always and in everything thank God; and I do not wish only to speak of the many graces he has deigned to give by allowing me, who am unworthy and without merit, to see all the places which I was unworthy to see, but also all these holy men whom I can never thank enough who deigned to welcome my humble person in their hermitages, and lead me to all the places I asked to see.

"When we got back to Pharan, which is 35 miles from the mountain of God, we had to remain there, to rest, for two days. On the third day, we came back to the desert of Pharan, where we halted on our way out. Next day, having taken on provisions of water, and walking between the mountains, we arrived at the seashore, where one comes out of the mountains, and where one walks quite close to the sea; suddenly the sea was around the feet of our mounts, and one is walking 100 or 200 feet from the water, and there is no road anywhere, one is walking in sand deserts.

"The inhabitants of Pharan, who customarily circulate there with their camels, put up signs which they follow in the daytime. At night, it is the camels who follow the signals. In short, because they are used to it, the inhabitants of Pharan circulate at night more precisely and safely than any man could do even in regions where there is a well-marked road. When we got back to Clysma we again had to rest, because we had marched long in the desert sands.

"Obviously, I already knew the land of Gessen; it was that way I went for the first time to Egypt. But in order to see where the children of Israel, after leaving Ramesses, had passed before reaching the Red Sea, at the place which today is called Clysmu because of the fort that is there, I wanted to go from Clysma to the land of Gessen, to the town called Arabia, which is in the land of Gessen . . . This is part of Egypt, but is much better than the rest of Egypt. From Clysma to Arabia, there are four stages through the desert. But though it is desert, at each stage there are posts with soldiers and officers who always escorted us from one fort to another. On the way, the holy men accompanying us, priests and monks, showed us all the places that I wanted to see. They showed us Etham, which is quite close to the desert, and also Socoth. Socoth is a little hill in the midst of a valley: it was close to this hill that the Israelites established their camp; it is here they were given the law of Pasch. Here they built the town of Pithom, which is now a fort. Hieropolis was a town in olden times, . . . it is now a village, but a big village with a church and a great number of *martyria* [3] and a great number of hermitages and of holy monks. This village is today called Hero, and it is sixteen miles from the land of Gessen, on Egyptian soil. It is a most agreeable place, for a branch of the Nile flows by there. Leaving Hero, we got to Arabia . . . from Arabia to Ramesses there are 4,000 steps [4 Km.]. At Ramesses now there is not a single habitation, though there are many ruins and a huge Theban stone, on which, in relief, are two gigantic statues which they say represent those holy men, Moses and Aaron. There is also a sycamore tree there, planted, it is said, by the patriarchs. It is very old now, and shrunken, but it still bears fruit. Anyone who is sick goes there, breaks off some twigs, and that does them good. The holy bishop of Arabia told us this; he told us the name of the tree; it is called in Greek: *dendros alethiae*, or 'tree of truth.' This holy bishop deigned to come to meet us at Ramesses; though he is quite old, he was formerly a monk, very friendly and welcoming to pilgrims; he knows the Holy Scriptures well.

"By great good fortune, the day we arrived at the stage of Arabia was the vigil of the Epiphany, so the holy bishop kept us with him two days. At this point, we dismissed the soldiers who had assisted us in the name of the Roman authorities while we were marching in suspect regions; but from now on it was the main public highway of Egypt which went through Arabia, the one which goes from the Thebaid to Pelusia, so it was no longer necessary for us to bother the soldiers.

"Leaving there, we crossed all the land of Gessen, always between vines which give wine, and vines which give balm, between orchards, well-cultivated fields, magnificent gardens on the banks of the Nile . . . in short, I don't think I have ever seen anywhere a more beautiful country than the land of Gessen. From the town of Arabia, after two days of march through Gessen, we arrived at the town of Tanis, where Moses was born. This town used to be the metropolis of Pharao. I had already seen these parts, as I have already noted, when I had been in going from Alexandria to the Thebaid; however, as I wished to follow the tracks of the Israelites as they went from Ramesses to the holy mountain of God, the Sinai, I had to come back by Gessen and Tanis. So leaving Tanis by a road I already knew, I came to Pelusia. Then I retraced my steps and arrived at the frontiers of Palestine. Then, in the name of Christ our Lord, still making several stages across Palestine, I returned to Aelia, otherwise said, to Jerusalem.[4]

"There after a certain time, and by God's will, I had another longing to go to Mount Nebo in Arabia from which God told Moses to look at the land of Canaan which 'I give to the children of Israel as their possession. And you will die on the mountain which you will climb.' Thus, in order to accomplish our enterprise, we began to hurry in order to reach Mount Nebo. On the way, we were informed by a local priest, that is, from Livias, that if we wanted to see the water which flowed from the rock,[5] which Moses gave to the children of Israel when they thirsted, you can see it but only on condition that you go out of your way at the sixth mile. So we immediately followed the priest who led us. At the place, there is a little church at the foot of the mountain, which is not Nebo, but another, not far away from Nebo; many monks live there, holy men who hereabouts are called ascetics. They even allowed us to enter to greet them. Once we had entered their dwelling, we prayed with them, and they deigned to give us *eulogies*,[6] which they habitually do to those to whom they extend their hospitality. Between the church and the hermitages, there flows from a rock a most abundant, beautiful and clear water, with an excellent taste. So we asked those holy monks who lived there, what was this limpid water with such a delicious flavor? They replied 'This is the water Moses gave to the children of Israel in this desert.' So there we made a prayer, and read from the books of Moses, and said a psalm. Then accompanied by those of the holy men who were up to the fatigue of the climb, we arrived at the foot of Mt. Nebo; most of the climb we could do on donkey back, but one part was so steep we had to make it on foot, painfully. So we arrived at the top of Mt. Nebo; there is a small church, within which, at the place where usually there is a pulpit, there was something higher, whose dimensions were that of a tomb. I asked our holy friends what it was, and they said: 'here Moses was placed by the angels. But, as it is written "no man knows his tomb" it is not shown, even today; only our forbears, who lived here showed us where he was placed, and we have shown you, and the ancient ones who told us got it from a tradition from those more ancient than they.' So we made a prayer, and left the chuch. From the chuch door we saw where Jordan enters the Dead Sea, and not only Livias, but also Jericho, and a great part of Palestine and to the left we saw So'ar, the only one of the five towns of the people of Sodom that is still standing. There is a *memorial* but the other towns were reduced to ashes. We were shown where had been the column of Lot's wife, but not the column itself, venerable ladies, for it is not visible, it has been covered by the Dead Sea.

"Some time later, I wished to go the land of Ausitis [Hus] to visit Job's tomb and pray there . . . on the way I saw on Jordan's banks a lovely valley, full of vines and trees, with excellent water. In this valley was a large village, called Sedima, with many ruins around. There was a hill there, and on top of the hill, a church, and I was told: 'Formerly this town was called Salem and it was the town of king Melchisedech, and where the church is now, is where Melchisedech offered to God pure sacrifices, of bread and wine.' Thereafter, walking along Jordan's banks, which is the way we had to follow for some time, suddenly we saw the town of the holy prophet Elijah, called Thesbis, from which he was called Elijah the Thesbite, and the holy men who were with us said: 'here in this valley of Corra, Elijah lived during the reign of King Ahab and here a crow came by God's command during a time of famine and brought him food and he drank from this spring.'

"A holy monk had been told to dig at a place which had been shown him near Carnea and a cave was found which they followed for a hundred yards; there they found a stone on which was written JOB. This was the place where he sat on his dung-heap, and where they found his body, but they did not move it, but built a church: the altar is where the body was. After going there to communion we returned to Jerusalem, praising and giving thanks to God.

"Then, as three full years had now passed since I had arrived in Jerusalem, and as I had seen all the holy places, and having as my intention to return to my own country, I went to Antioch, and from Antioch I came to Hierapolis . . . Leaving Hierapolis, at the 15th mile, I came, in God's name, to the river Euphrates . . . it is really terrible and enormous, with a current as impetuous as that of the Rhone, with this difference that the Euphrates is even bigger. There, as it is only possible to cross it on big boats, I had to wait more than half a day; then having traversed the Euphrates, I came into Syrian Mesopotamia."

Here Etheria met a bishop who told her she could not go to Nisibis, now occupied by the Persians, nor to Ur of the Chaldees, five stages further, but he led her to Charra, to the well where St. Jacob watered the flocks of St. Rachel. To honor this site, a big church had been built, and the pilgrims saw the huge stone Jacob lifted from the top of the well. All around the well, priests and monks were living and the good bishop described their life to Etheria. She visited many in their hermitages, and they gave her *eulogies* and showed her where Laban, St. Rachel's father, was burned and the place where Rachel stole the *theraphim* from him. Then the pilgrims went back to Antioch by the same way they had come. There Etheria spent a week preparing for her voyage, and then arrived in Cicilia, at Tarsus. Three stages from Tarsus was the *martyrium* of St. Thecla, St. Paul's disciple, who lived with a goup of women who followed the ascetic life under her saint, formerly a monk. All around St. Thecla's church were numberless monasteries of men and of women. Etheria found there one of her greatest friends, known throughout the East for her holy life: she was a holy deaconess called Marthana. Etheria had known her in Jerusalem; she was there in charge of several monasteries for virgins. When she and Etheria saw each other "what joy for both." Etheria then returned to Tarsus, where she spent three days, then went on to climb Mt. Tarsus, and arrived at Chalcedon, where she stopped to see the very celebrated *martyrium* of St. Euphemia. St. Euphemia had been martyred, devoured by wild beasts, at Chalcedon, probably in 307. A magnificent basilica was erected in her honor, in which, in 451, the Council of Chalcedon was held, memorable for declaring that if anyone became a monk or nun out of contempt for marriage, they should be declared anathema. Etheria then took a boat to Constantinople. Thence, Etheria proposed to go to Ephesus, to pray at the *martyrium* of St. John.

"After this, if I have not left my body, I will write you all about it. And you my friends, dear ladies, deign to remember me, whether I am in my body or already out of it."

Unfortunately, the rest of Etheria's first book is lost. The second is a long account of all the Christian ceremonies in Jerusalem, day by day, for the whole liturgical year, and is interesting only as a proof that women were as assiduous in public worship at that time as were men, and as aware of the meaning of all the various rituals.

More interesting is a long letter from a Galician monk, Valerius, who wrote in the 7th century, praising Etheria in order to excite his brethren to fervor. He relates how "at the time when the beneficent Catholic faith was arising and the immense luminous clarity of our holy religion arrived late here at these remote ends of the West, and had finally illuminated them, the blessed nun Etheria, burning with the flame of desire for divine grace, aided by the power of the majesty of our Lord, with intrepid heart, undertook an immense voyage across the whole world. Walking thus, after a certain time, guided by the Lord, she arrived at the holy and longed-for places of his birth, passion and death, and also at the graves of innumerable saints and martyrs, in many different provinces and towns, to pray beside them and be edified. The more she had acquired a knowledge of holy dogma, the more burned in her heart the inextinguishable flame of holy desire.

"Searching everywhere for all that is contained in all the books of the Old and the New Testaments, visiting all the places where the holy miracles had taken place in different parts of the world, provinces, towns, mountains and deserts, her voyages took many long years, and at last she arrived in the lands of the East, animated with a great longing to see the saints of the Thebaid, she visited the glorious monasteries of communities of monks there, and even the hermitages of the anchorites. From thence, she visited all the provinces of Egypt, seeking there the traces of the ancient journeys of the Israelites, remarking on the excellences of each province, their rich and extraordinary fertility, the varied construction and beauties of the towns, describing all in detail. Then, enflamed by her longing to see the holy mountain of the Lord, following the traces of the children of Israel as they came out of Egypt, she ventured into the vast deserts and those diverse solitary regions described in Exodus. There, where, because of their complaints, the Lord made water spring from a rock at the hand of Moses, there in the heart of this woman thirsting for the Lord, flowed a spring of living water rising to eternal life . . . Thus, aided by divine goodness, she arrived at the summit of the rocky mountain where the divine majesty itself, while giving the holy law to the blessed Moses, deigned to dwell. There, exulting with joy, in the midst of the unending praise of her prayer, she offered to God the victim of salvation, then continued her march to visit still other places.

"Indeed, she was not content to travel across almost all countries of this world, but she climbed other giant mountains: the height of Pharan, at whose summit Moses prayed, his arms outstretched, while his people fought, until they had obtained the victory; then also the enormous mountain of Thabor, where the Lord, accompanied by Moses and Elias, appeared full of glory to his disciples, then another, called Eremus, upon which the Lord taught his disciples the Beatitudes; and another equally high mountain, called the mountain of Elijah where he lived and where a hundred prophets hid; and still another mountain, which dominates Jericho.

"Who can tell what fear of the judgement to come froze her heart, what love expresessed in deepest charity made it overflow, what burning ardor of divine hope and faith consumed her? The roads of the whole world did not tire her, wild seas and giant rivers did not stop her, the hugeness of mountains and their steepness did not shake her, the bitter cruelty of impious nations did not scare her, until she had completely satisfied all her devotion desired.

"Thus, dear friends, should we not blush, we who have physical strength and perfect health, that a woman followed the holy example of the patriarch Abraham, striking bravely, like hammer on anvil, her fragile woman's body, in order to win the endless recompense of eternal glory? Starting from the furthest extremes of the ocean to the west, she became known in the east. Seeking a remedy for her soul, she gave to many admirable instruction on how to follow God. Here below she did not wish rest, in order to assure herself of eternal glory and the victor's palm; Here she tormented her terrestial body by laying upon it a terrestial burden, in order to prepare for the Lord in heaven a soul wholly celestial in its innocence; here below, she deliberately and voluntarily treated herself as a stranger, in order . . . to possess the inheritance of the celestial kingdom."

Valerius goes on to exhort his "beloved brethren" to avoid all earthly seductions, then abruptly ends: "Here ends the letter in praise of the virgin Etheria."

NOTES CHAPTER 2

1   "Et mulier peregrina Vertit in pulverem" Horace: Odes, Book III, Ode III, line 20.

2   The center of the prehistoric amber route and a busy market town thereafter.

3   *Martyria* were sanctuaries erected in honor of the martyrs, generally on their tombs.

4   Jerusalem, largely destroyed by Titus in A.D. 70, was rebuilt by Hadrian, who renamed it *Aelia Capitolina*.

5   Still called *Ayoun-Mousa* today.

6   Little presents—fruit, cakes, etc.

HYPATIA (370-415) AND ST. MONICA (332-388)

By the beginning of the fifth century, the "pale Galilean" had conquered, and what Dante called the "fatal gift of Constantine" had made the Church all-powerful throughout the Roman empire. The "sacred Emperors" after Constantine mercilessly fought the "old religion," as Paganism was now called. In 353 Constance issued an edict that ordered the closing of all the temples and the abolition of all sacrifices to the Gods, under pain of death and of confiscation. However, in remote provinces, such as Numidia and Egypt, the efficiency of the central power was slow and uncertain, and the local aristocracy, of birth or education, was overtly or clandestinely anti-Christian. In their immense villas and even in the universities, processions and feasts for the ancient gods took place. Two women, Hypatia, who occupied the chair of Platonic philosophy in Alexandria, and Monica, the mother of St. Augustine of Hippo, can be taken as representative of women's ways to God—the old and the new—at this time.

Hypatia was the daughter of a mathematician, Theon of Alexandria. She was pupil of Synesius of Cyrene, Bishop of Ptolomais, who around 411 wrote affectionate and admiring letters to her. In one he writes: "Time was when I could be useful to my friends, and when you, Hypatia, were wont to call me 'Other Good' as using for the good of others my influence with men in great authority, men whom I made to serve me. Now I am left destitute by all, unless you have any power for good, you, and virtue with you. I count you good indeed, a good of which none can rob me. For you have, and always will have, power, by reason of the wise use you make of your credit." Her answer to this appeal has not survived, but Synesius sent her his book, *Dion*, and his *Book of Dreams*, and Hypatia herself tried to induce dreams by lying down and willing herself to sleep. She also helped Synesius design a silver astrolabe. Hypatia was a devotee of Plotinus, whose last words were: "I am striving to bring the God which is in us into harmony with the God which is in the universe."

Unfortunately, St. Cyril, Bishop of Alexandria, was rabidly Christian, and loathed Hypatia. He stirred up the Christian mob in Alexandria to tear Hypatia to pieces in the street. All her works have been lost, but an Anglican clergyman, whose mother was Jewish, Charles Kingsley, wrote a sympathetic novel about her, which cost him his Oxford DCL (Doctorate of Common Law) in 1857.

St. Monica, born in 332 in Thagaste, North Africa, was a Christian. She was perhaps sixteen or seventeen when she was married to Patricius, who was over forty. He was a pagan, and when urged to become a Christian, smiled ironically and said, "When you have stopped squabbling over what is the truth, maybe I will be baptized." Monica's parents were both Catholic, and her ancestors had been so for several generations. Monica was brought up by a Kabyle slave, who was very stern with the children: she would not allow them to drink, even water, between meals. "If you drink water now, you will drink wine later," the old woman said. This proved true of Monica, who, when sent to get wine from the cellar, would always drink some. One day the slave caught her at it, and called her "Drunkard! Drunkard!" Monica never forgot. Married to Patricius, she bore him a son, Navigius, and a daughter who later became superior of a monastery at Hippo. And in 354, on November 13, another son, Augustine. Monica practiced her religion assiduously and ostentatiously, and this meant going out, alone or with a maid, to church, to visit the poor, to distribute alms, and to spend part of the night, on the vigils of feasts, in church. On Sundays she went to Mass and visited the cemeteries, where the Christians sat on the tombs and ate and drank, piously, in honor of the martyrs. Her husband's friends described her outings, and suggested to Patricius that she was unfaithful. (He was.) His old mother repeated to him all the gossip told her about his wife but Monica was so gentle, so patient under these gibes and innuendoes, that first her mother-in-law and then her husband were won over, and the servants who tittle-tattled were beaten instead of Monica. Everyone in Thagaste was surprised that Monica escaped being beaten!

Augustine was not baptized at birth, but was listed among the Christian catechumens. When he fell ill, quite young, he asked for baptism, and Monica was delighted; but he suddenly recovered, and his baptism was put off again. He loathed school, where he was often beaten, and when he got home both Patricius and Monica laughed at him. He began to pray, having heard from Monica about a powerful and good Being, kind to those in distress. His first prayer was: "My God, may I not be beaten at school." In spite of the beatings, he was so bright his parents decided to send him to Madaura, some thirty miles from Thagaste, to school. He went on horseback. In Madaura he got a wholly pagan education, the Iliad, the Odyssey, and, above all, Virgil. At sixteen he returned to Thagaste, to his parent's house, as Patricius had no longer enough money to keep his brilliant son in Madaura. One day, in the public baths, Patricius noticed that his son had reached puberty; he returned home, delighted, to tell Monica. She was horrified, worried about the dangers her son's virtue would confront. Augustine sneered at her "old woman's grumblings—who cares?" However, she told Augustine to avoid courtesans and above all not to commit adultery.

Finally, thanks to a rich friend, Romanianus, Augustine was sent off to Carthage to continue his studies. Monica stayed at home with Patricius and prayed. Augustine remained at Carthage until he was twenty: by that time his father had died, and his benefactor, Romanianus, called Augustine back to tutor his own son. So Augustine returned to Thagaste and to Monica. Monica, widowed, now spent *all* her time in church, going twice daily. She scolded Augustine for his wild ways and, when he became a Manichaean, threw him out of her house.

Manichaeanism was a doctrine invented by Mani, who was born of Persian parents in Babylonia around 216. His father probably belonged to a sect known as the Mandeans. Mani received his summons from the Living Paraclete in about 241: the Paraclete revealed to Mani "the Mystery of the Light and the Darkness, the mystery of the great war which the darkness stirred up." The basis of Mani's doctrine is that "before the existence of heaven and earth there were two natures, the one good and the other evil." The Persian Manichaeans called the Darkness Ahriman, the Arabs Iblis. Mani declared "Matter" itself to be evil, and its strivings "are evil lust." The realms of good and evil are coeternal; they are themselves the origins. Orthodox Zoroastrianism already admitted two principles, Light and Darkness, but Mani's doctrine added the union of the two here below, and the unending war between them. Since Light could not fight (for to strive, even against darkness, was evil), it called forth the Mother of Life, who called forth Primal Man. This Primal Man was to fight the darkness, but the Arch-Devil of Darkness overcame Primal Man. Then Adam was created but he too was, with the help of the demons, seduced by Eve. So Manicheans ate only vegetables, abstained from marriage and the begetting of children, and also from suicide. Mani deliberately included Buddhist, Zoroastrian and Christian elements in his teaching, and of these Zoroastrianism was most influential on his cosmogony, Christianity on his eschatology, and Buddhism on his ethics. Manichaeanism "stretched from the Atlantic to the Indian Ocean," (Hans Jonas, *The Gnostic Religion*, p. 207) and even into China. The ideas of Mani were revived by the Reformers ("total depravity" for example) and by Mary Baker Eddy, who, with her M.A.M.—Malicious Animal Magnetism—accepted as one of the bases of Christian Science the Manichaean dualism.

Augustine, cast out by Monica, calmly went to live with Romanianus, and soon converted his host. Then Monica had a dream. She was on a see-saw, and a luminous young man came to her and smiled at her. She was crying, and the shining adolescent asked the cause of her tears. She explained that she was fearful of Augustine's perdition. The young man said, "Don't be afraid; where you are, he will be," and suddenly she saw Augustine sitting beside her on the see-saw. Augustine said the dream meant Monica would become a Manichaean. "No," Monica said, "he didn't say I would be where you are, but that you would be where I am." Monica tried appealing to the local Catholic Bishop, who wisely refused to tackle the brilliant, bad boy. Bored by Monica's constant miauing, the bishop prophesied: "It is impossible that the son of such tears would be lost." Augustine at this time lost his best (male) friend, who died suddenly. Bereft, Augustine decided he couldn't bear Thagaste any more. Romanianus paid his fare and he returned to Carthage for the next nine years. Here he acquired an unnamed concubine, who bore him a son whom he named Adeodatus, "the gift of God."

One night Augustine decided to try his fortune in Rome; he had sent to Hierius, a powerful Manichaean there, his first book, a treatise on the Beautiful. In Carthage the Manichaeans were beginning to be persecuted by the Catholics; time to move. Monica tried to dissuade him, as did his mistress. Monica followed him to his ship; it was waiting for a wind, and Augustine persuaded his mother to take a little sleep in a nearby chapel. As soon as she dropped off, he got on board, and before morning, before she woke, he was gone.

A penniless professor in Rome, belonging to a proscribed sect, Augustine did not have an easy time of it. He collected a few students, but they left him without paying. So he decided to apply for the Chair of Rhetoric in Milan. Thanks to his Manichean friends, who intrigued with the pagan Prefect of Milan, Symmachus, Augustine got the job. He was now thirty. Arrived in Milan, he went to pay his respects to St. Ambrose, the Catholic bishop. But, just as the Manichaean bishop in Rome had disappointed him by his gross peasant ways, so St. Ambrose disappointed Augustine by his icy upper-class politeness. "Ambrose received me," Augustine wrote, "in a sufficiently bishoply manner" (*satis episcopaliter*).

Hardly established in Milan, Augustine sent for his mistress and his son. He had acquired a small house and a garden. Soon Monica, unasked, joined them. On the boat, crossing from Africa, a storm arose. Everyone was scared, except Monica. God, she told the captain and the crew, has assured her they would arrive safely. Which they did. Augustine now had his mistress, his mother and his son living with him and a group of friends around him: Alypius, Nebridius, Romanianus, and Manlius, a rich friend with a lovely villa. Augustine began at this time seriously to consider marriage, and Monica found him a suitable girl, with a good dowry. Preparing for marriage, Augustine dismissed his mistress but kept her son. She was a Christian who quietly returned to Africa and never took another lover. Augustine, on the other hand, having to wait two years before his promised bride would be old enough to marry, took another mistress at once.

Augustine was by now sick of himself and of Manichaeanism. One day a Christian friend, Pontitianus, came to visit. A fellow-African too, like Alypius, who was sitting with Augustine, the three talked. Pontitianus left, accompanied to the door by Alypius. Meanwhile Augustine rushed out into the garden and fell on his knees under a fig-tree. A child's voice next door kept repeating "take and read, take and read." Augustine went back into the house and told Alypius his struggles were over: he would be baptized. Then he went and told Monica. She was not surprised, only pleased. Romanianus came once more to Augustine's aid. Would he tutor his son Licentius, again? Another pupil, Tygetius, was found, and the grammarian Verecundus, who had a villa in the suburbs of Milan, Cassiciacum. Why shouldn't Augustine spend the summer holidays there, with his pupils, and Alypius and Monica, and take care of the Verecundus estate?

The following summer, fall, and winter were the happiest times in the lives of Monica and Augustine, even though he had sole financial responsibility for his mother, his son, his brother Nebridius, his students, his friend Alypius—there were nine of them daily at table. Alypius took care of the farm, of sales and purchases, stock and produce. Monica "looked after us as if every one of us was her child, and served us, as if every one of us was her father." Yet she could still scold. One evening Licentius had gone to the john, and there was heard singing a verse from a psalm. Over and over. Monica, shocked, told him off when he came out. But he replied, "Suppose that an enemy had shut me up in that place, or that I was overcome with sickness and dying there: should I not still give God praise and sing Him psalms?" Augustine agreed with his pupil, not his mother. Another time Augustine couldn't sleep. He and his pupils slept in the same room. He wanted to talk, so he listened hopefully. Then he heard Licentius knocking a piece of wood against his bed to chase away the mice. Augustine, delighted, asked: "Why are there intermittences in the course of a stream? Do they obey a secret law?" Then Trygetius, now awake, joined in the talk, which lasted until daylight.

Sometimes Monica would come into the room where they were all talking, Augustine, Alypius, his brother, cousins, etc. She would announce dinner was ready, and then Augustine would invite her to remain with them. Embarrassed, she would refuse. But Augustine told her, "You love truth even more than you love me—and the Lord knows how much you love me. How can I not call myself your disciple?" Monica, now even more embarrassed, told him, "You've never before told such awful lies." The tradition of Socrates talking with his disciples under the plane trees of Illisus ended with Augustine under the chestnut trees of Cassiciacum.

The group at Cassiciacum only broke up at Easter 387 when, on April 25, Augustine, his son Adeodatus, and his friend Alypius were baptized by St. Ambrose. The legend that the *Te Deum* (We Praise Thee, O God) was written by the two of them together on that occasion is, alas, but a legend. The baptism over, they all prepared to return to Africa: Augustine's one idea was to go back there, with his mother, friend and son, and lead a monastic life in his native land. After he had resigned his job, they set off. When they got to Ostia, they had to wait for a boat going to Africa and stayed with some Christian friends. There, one day, Augustine and Monica were looking out of a window into a garden. They had been talking of earthly things, including the sky. It was evening, and Augustine wrote, "We were admiring the beauty of your works, my God, and then we lifted out hearts higher, and we reached our souls, but passed beyond them to reach, o Lord, to that region of inexhaustible abundance where you feed Israel eternally with the bread of truth. As we talked, and, as starving, we sought to reach that divine region, with a leap of our heart, we did reach it for a moment. Then sighing we fell back, and returned to these movements of our lips, that human mortal speech, which has a beginning and an end."

Then Monica said: "Son, nothing more in this life has any charm for me. I don't know, indeed, what I'm doing here, nor why I am still here." Five or six days later, she fell ill with fever. Coming to after having lost consciousness, she said, "You will bury your mother here." Navigius, her devoted elder son, replied "No, mother—you'll recover. You'll see your own country again; you won't die in a strange land." But she turned to Augustine and asked him, "Do you hear what he says?" Then to them both she said, "Bury this body wherever you will, and don't bother about it. All I ask of you is that, wherever you may be, you will remember me at the Lord's altar." She died on the ninth day of her illness, at the age of 56.

ST. RADEGUND
(523–587)

For woman, the ways to God have always been an assertion of her freedom: freedom to lead the kind of life she liked, but also freedom from the total control of the male, whether father or husband. Certainly, in Christianity, the woman religious was to some extent generally controlled by priest, bishop or confessor, but from its beginning the Church upheld the absolute right of both men and women to choose and to change their confessor. When the barbarians took over the decomposing Roman Empire, the lives of both men and women became, more perhaps than at any other time in the history of the West, nasty, brutish and short. So it is not surprising that many women sought the cloister as an agreeable alternative to life in courts or castles. Peasant women had no choice, and the bourgeoisie arose only when the towns began to be safe, after the Church had established some sort of order, a time that varied from locality to locality, not merely from country to country.

Initially, Christianity spread through the Roman Empire largely because of great Roman ladies who, converted to the new faith, converted their husbands and freed their slaves. So too, after the fall of the Roman Empire, the barbarians were often converted by their wives. Queen Clothilda, for example, the wife of the Frankish king Clovis, disapproved of the pagan gods because of their indecent behavior. She was Christian and urged Clovis to worship the one God who had ceated all things out of nothing. Clovis said "nonsense," yet

39

allowed his first son to be baptized. The infant died in his baptismal robes, and when another son was born, Clovis declared baptism would kill him too, but Clothilda prayed and the child survived. Fighting the Alemanni (Germans), Clovis was about to be beaten. He prayed: "Jesus Christ, Clothilda says thou art the Son of the living God and can give me a victory. If you do, I will be baptized." Jesus Christ obliged, and Clovis was baptized by St. Remi of Rheims, who told him, "Bend your neck. Burn what you worshipped, and worship what you burned." He then anointed Clovis with the holy oil, and thereafter all the kings of France were anointed at Rheims. Three thousand of Clovis' army were baptized with him. It was another queen, Theodolinda, who induced her Lombard Arian husband, Agilulf, to accept Nicene orthodoxy at the time of Pope St. Gregory I.

In this brutal age, St. Radegund shines out, as much for her sense as her sanctity. She was the daughter of the Thuringian King Berthar, and was taken prisoner by the Franks when they overran her country. King Lothar, a son of that Clovis whose conversion to Christianity provided Christ with one of his less pleasing followers, received her in booty, killed Berthar and so many other Thuringians that, according to Legend, the river Unstrut was piled high with corpses and the Franks walked over them as though over a bridge. Lothar got Radegund as part of his booty, and in 540 married her. She had attempted to escape but had been caught. Lothar, after fifteen years of married life, killed Radegund's brother as he had killed her father previously. That same day she left him, with his permission, and withdrew to her villa of Saix in Poitou, where she took the veil of a deaconess of St. Medard, then built herself an abbey near Poitiers, which was very civilized. The nuns were encouraged to take baths, to play dice and to have male visitors. When King Chilperic wanted his daughter by Audovera, Basina, disposed of, he shut her up in Radegund's convent; later he wanted to send Basina to Spain to marry, but Basina was unwilling, and the blessed Radegund backed her up. "It is not seemly," she declared, "for a nun dedicated to Christ to turn back once more to the sensuous pleasures of the world."

St. Radegund, who wrote poetry, is best known and remembered for her friendship with the last, and one of the best, silver Latin poets, Venantius Fortunatus, who came from Italy to the court of King Sigibert in 566. He was a cleric and, later in life, a bishop. He wrote a large number of letters, and among his correspondents was the Patriarch Dynamius of Marseilles. His letters to St. Radegund are amusing and quite worldly. He retired to her monastery of St. Croix (Holy Cross) at Poitiers and wrote for her two of the greatest Latin hymns still in use. The occasion was St. Radegund's sending to the East for "pieces of wood from the true cross and for relics of the Holy Apostles and other martyrs." She had King Sigibert's written permission to do this. The churchmen set out and eventually they brought back some relics. As soon as these arrived, the Queen asked Bishop Maroveus if he would deposit them in her nunnery with all due honor and a great ceremony of psalm chanting. He refused point-blank; instead, he climbed on his horse and went off to visit one of his country estates. Then the Queen wrote a second time to Sigibert, begging him to order one of his bishops to deposit the relics in the nunnery with all the honor due to them, in compliance with her vow. Sigibert deputed Saint Eufronius, bishop of Tours, to do what Radegund had asked. Eufronius came to Poitiers with his clergy. Maroveus deliberately stayed away, while Eufronius deposited the sacred relics in the nunnery with much chanting of psalms, with candles gleaming and with great burning of incense"[1] The two hymns Venantius Fortunatus wrote for the occasion are *Vexilla regis prodeunt* ("the royal banners forward go, the Cross shines forth in mystic glow"), still used on Palm Sunday, and the Good Friday hymn with the splendid refrain: *Crux fidelis, inter omnes arbor una nobilis* ("Faithful cross, above all other, one and only noble tree").

Since Radegund got nowhere with her own bishop, she turned instead to Arles, from whence she and her nuns received the rule of Saint Caesarius and of the blessed Caesaria. The letter of St. Radegund to seven bishops announcing the foundation of her monastery follows.[2]

To the holy fathers in Christ and to the Lord Bishops, worthy occupants of their apostolic sees, Radegund of Poitiers [sends greetings].

In its first beginnings a new project such as this can only move forward towards fruition with any hope of success if it is explained in full detail to the common fathers, the physicians and the shepherds of the flock, and if it then gains their support. It can only be realized if in their loving kindness they are prepared to cooperate, if they give it the benefit of their valuable advice, if they support it in their prayers.

Some time ago, when I found myself freed from earthly cares, with Divine Providence and God's guidance, to the religious life. I asked myself, with all the ardour of which I am capable, how I could best forward the cause of other women, and how, if our Lord so willed, my own personal desires might be of advantage to my sisters. Here in the town of Poitiers I founded a convent for nuns. Lothar, my lord and King of glorious memory, instituted this and was its benefactor. When it was founded, I made over to it by deed of gift all the property which the King in his munificence had bestowed upon me. For the community which, with Christ to help me, I had myself assembled, I accepted the Rule in accordance with which Saint Caesaria had lived, and which in his loving care Saint Caesarius had drawn up from the writings of the holy Fathers to suit her very needs. With the full approval of the Bishop of this city and of his fellow-prelates, all of them holy men, and after proper election by our community, I appointed as Mother Superior the Lady Agnes, who became like a sister to me, and whom I have loved and brought up as if she were my daughter from her childhood onwards. I submitted myself in regular obedience to her authority, after God. The other nuns and I followed the example of the Apostles in making over to her by deed whatever earthly property we possessed at the moment we entered the nunnery, reserving nothing at all for ourselves, for we feared the fate of Ananias and Sapphira. However, since the affairs of human beings are unpredictable, and because our times and our circumstance are always changing, for the world is running to its end and some people now prefer to follow their own desires rather than the dictates of God, while I am still alive, and in full devotion, in Christ's name and with God to guide me, I send to you, apostolic fathers, this document in which I have set out all my plans.

Seeing that I have not been able to come to you in person, I make obeisance to you vicariously through this letter, throwing myself at your feet. I conjure you, in the name of the Father, the Son and the Holy Ghost, and by the awful Day of Judgement, just as if I stood before you, to ensure that no tyrant may stand in my way, but that the rightful king may crown my wishes. If perchance after my death any person whatsoever, either the bishop of this city, or some representative of the king, or any other individual, should attempt, in a spirit of malevolence or by some legal subterfuge, to disturb the community, or to break the Rule, or to appoint any Mother Superior other than Agnes, my sister in God, whom Saint Germanus, in the presence of his brother churchmen, consecrated with his benediction; or if the community should rise in revolt, which is surely impossible, and wish to make a change; or if any person, possibly even the bishop of the diocese, shall wish to claim, by some newfangled privilege, jurisdiction of any sort over the nunnery, or over the property of the nunnery, beyond that which earlier bishops, or anyone else, have exercised during my lifetime; or if any nun shall wish to break the Rule and go out into the world; or if any prince, or bishop, or person in power, or even individual from among the nuns themselves, shall attempt with sacrilegious intent to diminish or to appropriate to his or her own personal possession any part or parcel of the property which our most noble Lothar and the most glorious kings his sons have bestowed upon me, and which I, with his express permission and injunction, have made over to the nunnery, for which conveyance I obtained confirmation by letters from our noble lords and Kings Charibert, Guntram, Chilperic and Sigibert, by the swearing of an oath and the subscribing of their sign manual, or which others have donated for the saving of their souls, or which the nuns themselves have made over from their own property, may that person incur the wrath of God and that of your holiness and of those who succeed you, and may all such persons be shut off from your grace as robbers and despoilers of the poor. With you to block the way, may no change ever be brought about in our Rule and may no alienation of the nunnery's property be permitted.

With God to watch over me, on bended knee I commend my cause to those rulers and to those princes of the Church, in the name of Him who redeemed all peoples. May they dwell for ever in the Kingdom which has no end, together with the Defender of the poor and the Husband of all cloistered nuns, in whose name they protect the handmaidens of God.

I also beseech you, saintly bishops, and you, lords and kings omnipotent, and the whole Christian people, by that Catholic faith in which you are baptized, that, when God shall ordain that the time has come for me to die, my poor body shall be buried here, in this church which I have begun to build in honour of the Blessed Mary, Mother of God, where so many of my nuns have been laid to rest, no matter whether that church is finished or not. If anyone wishes or attempts anything to the contrary, may he incur the wrath of God, through the mediation of the Cross of Christ and of the Blessed Mary. I pray that I may be held worthy, with you to intervene for me, to find a resting-place in this church, with the nuns of my own community all around me.

With my face suffused with tears, I beg that this petition, which I have signed with my own hand, may be preserved in the archives of our cathedral church.

It was.

St. Radegund died on August 13, 587, and St. Gregory of Tours noted, "I myself was present at her funeral."[3]

There were other learned ladies at this time. Vilihuta, the Parisian wife of King Daganulf, studied letters, and was considered "Roman by her studies, barbarian by her birth." She died in childbirth at the age of seventeen. Brunehild, the wife of Sigibert, a Visigothic princess, was also educated, as was Bandinivia, who wrote a life of St. Radegund in Latin. In England, too, there were educated holy women, among whom were the daughter of Caribert, a Frank who married the King of Kent; Lioba, a nun of Wimborne, who had been taught to write poetry by Eadburg; and Eangythe and her daughter Bugga. There were also at this time great double monasteries, for men and women, headed sometimes by women; of these women abbesses, St. Hilda of Whitby in England and St. Gertrude in Gaul were outstanding examples. Even in the darkest of the so-called Dark Ages, monks and nuns had to be able to read and to follow the psalter. St. Caesaria wrote to St. Radegund, warning her that illiterate nuns were to be avoided at *all* costs!

NOTES CHAPTER 4

1   Gregory of Tours, *History of the Franks* (Harmonsworth, England: Penguin, 1974), p. 530.

2   *Ibid,* p. 535 et seq.

3   *Ibid.,* p. 481.

5

FATIMA AND RABI'A AL ADAWIYA

Mohammed (570–632), the prophet founder of Islam, was strongly supported in his mission by his first wife, an elderly widow, Khadijah, by whom he had his only child, a daughter, Fatima. Mohammed remained monogamous until Kadijah's death, then took several wives at once. He elevated the physical and spiritual status of women in Arabia by forbidding female infanticide, then widely practiced, and by insisting, in the Koran, that women be given dowries, and that divorced women and widows be provided for. The word "Islam" means "surrender," and a person who practices Islam is called a Muslim, "one who has surrendered" to God. The feminine form of Muslim is Muslimah. In Islam there is no such thing as an illegitimate child; each Muslim male is responsible for whatever child he begets, and every child is equally legitimate, whether the mother is a wife, a concubine, or a slave.

Fatima married Ali, Mohammed's most faithful disciple, and had two sons, Husain and Hassan. She died, after giving birth to a still-born third son, 75 days after Mohammed's death. The succession was fiercely contested. Some of Mohammed's followers sided with Omar, who became the second Khalifa (head) of Islam, while others thought the elder of Fatima's sons should have inherited. Husain and Hassan were put to death, and Islam broke into two factions, the Sunnis, or orthodox, who sided with Omar, and the Sh'iah, or partisans of the murdered "Fatimite" brothers.

Fatima became, and still is, a cult figure for the Shi'ites.

She has been elevated by them to a position not unlike that of the Virgin Mary in Christianity. She is the only "carnal" link between her father, her husband and her sons. Of her two murdered sons, Husain was poisoned, Hassan killed by the sword. After the birth of her still-born third child, Muhsin, seventy-five days after her father Mohammed's death, she refused to leave her tent and her mourning to make her vow of allegiance to Omar, the second caliph, who succeeded her father. She unbound her long hair in a supreme gesture of distress. After her own death, she was secretly buried, and she is the only woman to whom prayers are addressed in the "tawassul," the recourse to the imams. The Shi'ite prayer goes: "O our God, honor and salute, enrich and bless the glorious lady, the beautiful, generous and noble, the sorrowful, the sick, the immaculate, the persecuted lady of so many afflictions, during her brief existence here, secretly buried, publicly despoiled, her rank unrecognized, the queen of women, she of the great dark eyes, the daughter of the best of prophets, Fatima, the pious, the unpolluted, on her be the honors and the salvation of God." This prayer was traditionally ascribed to Nasir Tusi (d. 672). In Mecca, the room where she was born is still shown, and she is often invoked as a martyr. Fatima, at the meeting between the Prophet and the Christians called the Mubahala (still celebrated as a feast), was offered as a hostage by the prophet to prove his sincerity.

She is surrounded, throughout Shi'ite history, with miracles; before her conception, Gabriel brought a fruit from Paradise to Mohammed; she is invoked, or thanked, by women and girls who wish to obtain, or have obtained, favors through her intercession. Fatima gradually acquired many physical characteristics of the Virgin Mary: she is credited with having escaped menstruation or the loss of blood after childbirth, and some even say she gave birth through her navel. Many other legends involve Fatima: in the Umm al-Kitab (circa 1307) she is shown to Adam and Eve as a girl more beautiful than they, wearing a diadem (her father, Mohammed), two earrings (her sons) and a sword (her husband, Ali). She is, Louis Massignon concludes, the human hostage of the affirmation of the divine inaccessibility, in contrast to the Christians' Mary, the superhuman hostess of the divine immanence. (*Opera Minor*, Tome 1, p. 567.)

From Fatim's defenders, the Shi'ites, arose the Sufis, the Muslim mystics who came mostly from Persia (Iran); neither Mohammed himself nor most of his Arab followers were mystically inclined. Many of the Muslim mystics were persecuted. Some, like al-Hallaj, were put to death; he was crucified in 922 for having cried out, "I am He." But the one great female muslim mystic, Rabi'a, was never persecuted and died peacefully in her bed.

Rabi'a al Adawiya (752?–801?)

Rabi'a bint Esma'il al-Adawiya was born in Basra of parents who were very poor. The night she was born, there was nothing in her father's house, not ever a drop of oil to anoint the child's navel, no lamp nor clothing for her. Her father already had three daughters. His wife asked him to go and beg a drop of oil from a neighbor so she could light the lamp. The man had made a vow that he would never ask anyone for anything. So he went out, laid a hand on the neighbor's door, and came back. "They will not open the door," he told his wife, and she wept bitterly. Her husband went to sleep. He dreamed he saw the Prophet Mohammed. "Be not sorrowful," the prophet told him. "The girl child who has just come to earth is a queen among women, who shall be an intercessor for seventy thousand of my community. Go tomorrow to the governor of Basra. Write on a piece of paper the following: 'Every night you send upon me a hundred blessings, and on Friday night four hundred. Last night was Friday night, and you forgot me. In expiation, give this man four hundred dinars lawfully acquired.' " On waking, Rabi'a's father burst into tears. He wrote as the Prophet had bidden him, and sent the message to the governor by the hand of a chamberlain. "Give two thousand dinars to the poor," the governor commanded when he had read the message, "as a thanksgiving to the

Master for remembering me. Give also four hundred dinars to the shaikh who brought the message and adjure him, by God, to let me know whatever he may need." So Rabi'a's father took the gold, and bought all he needed.

When Rabi'a had become a little older, and her mother and father were dead, a famine came upon Basra, and her sisters were scattered. Rabi'a ventured out and was seen by a wicked man who seized her and then sold her for six dirhams. Her purchaser put her to hard labor.

One day she was passing along the road when a stranger approached. Rabi'a fled. As she ran, she fell headlong and her hand was dislocated.

"Lord God," she cried, bowing her face to the ground, "I am a stranger, orphaned of mother and father, a helpless prisoner fallen into captivity, my hand broken. Yet for all this I do not grieve; all I need is Thy good pleasure, to know whether Thou are well-pleased or no."

"Do not grieve,,' she heard a voice say. "Tomorrow a station shall be thine such that the cherubim in heaven will envy thee."

So Rabi'a returned to her master's house. By day she continually fasted and served God, and by night she worshipped standing until day. One night her master awoke from sleep and, looking through the window of his apartment, saw Rabi'a bowing prostrate and praying.

"O God, Thou knowest that the desire of my heart is in conformity with Thy command, and that the light of my eye is in serving Thy court. If the affair lay with me, I would not rest one hour from serving Thee; but Thou Thyself hast set me under the hand of a creature."

Such was her litany. Her master perceived a lantern suspended without any chain above her head, the light whereof filled the whole house. Seeing this, he was afraid. Rising up, he returned to his bedroom and sat pondering till dawn. When day broke he summoned Rabi'a, was gentle with her and set her free.

"Give me permission to depart," Rabi'a said.

He gave her leave, and she left the house and went into

the desert. From the desert she proceeded to hermitage where she served God for a while. Then she determined to perform the pilgrimage, and set her face towards the desert. She bound her bundle on an ass. In the heart of the desert the ass died.

"Let us carry your load," the men in the party said.

"You go on," she replied. "I have not come putting my trust in you."

So the men departed, and Rabi'a remained alone.

"O God," she cried, lifting her head, "do kings so treat a woman who is a stranger and powerless? Thou hast invited me unto Thy house, then in the midst of the way Thou hast suffered my ass to die, leaving me alone in the desert."

Hardly had she completed this orison when her ass stirred and rose up. Rabi'a placed her load on its back, and continued on her way.

A party of men once visited her to put her to the test, desiring to catch her out in an unguarded utterance.

"All the virtues have been scattered upon the heads of men," they said. "The crown of prophethood has been placed on men's heads. The belt of mobility has been fastened around men's waists. No woman has ever been a prophet."

"All that is true," Rabi'a replied. "But egoism and self-worship and 'I am your Lord, the Most High' have never sprung from a woman's breast. All these things have been the speciality of men."

One day Rabi'a's servant girl was making an onion stew; for it was some days since they had cooked any food. Finding that she needed some onions, she said, "I will ask of next door."

"Forty years now," Rabi'a replied, "I have had a covenant with Almighty God not to ask for aught of any but He. Never mind the onions."

Immediately a bird swooped down from the air with peeled onions in its beak and dropped them into the pan.

"I am not sure this is not a trick," Rabi'a commented. And she left the onion pulp alone, and ate nothing but bread. Rabi'a had gone one day into the mountains. She was soon surrounded by a flock of deer and mountain goats, ibexes and wild asses which stared at her and made to approach her. Suddenly Hasan of Basra came on the scene and, seeing Rabi'a, moved in her direction. As soon as the animals sighted Hasan, they made off all together, so that Rabi'a remained alone. This dismayed Hasan.

"Why did they run away from me, and associated so tamely with you?" he asked Rabi'a.

"What have you eaten today?" Rabi'a countered.

"A little onion pulp."

"You eat their fat," Rabi'a remarked. "Why then should they not flee from you?"

Once Rabi'a passed by Hasan's house. Hasan had his head out of the window and was weeping, and his tears fell on Rabi'a's dress. Looking up, she thought at first that it was rain; then, realizing that it was Hasan's tears, she turned to him and addressed him.

"Master, this weeping is a sign of spiritual languor. Guard your tears, so that there may surge within you such a sea that, seeking the heart therein, you shall not find it save *in the keeping of a King Omnipotent*."

These words distressed Hasan, but he kept his peace. Then one day he saw Rabi'a when she was near a lake. Throwing his prayer rug on the surface of the water he called, "Rabi'a, come! Let us pray two *rak'as* here!

"Hasan," Rabi'a replied, "when you are showing off your spiritual goods in this wordly market, it should be things that your fellow-men are incapable of displaying."

And she flung her prayer rug into the air, and flew up on it.

"Come up here, Hasan, where people can see us!" she cried.

Hasan, who had not attained that station, said nothing. Rabi'a sought to console him.

"Hasan," she said, "what you did fishes also do, and what I did flies also do. The real business is outside both these tricks. One must apply one's self to the real business."

One night Hasan with two or three friends went to visit

Rabi'a. Rabi'a had no lantern. Their hearts yearned for light. Rabi'a blew on her finger, and that night till dawn her finger shone like a lantern, and they sat in its radiance.

Once Rabi'a sent Hasan three things—a piece of wax, a needle, and a hair.

"Be like wax," she said. "Illuminate the world, and yourself burn. Be like a needle, always be working naked. When you have done these two things, a thousand years will be for you as a hair."

"Do you desire for us to get married?" Hasan asked Rabi'a.

"The tie of marriage applies to those who have being," Rabi'a replied. "Here being has disappeared, for I have become naughted to self and exist only through Him. I belong wholly to Him. I live in the shadow of His control. You must ask my hand of Him, not of me."

"How did you find this secret, Rabi'a?" Hasan asked.

"I lost all 'found' things in Him," Rabi'a answered.

"How do you know Him?" Hasan enquired.

"You know the 'how'; I know the 'howless'," Rabi'a said.

Malek-e Dinar relates as follows:

I went to visit Rabi'a, and saw her with a broken pitcher out of which she drank and made her ritual ablutions, an old reed-mat, and a brick which she occasionally used as a pillow. I was grieved.

"I have rich friends," I told her. "If you wish, I will get something from them for you."

"Malek, you have committed a grievous error," she answered. "Is not my Provider and theirs one and the same?"

"Yes," I replied.

"And has the Provider of the poor forgotten the poor on account of their poverty? And does He remember the rich because of their riches?" she asked.

"No," I replied.

"Then," she went on, "since He knows my estate, how should I remind Him? Such is His will, and I too wish as He wills."

One day Hasan of Basra, Malek-e Dinar and Shaqiq-e Balkhi went to visit Rabi'a on her sickbed.

"He is not truthful in his claim," Hasan began, "who does not bear with fortitude the lash of his Lord."

"These words stink of egoism," Rabi'a commented.

"He is not truthful in his claim," Shaqiq tried, "who is not grateful for the lash of his Lord."

"We need something better than that," Rabi'a observed.

"He is not truthful in his claim," Malek-e Dinar offered, "who does not take delight in the lash of his Lord."

"We need something better than that," Rabi'a repeated.

"Then you say," they urged.

"He is not truthful in his claim," Rabi'a pronounced, "who does not forget the lash in comtemplation of his Master."

A leading scholar of Basra visited Rabi'a on her sickbed. Sitting beside her pillow, he reviled the world.

"You love the world very dearly," Rabi'a commented. "If you did not love the world, you would not make mention of it so much. It is always the purchaser who disparages the wares. If you were done with the world, you would not mention it either for good or evil. As it is, you keep mentioning it because, as the proverb says, whoever loves a thing mentions it frequently."

When the time came that Rabi'a should die, those attending her deathbed left the room and closed the door. Then a voice was heard saying, *O soul at peace, return unto thy Lord, well-pleased!* A time passed and no sound came from the room, so they opened the door and found that she had given up the ghost.

Herewith follow three of her prayers:

O God, whatsoever Thou hast apportioned to me of worldly things, do Thou give that to Thy enemies; and whatsoever Thou hast apportioned to me in the world to come, give that to Thy friends; for Thou sufficest me.

O God, if I worship Thee for fear of Hell, burn me in Hell, and if I worship Thee in hope of Paradise, exclude me from Paradise; but if I worship Thee for Thy own sake, grudge me not Thy everlasting beauty.

"I love you with two loves: a love aiming at my own happiness, and a love truly worthy of You. As for this love of my own happiness, it causes me to think only of You and of no one else. And as for the love that is worthy of You, it causes your veils to fall that I may see You. No glory to me, for the one or the other, but glory to You, for both the one and the other."

A life-long celibate, Rabi'a brought into Islamic mysticism the theme of divine love. She is buried near Jerusalem.

6

HROSTWITHA
(935-1002)

The earliest poet known in Germany was a canoness of the Benedictine monastery of Gandersheim in Saxony. She also wrote the first post-classical plays, in Latin, and Cardinal Gasquet (1846-1929) wrote of her eight legends in verse, six dramas, two historical poems, three prose prefaces and a précis in thirty-five lines of St. John's *Revelation*—all of which have survived—that: "they have a claim to an eminent place in medieval literature, and do honor to her sex, to the age in which she lived, and to the vocation which she followed."

Her abbess, the Princess Gerberga, five years younger than she, was the granddaughter of Henry the Fowler, a Saxon king, who ruled from 919–936. His son Henry, Gerberga's father, was Duke of Saxony; his brother was Otto I, who, after restoring order in Italy, received the Imperial Crown from Pope John XII and was the founder of the Holy Roman Empire which Gibbon so rudely apostophized as "neither Holy, nor Roman, nor Empire." Hrostwitha wrote a history of Otto's reign, the *Gesta Ottonis*. Hrostwitha probably entered the monastery in 935; later, she and Otto II, born that year, became great friends. The Abbess Gerberga who learned Greek (probably Hrostwitha did too) had enormous privileges: she had her own court of law, sent her men-at-arms into battle, coined her own money, and had a seat in the imperial Diet. The canonesses over whom she ruled took vows of chastity and obedience, but not of poverty: they received guests, traveled with permission, owned books and property, and had servants. Hrostwitha must have been of noble birth because no canoness was received who was not, and she was trained in Gandersheim to write excellent Latin verse and prose. She read Virgil, Ovid and Terence, and admired Boethius enormously. She describes how she came to write in a preface translated by Sister M. Gonsalva Wiegand, O.S.F.:

"Unknown to others and secretly, so to speak, I worked alone. Sometimes I composed with great effort, again I destroyed what I had poorly written; and thus I strove according to my ability, scarcely adequate though that was, none the less to complete a composition from the thoughts in the writing with which I had become acquainted within the confines of our monastery at Gandersheim: first through the instructive guidance of our learned and kindly teacher Rikkardis, and of others who taught in her stead; and then through the gracious considerations of the royal Gerberga, under whose rule as Abbess I am living at present. Though she is younger in years than I am, yet, as befits a niece of the Emperor, she is farther advanced in learning, and she it was who right kindly instructed me in those various authors whom she herself studied under the guidance of learned teachers.

Even though the art of prosody may seem difficult and arduous for one of my feeble sex, nevertheless, relying in my own strength, I have attempted to sing the songs of this little collection in the dactylic strains, solicitous that the slight talent of ability given me by Heaven should not lie idle in the dark recesses of the mind and thus be destroyed by the rust of neglect, I submitted it under the mallet of ready devotion, so that thus it might sound some little cord of Divine praise. Thus, though I had not the opportunity to achieve any other gain through use of that talent, it might at least be transformed into an instrument of value at the end.

Wherefore, gentle reader, whosoever thou mayest be, if thou art truly wise before God, do not hesitate to lend the assistance of thy correcting power to the poor page which lacks the skill of a master hand. If, however, thou findest something which is worthy of approval, give credit to God for this success and at the same time ascribe all the blemishes to my lack of care.

Let this be done, not in spirit of censure, but of kindliness; for the keen edge of censure is blunted when it encounters the humility of self-deprecation."

The Abbess Gerberga took great pride in the writings of her friend and pupil, Hrostwitha, and brought them to the attention of the scholars who visited the monastery, especially to the Archbishop William of Mainz, the illegitimate son of Otto I, and to her sympathetic young friend, Otto II. (later Hrostwitha was to write the life of the Ottos at the request of Gerberga.)

Hrostwitha's second preface is addressed to her readers, "Epistle of the Same to Certain Learned Patrons of this Book":

To you, learned and virtuous men, who do not envy the success of others, but on the contrary rejoice in it as becomes the truly great, Hrostwitha, poor humble sinner, sends wishes for your health in this life and your joy in eternity.

I cannot praise you enough for your humility or pay an adequate tribute to your kindness and affection. To think that you, who have been nurtured in the most profound philosophical studies, and have attained knowledge in perfection, should have deigned to approve the humble work of an obscure woman! You have, however, not praised me but the Giver of the grace which works in me, by sending me your paternal congratulations and admitting that I possess some little knowledge of those arts the subtleties of which exceed the grasp of my woman's mind. Until I showed my work to you I had not dared to let anyone see it except my intimate companions. I came near abandoning this form of writing altogether, for if there were few to whom I could submit my compositions at all there were fewer still who could point out what needs correction and encourage me to go on. But now, reassured by your verdict (is it not said that the testimony of three witnesses is "equivalent to the truth?"), I feel that I have enough confidence to apply myself to writing, if God grants me the power, and that I need not fear the criticism of the learned whoever they may be. So I will not deny that through the grace of the Creator I have acquired some knowledge of the arts. He has given me the ability to learn—I am a teachable creature—yet of myself I should know nothing. He has given me a perspicacious mind, but one that lies fallow and idle when it is not cultivated. That my natural gifts might not be made void by negligence I have been at pains, whenever I have been able to pick up some threads and scraps torn from the old mantle of philosophy, to weave them into the stuff of my own book, in the hope that my lowly ignorant effort may gain more acceptance through the introduction of something of a nobler strain, and that the Creator of genius may be the more honored since it is generally believed that a woman's intelligence is slower. Such has been my motive in writing, the sole reason for the sweat and fatigue which my labors have cost me. At least I do not pretend to have knowledge where I am ignorant. On the contrary, my best claim to indulgence is that I know how much I do not know.

Hrostwitha composed "arguments" to explain each of her plays. What follows is the "argument" to the play *Dulcitius*: The martyrdom of the holy virgins Agape, Chionia and Irena. The Governor Dulcitius seeks them out in the silence of the night with criminal intent, but hardly has he entered their dwelling than he becomes the victim of a delusion, under which he mistakes for the objects of his passion the saucepans and frying-pans in the kitchen. These he embraces and covers with kisses until his face and clothes are black with soot and dirt. Later, by order of Diocletian, he hands the maidens over to the care of Sisinnius who is charged with their punishment. Sisinnius in his turn is made the sport of the most strange delusions, but at length succeeds in getting Agape and Chionia burnt, Irena shot to death with arrows.

Here follows a sample scene (Scene II of Dulcitius), in Hrostwitha's own words, ably translated by Dr. Larisa Bonfante of New York University.

A courtyard of the great palace. A door, stage left, leads to the prison: stage right, the entrance to the kitchen and pantry building. This connects with the building in back, which has only a high window with a grating. Dulcitius and a half dozen soldiers are standing center stage. Dulcitius, the governor, is a hearty figure, lecherous in a conventional manner. His lack of dignity makes him take his soldiers into his confidence, and treat them with a familiarity quite out of keeping with his position as governor. The contrast with the quiet dignity of the girls is striking. At the moment, Dulcitius is very excited at the thought of the pleasure he will enjoy with all three girls. It is possible that rumors he has heard about exotic Christian practices and orgies lead him to believe they will be cooperative. He is rubbing his hands in anticipation.

DULCITIUS: All right men, quickly now, let's see these girls you have been guarding in this prison. *(Soldiers bring out the three girls, stage left. Having saluted, they stand at attention, impassive, during the whole scene).*
SOLDIERS: Here are the girls you called for, sir.
DULCITIUS: Good, very good! *(Looks at them*

each in turn). Oh, how beautiful, how delectable!
What perfectly exciting girls!.

SOLDIERS: They *are* lovely, sir.

DULCITIUS: I am overcome by the sight of
them!

SOLDIERS: We do not wonder, sir.

DULCITIUS: I must make them want me!

SOLDIERS: We do not believe you'll succeed,
sir.

DULCITIUS: Why not?

SOLDIERS: Because, sir, their faith is too strong.

DULCITIUS: Suppose I were to coax them, lure
them on with promises?

SOLDIERS: They don't care for things like that,
sir.

DULCITIUS: Well, suppose I were to scare them
with threats of dreadful punishment?

SOLDIERS: It would not make much difference
to them, sir.

DULCITIUS: What can I do, then?

SOLDIERS: We suggest you think of some plan,
sir.

DULCITIUS: *(Thinks a while. Then, as if struck
by a sudden idea).* I know. Lock them up in the
pantry—there beside the kitchen, where the cooking
utensils are kept.

SOLDIERS: Why in there, sir?

DULCITIUS: So I can visit them alone as often as
I want.

SOLDIERS: Just as you say, sir!. *(Take girls into
door at stage right. Dulcitius exit stage left.)*

Scene III

*The courtyard at night. Dulcitius enters stage left. He
wears a handsomely decorated robe. The soldiers are
seated in a circle, playing cards. They get up when he
enters.*

DULCITIUS: *(Whispers.)* What are our pretty little prisoners doing at this hour of the night?

SOLDIERS: They're keeping themselves busy singing hymns, sir.

DULCITIUS: *(Moving closer to stage right, door.)* Let's get a little closer so we can hear them. *(Sound of singing.)*

SOLDIERS: The sound of their high pitched voices carries even from afar.

DULCITIUS: Keep a light by the door. You wait for me here. As for me, I'm going in there to claim those kisses and feel about me those arms I've been craving for.

Scene IV

The pantry in which the girls are kept. Irena, from the window, sees Dulcitius going in the kitchen door.

AGAPE: *(Interrupting her singing.)* What was that noise outside the door?

IRENA: That wretched man Dulcitius is coming.

CHIONIA: *May the Lord help us and keep us safe!*

AGAPE: Amen!

(A pause, as they wait for him tensely. Then, as a loud sound of rattling and clattering is heard, Irena runs to the wall separating the two rooms, and looks through a crack at Dulcitius on the other side.)

CHIONIA: *Why is he clattering around the pots and pans?*

IRENA: Let me see. Oh, hurry, come, look through this crack. *(Steps aside to let Chione look; she in turn gasps in amazement.)*

AGAPE: *(Feeling left out.)* What is going on? What is he doing?

IRENA: *(Back at her crack.)* Look at him, the fool. He's completely out of his mind! He thinks he is embracing us!.

AGAPE: What is he doing now?

IRENA: Now he is fondling the pots and hugging the frying pans to his eager breast, bestowing long, lustful kisses upon them!

CHIONIA: *It's the funniest thing I have ever seen!*

IRENA: His face and hands and clothes are filthy, all covered with soot from the pots he's hugging. He looks just like an Ethiopian, all black from head to toe!

Hrostwitha, her beloved Abess Gerberga and Otto III (son of Hrostwitha's friend Otto II) "probably all died within a few months of each other during 1001–1002." Hrostwitha was then about sixty-five, and had spent forty-five happy years studying and writing. She is a splendid example of a truly fulfilled human being.

Bibliography

Bonfante, Dr. Larisa, trans., *Dulcitus*. New York University. Extracts published with her kind permission.

Haight, Anne Lyon. *Hrostwitha of Gandersheim: Her Life, Times, and Works and a Comprehensive Bibliography.* New York: The Hrostwitha Club, 1965.

7

HELOISE
(1100-1164)

In one hundred years, between 632 and 732, Islam conquered the lands between Persia and Spain: the Mediterranean became a Muslim lake, and the lands bordering it became, and remained for centuries, the Islamic world. As the Roman Empire and Roman civilization crumbled under the attacks of the Goths, the Huns, the Vandals, the Franks, the Burgundians and the Lombards, it was the Saracens, in North Africa and, above all, in Spain, who represented civilization, and through whom it gradually returned to Western, and finally, Northern Europe.

The eleventh century saw, in 1033, the election of Benedict IX as Pope, aged 12, who proceeded to lead "a life of infamy." It also saw, in 1037, the death of Avicenna, one of the greatest of Muslim philosophers. Averroes' ideas spread all over Europe, influencing Paris particularly. In Paris the most brilliant young teacher (professor) was at that time Abelard.

"Now there was living in that city of Paris a young girl called Heloise." So Abelard (1079–1142) introduces her in his autobiography.[1] She was sixteen when he first saw her, and was living in the house of her uncle, Canon Fulbert, a canon of Notre Dame in Paris. Abelard set out to seduce her. She had been raised by the nuns in Argenteuil and was their pride and joy; she knew Greek and Latin, and was as beautiful as she was wise. Abelard, almost twice her age proposed to her uncle, Fulbert, that he lodge in Fulbert's house and give

Heloise lessons. Fulbert doted on his niece (whom some say was a scion of the great house of Montmorency, others that she was the illegitimate daughter of a priest) and was delighted to accept. Abelard described what happened: "There was more kissing than teaching, my hands were at her breasts more often than on the book. No sign of love was omitted by us in our ardor, and whatever unusual love could devise, that was added too." As a contemporary wrote, "He that should have been her friend became her lover." And lazy. Abelard no longer bothered with his students, nor prepared new lectures: all he wrote were "pop songs" celebrating Heloise's beauty, and these were eagerly sung all over France by the teenagers, and carried all over Europe.

Abelard had no shame. He wrote that Fulbert entrusted his niece, "his lamb, to the care of a hungry wolf. He committed his niece to me, to be taught, and to be corrected, as I pleased, . . . likewise with a power of forcing her, by chastisement, to comply with my desires." Heloise, remembering later this first flowering of their love, wrote of his songs: "You possessed a tone of voice and a grace in singing, which gave you the control over every female heart. . . . Thus was my name soon carried to distant nations, for our loves were the theme of all your songs. Women envied my happiness." Everyone knew the lovers' story; finally Fulbert, last of all, twigged, threw Abelard out of the house, and reproached Heloise. She thought only of letting Abelard know "with exaltation" that she was pregnant. Abelard came by one night when Fulbert, quieted by his niece's meek acceptance of his reproaches, had gone to the country. Abelard brought a nun's robe to disguise her, and together they rode to Britanny, to Abelard's sister Dionysia, at whose home Heloise was delivered of their only child, a boy named Astrolabe. His son's birth made Abelard realize the sufferings of Fulbert, and his own shabby behaviour. "I felt indeed for his situation, and my shameful abuse of his confidence struck me on the heart."

Abelard went to see Fulbert, asked his forgiveness and offered any reparation he could make. He offered to marry Heloise, but secretly. Fulbert agreed, and Abelard went off to

Brittany to fetch Heloise, telling her "I am come to take you back to Paris to marry you." Heloise laughed, thinking he was joking, but he declared he had been reconciled to Fulbert. Heloise then told him: "I can never consent to be your wife," and explained why. "If you imagine this step will appease my uncle's anger, you are deceived. I know him well, and he is implacable. If to save my honor is your object, you mistake the means. Is it by disgracing you I must be exalted? What reproaches should I merit from the world, from the church, from the schools of philosophy, were I to draw from them their brightest star, and shall a woman dare to take to herself that man whom nature meant to be the ornament and the benefactor of the human race? No, Abelard, I am not yet so shameless." And she went on to describe the miseries of the married state, and to cite Socrates and Xantippe as sad examples. And then added: "The hidden feelings of my soul shall be open to you. I look for no wealth, no alliances, no provision, I have no pleasures to gratify, no will to service but yours . . . I vow to heaven, should Augustus, master of the world, offer me his hand in marriage . . . I would prefer to be called the mistress of Abelard, than the wife of Caesar." Abelard replied that his honor was pledged to Fulbert, it must be done. "If it must be done, it must, but God grant that the consequences of this fatal step be not as painful as the joys which preceded it were great," she said.

They arrived in Paris by night; the marriage took place in a neighboring church, privately, and Heloise returned to live with her uncle. But Fulbert's friends declared the marriage must be made known, and bruited it abroad. Heloise denied it, said it was a silly rumor. Now her uncle was really furious, and reproached Heloise for letting down the family, while she reproached him with breaking his word to Abelard. "Abelard is my husband," she told Fulbert. But Fulbert was so beastly to her that Abelard removed her to the convent of Argenteuil, where Heloise put on conventual dress. Fulbert was now convinced Abelard had stuck her there to get rid of her and resolved to rid himself of his incumbrance. As Heloise could not be dragged from the cloister (an act of sacrilege), Fulbert got five young friends to bribe Abelard's servant, who let them in at dead of night when he was asleep, and they castrated him in his bed. The news of this event made the rounds, and Abelard declared that the lamentations of his friends "irritated and disturbed me. The churchmen chiefly, and more than these, my scholars, pained me with their sighs and wailing. It was their compassion which afflicted me, and not the smart of my wounds. I hung my head and blushed." The selfish Abelard gives no indication of Heloise's reaction to his castration. Now he could hope for no clerical office, for, as he put it, "I had read in the book of Numbers, that such animals as myself were not to be received, even as victims, in the sacrifices of the Lord." No eunuch can, in fact, be a priest, though later, in Abelard's case, this rule seems to have been waived.

Abelard's only hope was the cloister; he could still be a monk. He "looked to the cloister as the only place which could bury his shame and hide him from the observation of mortals." But Heloise, he insisted, must go *first* into the cloister; she who had been his must hereafter belong only to God. Heloise obeyed. "It was not religion which called me to the cloister: I was then in the bloom of youth (she was not yet twenty) but you ordered, and I obeyed. . . . It seems you had the image of the patriarch's wife before your eyes: you feared I might look back, and therefore before you could surrender your own liberty, I was to be devoted. In that one instance, I confess, your mistrust of me tore my heart: Abelard, I blushed for you."[2]

When the day came, the Bishop of Paris officiated at Heloise's taking of the veil. Speaking the words the Roman poet Lucan wrote for Cornelia, she advanced to the altar steps and took the veil with which she covered her face, pronouncing distinctly the fatal vows which were to sever her from the world and Abelard forever.

It is difficult today, nearly nine hundred years later, to realize the impact of Abelard's mind and thought on his generation. He was completely contemporary; his sermons were directed against the corruptions of the Church of his day, against the superstitions of the monks, against the ambition of prelates "playing at power politics," while his theological and philosophical ideas were almost two hundred years in advance of his time. Instead of a savage God listing sins and lying in wait to catch and punish his creatures, Abelard taught God to be pure spirit, whose presence was manifest in His two great gifts to mankind, reason and love. As Friedrich Heer has written, "Abelard's intentions were creative; he was a master builder of man's inner kingdom, for him primarily a kingdom of the mind. . . . Abelard taught that everything depended on conscience, or inner conversion; intention and not deeds was what mattered."[3]

Abelard retired to the abbey of St. Denis, but his quarrelsome nature soon made it necessary for him to leave; he became a hermit at Troyes on land belonging to the Count of Champagne. Students flocked to him there, and built a neat convent of wood and stone which they called the Paraclete. In 1121, after Abelard's book on the Trinity was condemned unheard, he was elected abbot of St. Gildas, a remote monastery in his native Brittany. He was there for six miserable years, and his fellow monks, after doing everything else they could think of to get rid of him, tried poison in his chalice.

In 1128 Heloise was elected prioress of Argenteuil, but the convent was taken over by St. Denis, so Heloise and her nuns came to the Paraclete. Here they were abjectly poor, but such was the charm of Heloise and her nuns that very soon neighbours pitched in; one gave the nuns three farms, another gave fishing and forestry rights, and even Louis, the King of France, allowed them to buy and sell without tax. "In a single year," writes Abelard grouchily, "they acquired greater possessions than would have fallen into my hands had I labored a hundred years on the spot. . . . So many attractions did divine providence give to Heloise, that bishops viewed her as a daughter, abbots as a sister, and the laity loved her as a mother. Her piety, her prudence, her patience, her gentleness of character, commanded universal admiration. She appeared in public; the retirement of her cell was better adapted to holy meditation and to prayer, but her society was ardently sought for, and even strangers wished to be improved by her edifying conversation." Unfortunately, gossip found fault with Abelard's proximity to the Paraclete, and in his interest in Heloise and her nuns, so he moved again: luckily for prosterity, for the new separation occasioned Heloise's letters to Abelard, which are unique.

In her first letter Heloise reproaches Abelard for neglecting her and her nuns:[4]

You cultivate the vineyard of another, which you did not plant and which has turned to your own bitterness. Your admonitions are often fruitless, your sermons preached in vain. You who expend your care on another's vineyard, think what you owe to your own. You teach and admonish rebels, achieving nothing. In vain you cast before swine the pearls of your God-given eloquence. You who expend much thought on the obstinate, think what you owe to the obedient. You who shower gifts on your enemies, reflect how you are indebted to your daughters. The others apart, think by how great a debt you have bound yourself to me—that what you owe to a community of women consecrated to God you may pay with greater devotion to her who is yours in a manner that is unique.

With your superior knowledge you know far better than do we in our nothingness, how many long and serious treatises the Fathers of the Church compiled for the instruction, the encouragement and even the consolation of women, and with what care they compiled these. And so since we in this community are but the first frail shoots that you planted, it is astonishing that all this time (so forgetful of us are you) neither out of reverence for God nor love of us nor to follow the example of the Fathers of the Church have you attempted either by word of mouth when you were here or by letter when away to comfort me, harassed as I am and crushed by prolonged grief. And yet you know that you are bound to me by a debt which is the greater because you are united to me in the bond of the marriage sacrament; and that you are the more beholden to me because I have loved you always, as all know, with a love to which I have set no limit. You know, my beloved, the whole world knows, by what a cruel stroke of fortune that most shameful, public act of treachery, in robbing me of you, robbed me of my very self; and that I grieve incomparably more for the manner in which I lost you than for the loss itself. The greater the cause of grief, the greater the need of solace. And this must come from none but you, since you, who are alone the cause of my grief, alone can confer the grace of solace. For it is you alone who can make me sad, make me joyful or comfort me. It is you alone who owes me this immense debt. All your orders I fulfilled—to such a degree that, unable to gainsay you in anything, I found strength at a word from you to bring ruin upon myself. More than that (it is a strange story) my love reached such a pitch of madness that it robbed itself beyond hope of recovery of what it most desired—when straightway at your bidding I changed both my manner of dress and my purpose to prove that you alone were the master of my body and soul alike.

Tell me one thing, if you can—why, after our entry into religion which you alone decided upon, am I so neglected, so forgotten, that I have neither the encouragement of your words and presence nor the consolation of a letter in your absence. Tell me, I say, if you can. No, I will tell you what I believe and what moreover all suspect. It was lust not affection that bound you to me, the heat of passion not love. When, therefore, what you wanted ceased, all your show of tenderness vanished too. This, my beloved, is not merely my view but that of everyone. It is not a private but a general belief; not a personal sentiment but widely held. Would to God it were mine alone and that the love you profess could find someone to defend it, for that would comfort me a little. I only wish I could invent reasons to excuse you and in some measure conceal my dejection.

Listen, I beg you, to what I ask. You will see that it is a small favour and one that will cost you little. While I am robbed of your presence grant me at least through your words (these you have in plenty) the happiness of being with you. In vain can I hope to find you generous in deeds if you are niggardly in words. Up to now I had thought that I deserved much of you; for I have fulfilled all for your sake, persevering to this day only in obedience to you. It was not a vocation to the religious life but your bidding alone which made me submit as a young girl to the austerities of the cloister. If from you I deserve nothing, then my labour is indeed vain. For I can expect in return no reward from God, since it is certain that to this day I have done nothing for love of him. When you were hastening on your way to God I followed you. I did more, I went ahead. For me. While I enjoyed with you the pleasures of the flesh, many wondered whether I acted from love or from passion. Now the end is proof of the beginning. I have denied myself all pleasures to obey your will. I have kept nothing for myself except to be now, more than ever, yours. Consider then your injustice if when I deserve more, you give me less, indeed nothing at all, especially when it is small favour I ask and one easy to grant.

And so in the name of God to whom you have dedicated yourself I beg you that, in such way as you can, you restore to me your presence; by writing me, that is, some word of consolation, that thus refreshed I may give myself more readily to God's service.

Abelard's reply was chilly, to say the least. He asked her to remember in her prayers "him who, in a particular manner, is yours" and asked that at his death he should be buried at the Paraclete. "Heloise, live and farewell," he ended.

She replied:

I am surprised, my dearest Abelard, that, contrary to the usual style of epistolary correspondence, and even contrary to the obvious order of things, you would presume, in the very front of your salutation, to put my name before your own. It was preferring a woman to a man, a wife to her husband, a nun to a monk and a priest, and a deaconess to an abbott.—Decency and good order require that, when we write to our superiors or our equals, the names of those to whom we write, should have the first place. But in writing to inferiors, they are first mentioned who are first in dignity.

It was also to us a subject of much astonishment that, at the moment we expected consolation from you, then was our sorrow to be augmented. You should have dried our tears; but you rather chose to make them flow in larger streams. For which of us with dry eyes could read those concluding words of your letter: "But if, by the permission of heaven, my enemies should so far prevail as to take away my life?" &c. Oh, Abelard! how could your mind suggest such ideas; how could your hand write them?

She begged him not to praise her, since:

Before God, I am worthless. He is the searcher of hearts, and His eye penetrates into inmost thoughts. Through the whole course of my life, heaven knows what have been my dispositions! It was you, and not God, I was most anxious to please. My mind is still unaltered. It was not love of him, but solely your command, that drew me to the cloister. How miserable then my condition, if, undergoing so much, I have no prospect of a reward hereafter! By external show, you, like others, have been deceived.

So fascinating were the pleasures we once indulged; the thought of them cannot give me pain, nor can I efface their impression. Wherever I turn my eyes, in all their charms, there are they present to me. Even in my dreams the dear phantoms hover round me.

During the celebration of the august mysteries, when the soul, on the wings of prayer, should rise more pure to heaven, the same importunate ideas haunt my wretched soul: they seize every avenue to my heart. When I should grieve for what is past; I only sigh that the same pleasures return no more. My mind has been too faithful to its impressions: it holds up to the imagination every circumstance of pleasure, and all the scenes of past joys play wantonly before me. And it is not only what we did, the very places and moments we shared are so graven on my mind that I live the past over again in your company. Not even in sleep have I respite. Sometimes my thoughts are betrayed by a movement of my body; or they reveal themselves in an unguarded word. Unhappy am I indeed. Well may I utter the complaint of a stricken soul: "O wretched that I am! Who shall deliver me from the body of this death?" I wish I could add with truth what follows: "I thank God through Jesus Christ Our Lord" This grace, my most beloved, came to you unsought; when, in healing you from these torments by a single wound to your body, it healed many wounds in your soul. God who seemed to be cruel to you is proved to have been kind. He is the good physician who does not shrink from causing pain if it is to heal. For me it is harder: I am young and passionate and I have known the most intense pleasures of love—and the attacks directed against me are the fiercer in that my nature is frail.

They say that I am chaste, not discerning the hypocrite in me. They turn the purity of the flesh into a virtue, when it is a virtue not of the body but of the soul. I win some praise among men, yet merit none in the sight of God who tries the heart and the reins and seeks out the hidden places. I am thought religious in this age in which there is little religion not tainted with hypocrisy.[6]

To this, Abelard replied that Heloise had "subjoined her tiresome and never-ending murmurs against Providence in her letter to him." He went on: "In the admirable order of Providence, by the very means the devil aimed to destroy us, was our salvation effected. We were just then united by the indissoluble bond of marriage. It was my wish never to be separated from you and, at that moment, God projected to draw us both to himself.[7] He then sent her a prayer he had written for her to say. Heloise took the hint, and her next letter is about the right ordering of her nuns. "It is now, Sir, your duty,"[8] she admonishes him, "while God gives you life, to make such regulations for us as may be binding on the Paraclete forever. You, under him, are the founder of this house." Abelard's reply is "dry, uninteresting and prolix." After many further miseries, Abelard, condemned by the Church, found refuge in Cluny whose abbot, Peter the Venerable, treated him with the greatest kindness and courtesy.

Heloise wrote to Peter to ask after Abelard's health; he had already been sent to a nearby monastery, St. Marcellus, in a milder climate as he was very ill. Peter wrote to Heloise:[9]

It is not just now, that I begin to love you: I remember what my heart felt for you many years ago. When first I heared your name, and fame reported the progress you had made in human literature, I was but a young man. Then, I recollect, it was said, that a girl, though engaged in the world, was busied in the pursuits of science, and in the thorny paths of worldly philosophy. This was rare; but it was added that, neither pleasure nor amusements could draw her, by their allurements, from the objects of her laudable inquiry. And at a time, when almost the whole world, shamefully indolent, had ceased from these laudable pursuits, and wisdom could hardly find where to rest its foot, not only in the company of the softer sex, which had totally renounced her, but even amongst men, you Heloisa, by your exalted studies left all the women far behind you, and but few men could enter into competition with you. But soon your pursuits were turned to a better object: the gospels took place of logic, Paul of philosophy, and Christ of Plato; to the academic grove succeeded the retired cloister. Now were you truly called the philosophic maid.

Abelard died on April 21, 1142, in his sixty-third year. Peter the Venerable wrote to Heloise to acquaint her with the news. He described Abelard's exemplary behaviour, and goes on:

"He whose learning was vast . . . became the disciple of him, who was meek and humble of heart. He is gone to his master. And you, dear sister, who were once his wife, but whom afterwards a purer tie united to him, repose now in the certain hope that the day will come when he will again be given to you."[10] Peter himself stole Abelard's body from the monks of St. Marcellus, who had buried it with solemn pomp, and escorted it to the Paraclete. Peter also pronounced the burial service at the Paraclete, and Heloise wrote to thank him, the last letter of hers which is preserved:[11]

It was the kindness of heaven, most venerable father, which lately directed you to the Paraclete. We rejoiced, and we had reason to glory in your visit. Others may recount the benefits they have derived from your presence; but I am at a loss to express, nor can my mind well tell, how useful, and how pleasing, it was to me. You were with us in the month of November last, when in our church you celebrated the sacred mysteries, and the Paraclete you recommended to the charge of the Holy Spirit. The discourse you delivered to us is warm on our memories;

and never can we forget the treasure you intrusted to us, of the body of our dear master. To me, in particular, whom you honor with the appellation of sister, as a pledge of your love and sincerity, was a singular favor then also granted: when it shall please heaven to call me hence, thirty masses, you promised me, should be said at Chini, for the repose of my soul; and you said, you would confirm that promise to me by a writing under your own seal. I now request you to fulfill that engagement.—Send me also, if you please, another written deed, containing the absolution of Abelard, in distinct and fair characters, signed by self, which may be hung upon his tomb, And for the love of God and me, remember my son Astrolabius: if you can procure a living for him from the bishop of Paris, or from some other prelate. May heaven watch over you.

Peter's reply is kind and courteous:

"I was pleased, dearest sister, and not a little, by your letter. From it I perceived that my stay at the Paraclete was not really so transitory, for the recollection of it seems tenaciously fixed upon your mind. How kind and indulgent you were to me. Nothing seems to have been lost of all I did, or said, not only when my discourses were delivered intentionally for your instruction, but also when I conversed with you on common and familiar subjects. It is the regard you have for me which has given so retentive a power to your memory. . . . I trust then that I shall never be forgotten at the Paraclete, and that, to the father of mercies, you and your sisters will ever raise up your hands for me. The return I can make to you, that I daily do. Long before I knew you, you possessed a place in my heart, and since I have known you, that place has been enlarged by all the influence of the most sincere affection. The promise I made of the masses, I now execute, and send you, and with it you receive, what you requested, the absolution of Abelard, written and signed by me. As to Astrolabe, whom I adopt, because he is your son, I will do all I can to place him in one of the great churches. But the thing is difficult, for I have often experienced that our bishops, when application is made to them, make many difficulties, which are not easily removed."[12]

Abelard's absolution follows:

"I, Peter, Abbot of Cluny, who received Peter Abelard into the number of my religious, and who, having taken his body, by stealth, from the grave, delivered it to Heloise the abbess and to her nuns at the Paraclete, do now, by the authority of God and His saints, absolve him, in virtue of my office, from his sins. May he rest in peace."

Heloise survived Abelard for 21 years, "held in the highest estimation, a pattern of every Christian and monastic virtue." She herself wrote and introduced the rule of the Paraclete. She thus begins:

"I. We strive, as far as in us lies, to imitate the lives of the first Christians, by having all things in common. What is given to us, that we divide as far as it will go. If there is not enough for all, they are first served who want it most. II. Our dress is ordinary and simple, made of the coarsest wool and flax. III. We eat the bread that is laid before us, sometimes wheaten, and sometimes made of other grain. In the refectory our common fare is legumes, or such roots as the garden gives us. Milk, eggs and cheese are rarely served, and fish only when the kindness of our neighbours supplies us. Our wine is mixed with water. At supper only salad or fruit is allowed us, and when these fail, we bear it without murmuring. IV. Only the abbess and prioress have any right to command. Without their permission no one can presume to go out of the enclosure, or to speak, or to give, or receive, the smallest trifle. V. Would our strength permit us, we would till our lands and live by labor. But we cannot. We therefore call in the aid of lay-brothers and lay-sisters. Any alms, which the piety of the faithful offers, we do not refuse."[13]

She then lists the church services, from mattins through compline, attended daily.

On Sunday, May 17, 1164, Heloise died, and was buried in Abelard's tomb. Legend has it that as her body was lowered, his skeleton arms opened to receive her.

NOTES CHAPTER 7

1 All quotes from Abelard's *Historia Calamitatum*, unless otherwise indicated.

2 Joseph Berington, *The History of the Lives of Abelard & Heloise, With Their Genuine Letters* (Basil: J.J. Tourneisen, 1793), p. 143.

3 Friedrich Heer, *The Medieval World* (New York: Mentor Books, 1961), p. 113.

4 Elizabeth Hamilton, *Eloise* (Hodder & Stoughton, 1966), pp. 102–103.

5 Berington, *Abelard & Heloise*, p. 251.

6 Elizabeth Hamilton, *Eloise*, p. 105.

7 Berington, *Abelard & Heloise*, p. 270.

8 *Ibid.*, p. 293.

9 *Ibid.*, p. 157.

10 *Ibid.*, p. 159.

11 *Ibid.*, pp. 166–67.

12 *Ibid.*, pp. 168–69.

13 *Ibid.*, pp. 226–27.

LALLA YOGISWARI
(1379?–?)

Lalla Yogiswari lived in India near the end of the four-teenth century. She was married and from a good family, but her mother-in-law detested her and tried to starve her. There is a saying that "whether they killed a big sheep or a small one, it was all the same. Lalla always had a stone for her dinner." For when she dined in the presence of others, her mother-in-law put a lumpy stone on her platter and thinly covered it with rice, so that it looked like quite a big heap. The mother-in-law tried to persuade her son, Lalla's husband, that Lalla was unfaithful to him, but when he followed her to what his mother said was an assignation, he found Lalla at prayer. Finally her mother-in-law managed to drive Lalla, in rags, from the house. Lalla then adopted a Kashmiri saint called Sed Boy as her *guru*, and went about the country sing-ing and dancing, half naked. One day she saw a famous con-temporary Muslim saint, Sayyid Ali Hamadani, who was in-fluential in converting Kashmir to Islam. Saying "I have seen a man" Lalla fled into a nearby baker's shop, jumped into the blazing oven, and disappeared. Legend said the Sayyid fol-lowed her, and asked the baker's wife if any woman had come into the shop, but the baker's wife said no. Suddenly Lalla jumped out of the oven, dressed in the green garments of Paradise.

Lalla's poems and sayings are still quoted verbatim in Kashmir, and she is still highly revered there. The most ex-traordinary story current about her is that before her birth, she, in another incarnation, had borne a son, and was dying in childbirth. She told the priest who was at her deathbed that she would be born again, and marry her own son, after six births as various animals. At the age of twelve, she told the same priest, who came to marry her to her own son, the same story: her former husband had married a shrew, and that is how she came to have such a horrible mother-in-law!

In some of her most famous poems, she relates her own spiritual odyssey; she wandered far and wide seeking truth, and made many pilgrages. All in vain. Then suddenly she found, in her own soul, her Self, and learned that this Self and the Supreme Self were one. Specimens follow here:

I, Lalla, first as a cotton bloom
    Blithely set forth on the path of life.
Next came the knocks of the cleaner's room
    And the hard blows of the carder's wife.

Gossamer from me a woman spun,
    Turning me about upon her wheel;
Then on the loom was I left undone,
    While the kicks of the weaver I did feel.

Cloth now become, in the washing stone,
    Washermen beat me to their content;
Whitened me with earths, and skin and bone
    They cleaned with soaps to my wonderment.

Tailors then with scissors worked on me,
    Cut me and finished me, piece by piece;
Garment at last, as a soul set free,
    Found I the Self and attained release.

Hard is the way of the Soul on earth
    Ere it may reach the journey's end.
Hard is the path of life in each Birth,
    Ere thou cans't take the hand of the Friend.

Absorbed within Thyself, Thou remainedst hidden
   from me.
The livelong day I passed seeking for 'me' and 'Thee'.
When I beheld Thee in my Self.
I gave to Thee and to my Self the unrestrained rapture
   of (our union).

My body befouled I with mud, and Thou remainedst
   hidden from me.
The livelong day I passed seeking for mud.
When I beheld the mud upon my body,
I gave my body the unrestrained rapture (of union)
   with the mud.

For a moment saw I a river flowing.
For a moment saw I no bridge or means of crossing.
For a moment saw I a bush all flowers.
For a moment saw I nor rose nor thorn.

For a moment saw I a cooking-hearth ablaze.
For a moment saw I nor fire nor smoke.
For a moment saw I the mother of the Pandavas.
For a moment saw I an aunt of a potter's wife.

But pleasures are like poppies spread,
You seize the flower, its bloom is shed;
Or, like the snow-fall in the river,
A moment white, then melts for ever.

9

ST. JOAN OF ARC
(1412-1431)

The greatest heroine in French history was born of prosperous Lorraine peasants, Jacques Tarc and Isabeau Romée, on January 6, 1412, in Domremy. Jeanne was baptized in Domremy Church, and learned the Pater, Ave and Credo from her mother, who also taught her to sew and spin. She never learned to read or write, but could sign her name. She went to confession every year to her parish priest, took communion at Easter and fasted all the days of Lent. She had two brothers, Pierre and Jean, who joined her after her mission was established. Her father represented his village in 1427, and she had a first cousin from whom she took her male clothes, so he must have had spare garments to provide. She was probably stocky, had black hair and was sunburned. The best any chronicler ever said of her looks was that she was "passably good-looking." She must have been surprisingly strong; she could stay six days in the saddle without taking off a single piece of armour and rode over three thousand miles on horseback in under two years. She had a well-formed body, said the Duc d'Alençon, who often slept beside her, but he added she never "aroused any carnal desire in him." When Robert de Baudricourt, before he admitted Joan's mission, suggested his men might take their pleasure of Joan, "desire left them."

The Hundred Year War was already eighty years old when Joan appeared on the scene. For eighty years the Kings of England had been attempting to conquer all of France in order to unite both crowns under the English sovereign. By the fact that William, Duke of Normandy, conquered England in 1066, Normandy was a fief of the English crown. By Matilda's (William's grand-daughter) marriage to Geoffroy of Anjou, her son Henry II acquired Maine, Anjou and Touraine; by Henry II's marriage to Eleanor of Aquitaine, he added Gascony, Poitou and, by conquest, Flanders, Paris, Artois and Picardy. France was moreover also in the midst of a civil war. In 1407, Louise d'Orleans had been assassinated by his cousin John of Burgundy, who himself was assassinated in 1419. Meanwhile, at the battle of Agincourt, the young Duke of Orleans was taken prisoner and shut up at Windsor, and by the Treaty of Troyes, in 1420, Henry V of England agreed to marry Catherine, daughter of the mad French king Charles VI and his wife, Isabeau of Bavaria. Isabeau was so dissolute that she declared her son, the Dauphin, a bastard, and he was written out of the succession. Instead, the son of Catherine of France and Henry V of England was to succeed to both crowns. This the Armagnacs (the Orleanist party) would not accept. The Dauphin was at this time 19 and had in his favor the south of France (except Guyenne, which was English) and his mother-in-law, Yolande d'Aragon. The Duke of Burgundy and his followers were collaborating with the English.

Two years after the Treaty of Troyes, Henry V died, and two months later, in October, 1422, Charles VI. That left a baby nine months old and a boy of nineteen as the rival kings of France. The baby, Henry VI, could only claim the throne of France through the female line; this claim was contrary to the Salic law, which forbade succession through women. Charles VII (as the uncrowned Dauphin claimed to be) was branded illegitimate by the English, the Burgundians and by his own mother, although his claim, were his legitimacy accepted, was valid.

At this time, France was the biggest Christian state, with a population of more than fifteen million people. Most of these people lived in the country; Paris, the biggest city, had a population of 100,000. The armies marching around and fighting such battles as Agincourt were small: some 25,000

French against 13,000 English. All spoke French; only in the south was another langauge, the *langue d'oc*, spoken. Travel was slow, horseback the fastest means except water; it took two days to go from Avignon to Lyons, four from Lyons to Orleans. From Vaucouleurs to Chinon, Joan and her companions, riding mostly at night, travelled a week and a half.

Joan, though before her judges she boasted of her skill with the spindle, denied having accompanied her father's cattle or sheep into the fields. Sometimes, when her parents thought she was in the fields, she was praying at the shrine of Our Lady of Bermont. One day, when she was twelve, a boy came up to her as she was playing with her companions and told her to go home, because her mother needed her. She went, but her mother told Joan she had not sent for her. Joan started to go back, when a "luminous cloud" appeared, and she reported hearing a voice say:

"Joan, you are destined to lead a different kind of life and to accomplish miraculous things, for you are she who has been chosen by the King of Heaven to restore the Kingdom of France, and to aid and protect King Charles, who has been driven from his domain. You shall wear man's apparel; you shall bear arms and become the leader of the army; all things shall be guided by your counsel." Then the cloud vanished, and the girl didn't know what to make of it. But the visions appeared to her daily, always saying the same thing.

For four years she told no one, with the exception of her priest. She decided, from the nature of his instructions to her, that the voice was that of St. Michael the Archangel. He told her to be a good girl, and that Saint Catherine and Saint Margaret would also appear to her, and that she must do as they said. Asked if St. Michael was "corporeally present," she said, of him and of the subsequent saints, that "I saw them with my bodily eyes as clearly as I see you," and when they left her, she wept and wished they had taken her with them. Asked at her trial if St. Michael was naked she replied "Do you think our Lord doesn't have the wherewithal to clothe him?" St. Michael had wings, she said, but asked whether SS. Catherine and Margaret had limbs or bodies, she said only that they smelt good and had beautiful crowns, and that she knelt before them, and embraced them around the knees. They appeared to her several times a day, and brought guidance and comfort. Meanwhile, her father had dreams that his daughter would go off with soldiers; he told his sons and their mother, "If I believed what I dreamed about her would happen, I should want you to drown her, and if you did not do so, I would drown her myself."

Joan now confided in her first cousin, Durand Laxart, whom she called "uncle," as he was much older than she. He lived with his wife near Vaucouleurs, the nearest place (about twelve miles away) to Domremy that was held by the Dauphin. Vaucouleurs was commanded by Robert de Baudricourt, who had married two wealthy widows in succession. Joan spent a week in 1428 with her "uncle" Durand Laxart, then about forty, and his wife Jeanne, when Joan was sixteen. How she persuaded her cousin to take her to the Governor of Vaucouleurs is itself one of the major miracles of Joan's astonishing career. The cousin's account of the visit is simplicity itself. "She asked me to go to Robert de Baudricourt who could cause her to be conducted to the place where the Dauphin was. The said Robert told me several times that I should take her back to her father's house, and give her a smacking." But when Joan got home it was war, not a hiding that awaited her.

Vaucouleurs was threatened by the Burgundians, and the inhabitants of Domremy took refuge within the walls of Neufchateau. Joan, her parents and their cattle spent two weeks here in exile. When she and her parents returned to Domremy they found their village and church in ruins. In January, 1429, Joan left Domremy and her parents forever. She went again to stay with her cousin, whose wife was expecting a child. She spent six weeks with her relations, and in that time was able to persuade Robert de Baudricourt that desperate situations needed desperate measures.

She acquired two supporters, Bertrand de Poulengy and Jean de Metz, both gentlemen soldiers in their thirties. Jean de Metz met her in the house of friends, in her poor red skirt, and she said to him: "I have come to this royal town (of Vaucouleurs) to ask Robert de Baudricourt either to lead or to send me under escort to the king. He takes no notice of me or of my words; nevertheless, before mid-Lent I must be on my way to the King, even if I must wear out my legs to the knees. There is no one in the world, neither king, nor duke, nor daughter of the King of Scotland,[1] nor any other, who can regain the kingdom of France; there is no help for the kingdom but in me. I should prefer to be spinning beside my poor mother, for these things do not belong to my station, yet it is necessary that I should go and do these things since God wishes that I should do them." Jean de Metz then took her hand and swore he would lead her to the king. When did she want to start? "Now, rather than tomorrow, and tomorrow rather than the day after," she replied.

Jean de Metz took her to Baudricourt, who had her exorcised. Joan told that "it was imperative she should go to the place where the Dauphin was," and asked him: "Have you not heard the prophecy that France shall be lost through a woman and shall be redeemed by a virgin from the frontiers of Lorraine?" Baudricourt now accepted her, and while waiting to go to Chinon, Joan went to Nancy because the Duke of Lorraine had asked for her to cure him. Her advice was to leave his mistress and return to his wife. Joan returned from Nancy to Vaucouleurs on February 12, told Baudricourt that the Dauphin had suffered a great defeat in front of Orleans that day and would suffer worse if he did not take her to him. On February 23 she set off at last for Chinon, dressed in man's clothes with a sword Baudricourt gave her, accompanied by a knight and four men. She was dressed in a black doublet, a short, dark-grey tunic, high boots and a black cap; she had cut her hair quite short. At Chinon, Joan recognized the Dauphin, who had concealed himself in the crowd. He kept her with him for six weeks; "publicly and secretly she spoke with everyone, but one cannot find evil in her but humility, virginity, devotion, honesty and simplicity." The King's confessor, Gerard Marchet, found only good in her, "*tout bien en elle.*" She told the king about the prayer he had made on All

Saints Day, 1429, when he agonized in doubt of his own legitimacy, and questioned his own right to the crown. "I tell you from God you are the true heir of France and the King's son," she assured him. This "secret" the judges at her trial could not drag from her, and it was the king who, long after her death, told his friends. The "weak, knock-kneed, pious little cad" as V. Sackville-West called Charles VII, was, according to Anatole France, "very ugly, with small grey wandering eyes, his nose thick and bulbous." After Joan had soothed his secret anxiety, she was given rooms within the precincts of the castle. She had a chapel to herself, and was allowed free access to the Dauphin. She was given the services of a page, but was examined by women and was "under constant surveillance." She told the assembled court that the English would be destroyed after Orleans had been relieved, that the Dauphin would be crowned at Rheims, that Paris would be restored to its allegiance and that the Duke of Orleans would be released from captivity. The first two prophecies were fulfilled by Joan's help; the last two, only after her death.

After her sex and her virginity had been established, she was given a suit of armour made for her by the king's armourer. Her standard was a representation of the world, with a protrait of our Lord and the word JESUS between two angels. For a sword, she asked for one that was hidden in the chapel of St. Catherine at Tours; no one but she knew of it. It was rusty and had five crosses on it, but the king's armourer fixed it for her. She kept it with her until one day she broke it across the back of a prostitute following the army, and it could not be repaired. She also had a small battleaxe and two rings given her by her family; one had JESUS MARIA engraved on it. Young Guy de Laval saw her set off for Orleans. "I saw her mount a great black charger, a little axe in her hand. The horse was making a great fuss before the door of her lodging and would not let her mount, so she said, 'Lead him to the cross' in front of the church on the way. And there she mounted and he never moved, as though bound. And then she turned back to her road and said, 'Go! Go on!' Her standard was furled and carried by a graceful page, and she had her little axe in her hand." The army left Blois on April 27, led by priests singing the *Veni, Creator*, followed by four thousand men, who included Joan's two brothers. She had made all the knights with her go to confession, and had told them they must leave their camp-following women behind. They obeyed, and La Hire even gave up his swearing.

On the evening of April 29, by torchlight, Joan entered Orleans in full armour on a white horse, her standard before her. She rode at the right hand of *"le beau Dunois,"* the bastard of Orleans. There was such a crowd pressed around her that a torch set fire to her pennant. Joan maneuvered her horse so skillfully that she put out the flame. The populace acclaimed her, and she was taken to her lodging, where she refused supper and would drink only a little wine cut with water. A child of nine, Charlotte, daughter of the treasurer, shared her bed. She had entered Orleans unopposed. On May 4 the French attacked with Joan leading them. They burnt and plundered the Bastille of St. Loup, killed one hundred fourteen English soldiers, and all the church bells of Orleans rang out the victory. Next day, Ascension Day, Joan said there was to be no fighting. She confessed and went to communion. On Friday, May 6, Joan led the attack and the English fled. Joan was wounded in the foot. She told her confessor at supper that the next day he must "stay near me all the time, for tomorrow I shall have much to do, more than I ever had yet, and the blood will flow from my body above the breast." The struggle for the fort of Tourelles lasted from 7 a.m. till 8 p.m. At midday, Joan was hit by an arrow just above her left breast; she was in pain and wept. The wound was staunched with olive oil and lard after she pulled the arrow out herself. The English were completely routed, and *Te Deum* of victory was sung.

Joan was taken back to her lodging, and her wound was dressed. "She refreshed herself with four or five slices of bread dipped in wine mixed with a great deal of water. It was all she had eaten or drunk all day." Joan then left Orleans and rejoined the Dauphin at Tours. He met her as she entered the city, standard in hand, on May 10. During the week of June 10–18, Joan with the Bastard of Orleans and the Duc d'Alençon attacked Jargeau. Joan warned d'Alençon, "Move from this place, or that piece of ordinance on the rampart will kill you." He did, and a few minutes later the Sieur de Ludes was struck and killed in that very same spot. It was Joan's second sight that most impressed her companions: to one, who was discourteous to her, she asked, "How can you speak like that, and you so near your death?" He was drowned the next day.

At Jargeau, Joan was mounted on the scaling ladder, standard in hand, when she was knocked backwards on the ground by a stone which first struck her flag, then her helmet. She jumped to her feet, crying out "Friends, friends, our Lord has condemned the English; they will be ours within the hour; be of good heart." The town fell to the French within the hour. The Earl of Suffolk was taken prisoner, and 700 English were killed. Joan and d'Alençon next took Meung, but let the town go free; then Beaugency, from which the English departed on June 17. Sir John Fastolf advanced on the French there with an army of 5,000 men, but was badly beaten at the battle of Patay, on June 18. Fastolf fled, and the English lost between two and four thousand soldiers. Joan and the Dauphin left Gien on June 29 and reached Auxerre on July 1. That city was spared on condition that it provided the French army with supplies. Joan and the Dauphin went on to Troyes, which gave in and was spared; then to Chalons, which received them in friendly fashion. Here clouds of white butterflies were seen around Joan's banner, and the following day Joan and the Dauphin entered Rheims.

Joan had insisted they go there, rather than to Paris, for the most important thing was for the Dauphin to be crowned king where Clovis had been. Until he had been crowned and anointed, no man could be King of France. They entered the town on Saturday, June 16, and in the splendid cathedral, then almost completed, at 9 a.m. on June 17, 1429, the Dauphin was anointed and crowned by the Archbishop of Rheims. Joan stood beside the king in armour, her standard in her hand. At last, he was the only true king. In five months Joan had raised the siege of Orleans, beaten the English in many battles and secured the crown for the Dauphin. She fell on her knees before the newly anointed king, and wept. This was her greatest moment; she had obeyed her voices, and they had fulfilled their promises and her prophecies. Unfortunately, the combination of her tender heart—she wept over the English dead—and her King's miserable nature, as unattractive as his physique, combined to lead Joan to the scaffold and Charles to ignominy. "He was poor; he was sometimes reduced to borrowing money from his cook"[2] and he was under the influence of "a quartet of advisers, two of them unscrupulous and despicable, one of them merely a cats-paw, and the fourth an obstinate, short-sighted old soldier."

Joan had written on the day of the coronation to the Duke of Burgandy to beg him to make peace. He, meanwhile, had sent envoys to Rheims to negotiate. So, instead of proceeding to Paris as was planned on June 18, four days were lost by Charles, "gullible, optimistic, and only too thankful for any excuse for delay," while the English sent an army to defend Paris. Joan was tired and dispirited. Riding between the Bastard and the Archbishop of Rheims, she told them she "wished God her Creator would allow her to lay down her arms and return to serve her father and mother." The king had given her money for her father, and at her request had remitted all taxes on her village of Domremy in perpetuity (demands ever therafter were cancelled with the words: *Néant, la Pucelle*.)

Joan and the king reached Soissons, then Compiegne, which the King refused to enter, concluding a 15-day truce with the Duke of Burgundy, who promised to deliver Paris to the French on the fifteenth day. Of course, he had no intention of doing this, but was merely playing for time. On August 17 the Duke wrote a rude letter to Charles VII, calling him a murderer who was implicated in the Duke's father's murder, and calling Joan a "disorderly woman dressed in man's clothes." Joan and the King were at Senlis on August 18; it fell into their hands, and Beauvais made its submission before they arrived at Compiègne, which welcomed them. On August 23 Joan and d'Alençon were installed at St. Denis; the King, playing a double game, remained at Compiègne for ten days negotiating with the Duke of Burgundy, signing another truce with him on August 28. D'Alençon threw a bridge of boats across the Seine and prepared to attack, but Charles had it destroyed by night. Joan and d'Alençon attacked Paris on September 8, but Joan's thigh was pierced by an arrow, and the attack was withstood by the Burgundians inside Paris. September 8 was a holy day, a feast of Our Lady, and Joan admitted later to her judges her regret at having allowed an attack to be made on such a day.

On September 18 Paris was included in a truce between Charles VII and the Duke of Burgundy. The army, for lack of funds, was disbanded, the royal government fell back into inertia, and d'Alençon, Joan's chief supporter, went safely back to his wife, as Joan had promised her he would. The King retired to Gien on the Loire, ordering Joan to join him there. This she did, leaving her armour lying at the feet of Our Lady's statue in the cathedral of St. Denis. Joan had been enobled by the King, and all her family and descendants, even female. But Joan remained, at 17, as simple as ever: when women brought their rosaries for her to touch she said "Touch them yourselves; they will benefit as much from your touch as from mine."

In December it was decided to attack La Chariet, but the French were defeated and the siege had to be raised. From December 1429 to April 1430, little is known about Joan's movements, except that at the end of March, Melun yielded to the French and she led the attack. And there Joan's saints came to her with bitter tidings: it was still Easter time, and they told her that before the feast of St. John (June 24) she would be taken prisoner. Joan begged she might die when captured and escape prison, but the voices made no reply. Joan reached Compiègne on the eve of the Ascension (May 23rd) and her troops had already got safely through the gates, when de Flavy, one of Joan's captains who was already inside, ordered the drawbridge raised and the gates shut. Joan, her brother and a very few men were left outside. She was torn off her horse by a Burgundian, and her brother and two knights were taken with her. The Duke of Burgundy was jubiliant; he met Joan, then wrote boastful letters to the Duke of Brittany and others.

Charles VII, her King, made no attempt to ransom Joan. She was shut up in the castle of Beaulieu, and tried to escape. She was then removed to Jean de Luxembourg's castle of Beaurevoir, where Jean's old aunt, his wife and his step-daughter were good to Joan. His aged aunt begged her nephew not to sell her to the English. Joan heard he was proposing to, and jumped from the flat roof of the castle, some seventy feet. She was found unconscious with a concussion but otherwise unhurt. Jean de Luxembourg then sold her to the English for 10,000 écus, and Joan was shut up in Rouen in an iron cage, heavily chained by her hands and feet and guarded by English soldiers who never left her by night or day. On May 26 the Vicar General of the Inquisition wrote asking the Duke of Burgundy to hand her over; at the same time, the University of Paris asked Burgundy to submit Joan to the judgment of the Church to be tried "for idolatry and other matters." Bedford charged Pierre Cauchon, the bishop of Beauvais and a devoted supporter of the English, to try Joan; Beauvais had lost his see through her, and personally loathed her.

The trial opened on January 9, 1431, with Cauchon presiding. Joan faced between 40 and 60 clerics. She was alone before her judges with not even a lawyer to defend her. She was examined on four points: her voices, the secret sign (or message) she gave Charles VII, the men's clothes she insisted on wearing and her submission to the Church. On February 21 there was the first public hearing. Joan asked to hear Mass, but Cauchon would not allow it. She knelt and with her two hands on a missal swore she would tell the truth but never tell the king's secret except to Charles her king. She complained of the irons on her hands and legs, but was told if they were taken off she would try again to escape. On Saturday, February 24, she declared she came from God, and had nothing more to do here; let them send her back to God from whom she had come. Asked if she were in a state of grace, she made the superb answer: "If I am not, may God bring me to it; if I am, may He keep me in it." She was asked if our Lord the Pope was the true Pope and she replied, "Are there two?" and asked to be taken to Rome and judged by the Pope: "You write what is against me and won't write what is for me." She was closely questioned as to magic practices in her village, and showed no interest or knowledge of them. Asked what she had done with her mandrake root, she said she never had one. She declared she had never killed anyone, in battle or out; when threatened with torture she told her judges she would retract anything she might say under torture. On February 27, 1430, she was asked how she had fared since the last questioning. She replied: "You see I am as well as I can be under these circumstances." Asked if she received the sacraments in men's attire she said yes, but never in armour. On March 14 she was asked why she had leapt out of the tower, and replied it was because she knew she had been sold to the English and would rather die than fall into their hands.

Asked whether she would submit herself in all her words and deeds, whether good or evil, to the determination of our holy mother, the Church, she replied: "I love the Church, and would uphold it with all my strength. It is not I who ought to be prevented from going to church or hearing Mass." And again she asked to be taken to the Pope for judgment.

Joan now fell ill, and the English were terrified she would die a natural death. "She must die only at the hands of justice, and must be burnt," Lord Warwick told the doctor who attended her. She recovered, and on May 24, 1431, she was preached to in public, being told her king was a heretic and a schismatic. Joan retorted "By my faith, I dare say to you and swear, on my life, that he is the most noble of all Christians, who best loves the faith and the Church, and he is not as you say." Joan was then told to be quiet. She was offered an act of recantation, which she signed with a cross. Cauchon ordered her taken back to prison. Warwick was furious. "The King is ill-served, since Joan has escaped," he told Cauchon, who said, "My Lord, do not trouble, we will soon have her again." And they did. She meekly put on woman's clothes as ordered, but her voices came back and she declared: "If I were to say that God had not sent me I would be damning myself, for it is true God did send me . . . . It was fear of the fire which made me say what I did."

On Tuesday, May 29, 1431, Joan was declared a relapsed heretic, and was "abandoned to secular justice, with the request that they shall act mercifully towards her." The bailiff of Rouen, an Englishman, without any further trial and without pronouncing any sentence against her, ordered that she be taken to the place where she should be burnt. When she was told what was to be the manner of her death she broke down, crying piteously, "Alas, that I should be treated so horribly and cruelly, that my whole body, never yet corrupted, should today be consumed and burnt to ashes—I would rather be beheaded seven times, than thus be burnt." Cauchon now came in to her prison and she said, "Bishop, I die—through you." She was lead to the marketplace, where three platforms had been erected, one for the judges, one for the priest, and one with a stake heaped around with wood. Before it was a board painted with the words: "Joan who called herself the Maid, liar, pernicious deceiver of the people, sorceress, superstitious blasphemer of God, presumptuous, disbeliever in the faith of Jesus Christ, boastful, idolatrous, cruel, dissolute, invoker of devils, apostate, schismatic and heretic." Joan prayed there for about an hour, and an English soldier gave her a little cross made out of two pieces of wood, which she kissed and put against her breast, under her gown. The English were getting impatient: "Well, priest," they called out, "do you mean us to dine here?" Then a tall paper cap, like a mitre, on it the words "Heretic, relapsed, apostate, idolatress," was put on Joan's head. After the fire was lighted she was heard to cry "Jesus" and John Tressart, secretary to the King of England, exclaimed: "We are lost; we have burnt a saint." She was seen naked, as the flames ate her clothes, and a chronicler noted: "Well or badly made, she was burnt that day." On June 8, 1431, Bedford informed the Emperor and the princes of Europe, in the name of King Henry VI of France, of the fate of the Maid.

On November 10, 1449, Charles VII entered Rouen as victor, and on February 15, 1450, the process of Joan's rehabilitation was begun, a purely political move, as her trial and condemnation had been. On June 11, 1455, Pope Calixte II accepted Joan's family's request to reopen her case, and on November 11 of that year her old mother, Isabeau Romée, supported by her son, asked justice for her daughter in the Cathedral of Paris. On July 7, 1456, the Pontifical Commissioners, under the presidency of Jean Jouvenal, Archbishop of Rheims, stated: "We declare that the trial and the sentence were fraudulent, calomnious, full in iniquity and contradictions, manifestly erroneous in fact and in law, including the abjuration, the execution and all its consequences, and all these are, and shall be, nul, invalid and without authority." On May 16, 1920, over five hundred years after her death, Joan of Arc was canonized by the same church that excommunicated her as a heretic and handed her over to the secular authorities to be burnt.

10

ST. TERESA OF AVILA
(1515–1581)

Teresa de Cepeda y Ahumada, the only female Doctor of the Church, was born on March 28, 1515, at Avila in Spain. Her father, Don Alonso Sanchez de Cepeda, had three children by his first wife; by his second, Doña Beatriz Davila y Ahumada, he had nine, of whom Teresa was the third. Teresa's parents were well-born and prosperous, though not rich. Teresa wrote of her father that he was a man of great charity to the poor, and "he could never be brought to keep slaves, because of his compassion for them." Her mother, she wrote, was extremely beautiful, but so virtuous she never took the slightest account of her beauty. As a child, Teresa and her nearest brother in age, Rodrigo, whom she "most loved," used to read lives of saints together, and discuss how they could become martyrs. One day the two children "left Avila and went on over the bridge, until they were met by an uncle who took them back home to their mother, greatly to her relief, she having searched for them everywhere with great anxiety." When they saw they could not go anyplace where they would be martyred, "we decided to become hermits, and we used to build hermitages, as well as we could, in an orchard we had at home." When Teresa played with other little girls, she used to love building convents and pretending they were nuns. Teresa loved reading; "unless I had a new book, I was never happy," she wrote.[1] And she and Rodrigo would talk about the pain and the glory that would last "for ever"; they would repeat again and again: "for ever-ever-

ever." Rodrigo emigrated to South America in 1535, and in 1537 he died fighting the Indians on the banks of the Rio de la Plata.

In 1528, when Teresa was thirteen, her mother died. In tears, she went to a statue of Our Lady (now in Avila Cathedral) and asked her to be a mother to her. About the time her mother died and her sister married, Teresa began "to take great trouble with her hands and hair," and had an older woman friend with whom she enjoyed gossiping. But these vanities lasted barely three months, before Teresa was taken to the Augustinian convent of Our Lady of Grace, just outside the city walls of Avila, and was there entered as a boarder.

Teresa was her father's favorite, and for the first week at the convent she suffered a great deal, as also from her removal from the older girl with whom, she wrote, "my intimacy was of such kind that I thought it might end satisfactorily with her marriage." Teresa remained in this convent for a year and a half, until a serious illness forced her return to her father's house. On her recovery she went to stay with her married sister, who was "so fond of me that if she had her way, I should never have left her." Her sister's husband too showed her every kindness. And an uncle, Don Pedro, a brother of Teresa's father, lived near her sister. He was a widower, and in his old age he became a friar. He made Teresa read aloud to him from good books, and "though I did not much care for his books, I acted as though I did," she wrote. She now began to suffer from serious fainting fits and fevers; her health was always poor. She read St. Jerome, who gave her the courage to tell her father that she intended to become a nun. Telling him this was going almost as far as taking the habit, "for my word of honor meant so much to me" that she would never turn back from anything she had said she would do. But her father was so fond of her he would not hear of it; the most Teresa could persuade him to allow was that she could do what she liked after his death.

Meanwhile, she had persuaded her younger brother Antonio to become a Dominican (poor health compelled him to

leave the order, and he died in the Indies in 1546). He and
Teresa set out very early one morning for the convent where
Teresa's friend "of whom I was so fond" lived. Teresa took the
habit on November 2, 1536, and made her solemn profession
a year later, when she was twenty-two. God "converted the
aridity of my soul into the deepest tenderness. Everything
connected with the religious life caused me delight." Even
sweeping floors brought her a new joy, which amazed her.
But the change in her life and diet affected her health, and
"though my happiness was great, it was not sufficient to cure
me." She had increasingly frequent fainting spells, in addition
to heart-trouble, and seemed rarely fully conscious. Her
father had her taken from the convent to stay with a half-
sister, where Teresa suffered the greatest tortures from the
drastic remedies applied to her. She saw again the uncle to
whom she had read aloud. He gave her Francisco de Osuna's
Third Alphabet, which describes the prayer of recollection.
Teresa was delighted with this book "and determined to follow that way of prayer with all my might." During this first
period of solitude, which lasted about nine months, she was
led to the prayer of quiet, and even occasionally to the prayer
of union.

She was then about twenty-three, and at this time she
began making her confessions to a priest who had a great
affection for her. There was, she wrote, nothing wrong in this
affection, but "it ceased to be good because there was too
much of it." He began to confide in Teresa. For seven years
he had been in love with a local woman; yet he continued to
say Mass. He had lost his honor and good name, but no one
dared reprove him. Rather luckily, exactly a year from his first
meeting with Teresa, he died very devoutly.

Teresa, meanwhile, got worse: her throat choked her so
she could not even take water; she was all doubled up, like a
ball, and she had much pain as well as terrible cold fits, and a
distaste for food. Her one desire was to return to her convent,
so they took her there, where her illness continued for three
years. "When I began to get about on my hands and knees I
praised God." This attack (which appears to have been

catalepsy) had effects which continued until the summer of 1542. During her illness, and "before I knew how to take care of myself, I used to have the greatest desire to be of use to others. This is a very common temptation in beginners." She practiced on her father and gave him books to read. He visited her often and derived great comfort from speaking of the things of God. When his last illness began, which lasted some days, Teresa looked after him. "Distressed as I was I forced myself into activity," she wrote, and believed she was able to "return him some part of all he had done for me when I was ill myself." She loved him so dearly that when she saw his life was ending, "I felt as if my very soul were being torn from me."

For the next twenty years, Teresa writes of herself as having been on a stormy sea, owing to her "having relations both with God and with the world." Yet during all this time she continued to practice mental prayer, though she was, over a period of several years, "more occupied in wishing my hour of prayer were over, and in listening whenever the clock struck, than in thinking of things that were good." The practice of recollection as a preliminary to prayer was worse than any penance, yet the straying of her attention was also torture, and she would keep a book at hand, quickly to recollect herself. "It also used to help me to look at a field, or water, or flowers." Yet, while seeking "Great handfuls of the love of God," Teresa warns us that we constantly try to wrest out of His hands our self-importance, which we supposedly abandoned to Him.

After twenty years' experience of prayer, Teresa was still experiencing "much inward strife and many fears," when she met some of the Jesuit Fathers who had founded the College of San Gil at Avila, and found among them some who were to be of considerable spiritual help to her. More help still was Gaspar Daza, who became Teresa's confessor, and also Don Francisco de Salcedo, a married man whose wife was a cousin of Teresa's uncle. This Don Francisco "seems to me to have been the beginning of my soul's salvation," Teresa wrote, in her *Autobiography* that was written at the command of Fray

Domingo Banez and Fray Garcia de Toledo. Another confessor (a Jesuit), Father Juan de Pradanos, also helped her greatly. At this time there came to Avila St. Francis Borgia (who had been Duke of Gandia before he entered the Society of Jesus), and he told Teresa she was being led by the spirit of God and must not worry or think it was the devil, nor fuss if the Lord "should transport my spirit."

Teresa's confessor was transferred and "my soul was as if in a desert. . . . I did not know what would become of me." But she went to stay for some days with a widow who had a great deal to do with the Jesuits, and arranged for Teresa to make her confessions to her own confessor. This was Father Baltasar Alvarez, who became Teresa's confessor for five years, from 1559 to 1564. He told her to recite the *Veni Creator* (the hymn *Come, Holy Ghost, our souls inspire*) and Teresa, after spending the greater part of a whole day in prayer, began to recite the hymn. "While I was reciting it, there came to me a transport so sudden it almost carried me away; I could make no mistake about this, so clear was it. This was the first time the Lord granted me the favor of any kind of rapture." From that moment Teresa obtained her freedom from worldly attachments: "in that moment God was pleased to make His servant another person. Since that moment I have been courageous enough to give up everything for the sake of God." Sometime between 1559 and 1562 Teresa experienced what has been called the "transverberation" of her heart, when it seemed to her that a cherubim with a long golden spear with a point of fire at the end of the iron tip came to her. With the spear's flaming tip "he seemed to pierce my heart several times so that it penetrated my entrails. When he drew it out I thought he was drawing them out with it and he left me completely a fire with a great love for God. The pain was so sharp that it made me utter several moans; and so excessive was the sweetness caused me by this intense pain that one can never wish to lose it, nor will one's soul be content with anything less than God." On May 27, 1726, Pope Benedict XIII appointed a festival on August 27 to celebrate this "transverberation," which is observed all over Spain.

Carmelite tradition has it that Teresa received the same favor again, between 1571 and 1574.

It now occurred to Teresa that the first thing she could do for God was to keep the Rule of her order (Carmelite) with "the greatest possible perfection." But since 1432 the Rule had been mitigated, and Teresa thought "the excessive amount of comfort we had, for the house was a large and pleasant one," was a disadvantage, as was the habit of going away frequently, which Teresa herself often did.

One day one of the sisters asked Teresa "why we should not become Discalced nuns, for it would be quite possible to find a way of establishing a convent?" Later, on another day, after Communion, the Lord explicitly told Teresa to work at this project with all her might. The convent should be called St. Joseph's and would be a guiding star. Teresa was very happy where she was, and loved her cell: she foresaw that "I was at the beginning of a very disturbing time." And how right she was! For hardly had news of the project filtered out than Teresa and her like-minded friends were subjected to severe persecution: "people talked about us, laughed at us, and said the idea was ridiculous." The Provincial said there was not enough revenue to support a new convent, and he refused to sanction it, although he had previously approved Teresa's plan. She was now, not unnaturally, very unpopular "throughout my convent for having wanted to found a convent more strictly enclosed. The nuns said I was insulting them." Also, rumor spread that Teresa had received some kind of revelation, and suggestions were made that she should go before the Inquisitors. Even her confessor told Teresa to pipe down, and for six months she dropped the whole idea. When a new Rector was appointed, her confessor told her to consult him concerning the idea of the Discalced convent again. Then a sister of Teresa's bought and furnished a house, which was tiny. Teresa herself did not think it was big enough to use as a convent, until the Lord told her, "O, the greed of mankind! So you really think there will not be enough ground for you! How often did I sleep all night in the open air because I had nowhere to lay my head." Teresa determined she and her sisters would imitate St. Clare, and live on alms; this principle, that they could never have any income, was only approved by the Holy Father after much difficulty. While all the discussions were going on about the new house, Teresa was sent, under obedience by the Rector, to live with a rich lady in Toledo for six months. Teresa was also assisted in her project by St. Peter of Alcatara, who persuaded the Bishop to sanction St. Teresa's idea.

The convent was finally founded, in great secrecy, on St. Bartholomew's Day, August 24, 1562. Teresa was, from the first, delighted with St. Joseph's. "It was like being in Heaven to me to see the Most Holy Sacrament reserved, and to find ourselves supporting four poor orphans (taken without dowries) . . ." But now what Teresa and her friends had done became known in their old convent and throughout Avila, and there was hell to pay. Her superior sent for her and laid the case before the Provincial, but the latter was quite satisfied, and promised Teresa if her foundation was a success, to give her permission to go and live there as soon as the city was quiet. In the city the new foundation caused such a commotion that people talked about nothing else. Teresa was astonished that twelve women and a prioress could be thought to do harm simply by living strictly. Gradually, however, people began giving alms and "we get on very well, then, and have no lack of necessities. . . . None comes to this house save to . . . speak only of God . . . We observe the rule of Our Lady of Carmel, and we keep it without mitigation, . . . the aim of our nuns is to be alone with Him only." And Teresa concludes her *Autobiography* with "It is thus, dear Sir and Father, that I live now."

It was not until March, 1563, that Teresa actually moved to St. Joseph's, and it was August before the Papal Nuncio confirmed permission for her transfer with three companions. At the end of 1565, she sent her completed autobiography to Father Garcia de Toledo, asking him, before he sent it to Father Master Avila, to have it copied, "otherwise someone might recognize the handwriting."

Teresa's Reform spread. In 1567 the General of the

Carmelites arrived in Avila in April, and authorized Teresa to found further convents. In 1568 she founded a convent at Malagon, about which she writes delightedly to her great friend Dona Luisa de la Cerda. "The sisters are extremely happy . . . my absence will not affect religious observance in the convent, for the sisters already perform there so well." Dona Luisa was a great help; in June, Teresa writes her that the Malagon nuns "in your Ladyship's convent are getting on very well, and making great progress."

At the end of September, 1568, she sent St. John of the Cross with a recommendation to Francisco de Salcedo: "small in stature though he is, I believe him to be great in the sight of God. . . . The Lord seems to be leading him by the hand, for, although we have had a few disagreements here over business matters, and I have been the cause of them, and have sometimes been vexed with him, we have never seen the least imperfection in him." 1569 saw Teresa founding convents at Valladolid and Toledo. In 1570 she founded a convent at Salamanca. In 1573 she wrote to King Phillip II entreating the King's protection for the Reform. That same year, two pious ladies thought of founding a girls' school and staffing it with Discalced Carmelite nuns. Teresa did not approve: "With regard to taking all these girls . . . the idea has always displeased me; for it seems to me that teaching young women is as different from teaching young men as black is from white."[2] In 1574, after she founded a convent at Segovia, she returned to St. Joseph's Avila, as prioress. Her letters are very practical: "If you know anyone . . . who would lend me a few *reales*, I don't want them as a gift but merely to borrow them until I am paid the money my brother has sent me . . . the fact is, I haven't a farthing. . . . The novice with fifteen hundred ducats is coming on Saturday; her fervor amazes everyone. . . . What you tell me is quite normal in those who have attained to contemplation. . . . You must realize that in the spiritual world, as in this world, there are different kinds of weather: that is quite unavoidable." Writing again to King Phillip in 1575, she urges him to make the Discalced Carmelites into a separate province, or much harm will be done: "I have lived among Carmelites for forty years," she told him.

She was always on the go, and at the same time wrote her great books: *The Interior Castle* (1577); the *Way of Perfection* (1579); the *Foundations* (1573–1582) and quantities of letters, some 240 of which still exist. These represent only about half of all she wrote, and many are several printed pages long. She was as merciless with herself as with others. In 1577, she writes to Don Lorenzo de Cepeda to thank him for sardines and sweets which have arrived in good condition, and goes on, "I have had raptures again, and they have been most distressing. Several times I have had them in public—during Matins, for example. It is useless to resist them, and they are impossible to conceal. I get so dreadfully ashamed that I feel I want to hide away somewhere . . . lately I have been going about almost as if I were drunk; but at least it is clear that the soul is well employed." And, like any mundane author, she admits to vanity; she quotes a poem she wrote "when I was deeply absorbed in prayer and seemed to be enjoying more than my usual repose." The first verse reads:

> "O loveliness, that does exceed
> All other loveliness we know;
> thou woundest not yet painst indeed
> and painlessly the soul is freed
> from love of creatures here below"

There are two more verses. After writing them down she notes: "I can't remember any more! What a brain for a foundress! But I can tell you I thought I had a great brain when I made this up."

Her health did not improve. She had "morning sickness" continually, and took purgatives in order to be able to fast. "We middle-aged people need to treat our bodies well so as not to wreck the spirit," she writes, but in 1580 she had a paralytic stroke. At last, in June, the Discalced Reform was recognized as a separate province by Pope Gregory XII. Though in August Teresa became dangerously ill, she was able to write: "God be praised who has granted us so great a favor; you will do well to give him thanks." In 1581 she was again elected Prioress of St. Joseph's Avila, but wrote to a priest, "God help me—the further I journey in this life, the less comfort I find."

She died on October 4, 1582, at Alba de Tormes. She was beatified in 1614, canonised in 1622 and declared Doctor of the Universal Church in 1960.

Bernini's famous statue of her ecstasy in St. Peter's has been described by Aldous Huxley as portraying a woman in sexual orgasm. It was an English seventeenth century recusant poet, Richard Crashaw, who came nearest to understanding Teresa in his poem *The Flaming Heart*:

O thou undaunted daughter of desires
By all thy dower of lights and fires
By all the eagle in thee, all the dove
By all thy lives and deaths of love
By thy large draughts of intellectual day
And by thy thirsts of love more large than they;
By all thy last mornings draught of liquid fire
By the full kingdom of that final kiss
That seized thy parting soul and sealed thee His
By all the heaven thou hast in Him
(Fair sister of the Seraphim)
By all of Him we have in thee
Leave nothing of myself self in me
Let me so read thy life that I
Unto all life of mine may die.

NOTES CHAPTER 10

1   E. Allison Peers, ed. and trans., *The Autobiography of St. Teresa of Avila* (New York: Doubleday, Image Books, 1960).

2   E. Allison Peers, ed. and trans., *The Letters of St. Teresa of Avila* (Maryland: The Newman Press, 1950).

ANNE HUTCHINSON
(1591–1643)

The Protestant Revolution abolished convents as it did monasteries, and John Milton, the Reformation's greatest poet, wrote that man was "for God only, is she for God in him." This, of course, did not apply to royalty: Queen Elizabeth I of England wrote some pretty prayers, and made a superb answer when asked what she thought became of the Eucharistic bread at the moment of consecration: "His was the word that spake it, His was the hand that break it, and what His love doth make it, that I believe and take it."

Some Protestants rather regretted the abolition of nunneries; "they were good shee schools," Fuller wrote in his Church History. And Luther declared that he and his ex-nun wife did not pray as fervently after as they used to before their marriage. It was not, however, either in Anglicanism nor Lutheranism, but in the minor sects that Protestant women first came to express their ways to God. One of the most courageous of these women was Anne Hutchinson.

Anne Hutchinson, the first woman of any distinction in New England's religious history, was born at Alford, near Boston, in Lincolnshire, England, the youngest daughter of Francis Marbury, a "minister by license," a preacher not ordained in the Church of England. She was baptized on July 20, 1591, and married on August 9, 1612, at St. Mary Woolnoth, Boston, to William Hutchinson, son of Edward Hutchinson of Alford, Lincoln, Mercer. It has been claimed that she was a cousin of John Dryden, but of this there seems to be no evidence. She was an admirer of the Reverend John Cotton, who had been driven as a dissenter from the pulpit of St. Botolph's in Boston, and when he "kept close for a time and fitted himself to go to New England," she made plans to follow him.

Anne Hutchinson's sister-in-law Mary married John Wheelwright, born in 1592 at Saleby, a suburb of Alford. Wheelwright took his degree at Cambridge in 1618, and he was probably a contemporary there of Oliver Cromwell, who later said of him: "I remember the time when I was more afraid of meeting John Wheelwright at football than an army in the field, for I was infallibly sure of being tripped up by him." William and Anne Hutchinson sailed for America on the ship *Griffin* and arrived at Boston on September 18, 1634. Also on board were the Reverend John Lothrop and the Reverend Zechariah Symmes. The Hutchinsons brought with them a son, Edward, who was the ancestor of Thomas Hutchinson, the last Royal Governor of the colony. On board the *Griffin* Anne Hutchinson had startled some of the other passengers with her opinions, alarming the Reverend Symmes with her "revelations," one of which related to the length of the passage across the Atlantic.

On arrival at Boston, the Reverend Symmes spoke about Anne to the governor, John Haynes, and deputy, Dudley. As a result her husband, "a man of very mild temper and weak parts, wholly guided by his wife," was admitted to church membership in Boston on October 26. Anne "a woman of a haughty spirit and fierce carriage, or a nimble wit and active spirit, and a very voluble tongue, more bold than a man, though in understanding and judgment inferior to many women" (so one of her detractors, the Reverend Thomas Weld, wrote of her) was only admitted on November 2, 1634.

Anne had wept when, from the deck of the *Griffin*, she first saw Boston. Only four years old, the settlement indeed must have looked dreary, consisting of low-lying fields, poorly treed with three small hills rising from salt-marshes. The houses, even the meeting-houses, were thatched clay cottages and huts: Mr. Coddrington's "new brick house" was the only one of its kind. The rivers almost cut off the peninsula from the rest of the continent. What now are streets were winding foot-paths, and all the inhabitants had to work very hard indeed.

In 1637 there were about 2,000 people in Boston. The meeting house was a "rude, one-story barrack." William Hutchinson took the freeman's oath on March 4, 1635, and was "at once received to honor and place as a representative of Boston in the 'General Court'." In January 1636 he received an allotment of 600 acres of land in what is now North Quincy. His brother-in-law, John Wheelwright, who sailed from England and followed Hutchinson to Boston, landed on June 5, 1636. His allotment was made in February 1637 and included 250 acres lying "south of Mount Wollaston," and extending into the country. This was contiguous to land held by the incumbent minister, the Reverend John Wilson. But from the first, as a contemporary record had it, "Wheelwright lives near Master Wilson, but is far from his opinion."

Anne Hutchinson "soon acquired a well-deserved popularity by her considerate spirit and skill as a nurse and adviser in cases of childbirth" and "female ailments." The Hutchinson's house was near the town spring and "nearly opposite Governor Winthrop's house." Here and in her neighbor's houses Anne began to hold meetings, at first of women only, later attended by men also. They were quite large meetings, up to eighty women attending. At first these gatherings were to 'recapitulate' for women unable, because of their recent lying-in, or because they had small children and could not take them to Sabbath services, the substance of the sermons, more particularly those of the Reverend John Cotton. These gatherings were all the colonists had in the way of relaxation, as there were no newspapers, no social functions and no libraries. The arrival from England of young Sir Harry Vane greatly increased Anne Hutchinson's prestige. Landing at Boston on October 6, 1635, he, aged twenty-four and handsome, was elected Governor of Massachusetts to replace Winthrop by the General Court on May 25, 1636. He assiduously attended Anne's meetings, together with John Cotton and John Wheelwright. Such meetings took place in the simplest surroundings. A wooden table, with on it a copy of the Scriptures, and two lamps; Anne, dark-haired, her head covered, sat between young Vane and John Cotton.

Vane had been converted from the Church of England while on a continental tour, and on his return home he had cut off his Cavalier locks, and withdrawn from the Court and from his father's company. Thus he came to New England with an aura of Puritan sanctity and was welcomed extravagantly, his election as Governor being signalled by a discharge of volleys from all the ships in the bay. He entertained ideas of religious liberty far in advance of his time, and certainly far in advance of the other New England colonists.

At first, Anne Hutchinson had been encouraged. Her "profitable and sober carriage made her well beloved," as John Cotton wrote, "and all the faithful embraced her conference and blessed God for her fruitful discourse." Even the Reverend Wilson "encouraged her meetings manifesting his good will." But then Anne took to leaving Church during his sermons, followed by her handsome friend Mary Dyer, and encouraged others to do so. As a result the Reverend Thomas Weld wrote: "now, after our sermons were ended at our public lectures, you might have seen half a dozen pistols discharged at the face of the preacher. I mean so many objections made by the opinionists in the open assembly against our doctrine delivered, if it suited not their new fancies, to the marvellous weakening of holy truths delivered."

Anne taught her own doctrine. "It was a wonder," wrote Governor Winthrop later, "upon what a sudden the whole church of Boston (some few excepted) were become her new converts, and many also out of the church, and of other churches also; yes many profane persons became of her opinion. . . . She had more resort to her counsell about matters of conscience than any minister (I might say all the elders) in the country." As Weld noted, "some of the magistrates, some gentlemen, some scholars and men of learning, some burgesses of our general court, some chief men in town, and some men eminent for religion, part and wit" were to defend and patronize her.

The colonists in 1636 were simple Congregationalists, midway between Independency and Presbyterianism. As Charles Francis Adams succinctly wrote, "Church and state were one; and the church dominated the state." Or as John Cotton put it, the minister could compel conformity to God's institutions: "Christ does not persecute Christ in New England . . . for though Christ may and doth afflict his own members, yet he doth not afflict (much less persecute) Christ in them, but that which is left of old Adam in them, or that which is found of the seed of the serpent in them." And again, "no man's course compelled the rejection of truth, therefore to force truth on him is no violation of conscience."

Ann Hutchinson professed what was then called the Covenant of Grace, as opposed to the Covenant of Works. Winthrop declared that "Mrs. Hutchinson brought over with her two dangerous errors: 1. That the person of the Holy Ghost dwells in a justified person; 2. That no sanctification can help to evidence to us our justification. From these two grew many branches, as (1) Our union with the Holy Ghost." Anne contended that the divine spirit dwelt in every true believer. But she insisted that this divine presence could not be inferred from "demeanour of sanctity or from conduct in life"—both of which only witnessed to the Covenant of Works. She was, in fact, very near the Quaker belief in the "inner light" or "true inwardness." Only a person in whom the Spirit dwelt was within the Covenant of Grace. All others were under the Covenant of Works, and of the preachers in Boston, Anne thought only John Cotton and John Wheelwright to be "walking in a Covenant of Grace."

On Sunday, October 23, 1636, some of the members left the Boston Church and called upon Wheelwright to be their teacher, agreeing with what Wheelwright had said in a sermon, that "A believer was more than a creature" and "that the indwelling of the person of the Holy Ghost produced a personal union with the Holy Ghost" in a believer. The dispute now raged between Governor Vane, Mr. Cotton, Anne Hutchinson and John Wheelwright, on the one hand, and Deputy Governor Winthrop and the Reverend Wilson, on the other hand. In the midst of it, the Pequot Indians attacked.

On January 29, 1637, a public fast was observed in Boston "for strife and debate" because of the religious dissensions and the trouble with the Pequot Indians. Wheelwright on this day preached the single most famous sermon ever preached in North America. On the first Sunday in February, in his turn Cotton preached "that all the strife was about magnifying the grace of God, for which both parties contended; the one party seeming to advance the Grace of God within us (justification), the other, to advance the Grace of God towards us (sanctification)." He spoke thus "to soften and relieve the melancholy and disgraceful report," which some of the passengers about to sail to England would carry with them back home. The strife was indeed bitter; those who sided against Anne called her a "she-Gamaliel" and "American Jezebel."

Seven weeks later a General Court was held. This court declared Wheelwright in the fast-day sermon to have been guilty of "contempt and sedition." This General Court, which in 1637 consisted of all the magistrates and thirty-two deputies, was also solidly opposed to Anne Hutchinson. The following August, Vane sailed back to England, which left Wheelwright and Anne at the mercy of the Court. The last Pequot Indian had now been destroyed. True to their Old Testament training, the Bostonians treated the Indians as the Jews had the Amalekites. The magistrates "brought back the skins and scalps of Sassacus and his sachems."

To celebrate their victory, the anti-Hutchinson faction decided to hold a synod, the first in America. As John Milton had written, "New Presbyter is but old Priest writ large," and these New England worthies, having killed off the Indians, proceeded to disenfranchise and exile Wheelwright on account of the "sedition and contempt" he had supposedly expressed in his fastday sermon. He could have stayed in Boston until March, as it was already winter, but after preaching a "farewell sermon to his little congregation" he went out alone into the snow, and turned northward. He walked until he came to what is now Exeter, and there halted. The following April his wife and children, with her mother, joined him.

Anne, meanwhile, had bravely continued her interpretations of the preachers' sermons even after the convening of the General Court. But as soon as Wheelwright had been condemned, she was arraigned "for traducing the ministers and their ministry in this country." She was not accused of preaching sedition, nor, as a woman, was she suspected of preparing to take part in any possible uprising. But she had criticized the clergy and that was enough.

The Court was sitting at Newton (now Cambridge) and the trial was held "in a rude frame building, built of rough-hewn boards, the crevices of which were sealed with mud. Its roof, sloping down from a long ridge, had at first been thatched, but was now covered with slate on boards". The whole settlement was made up of some seventy log cabins. There was no attempt to heat the barrack-like building. The furniture was crude; wooden benches with a table and chair for Governor Winthrop and the magistrates. Anne, now forty-six, was pregnant, and was made to stand until "her countenance discovered some bodily infirmity" and a chair was found for her. Accused of failing in the observance of the commandment to honor her father and mother, by not honoring the fathers of the Commonwealth, she replied, "I do not think that I every put any dishonor upon you."

The following conversation then took place:

Governor Winthrop sneered at her: "It is well discerned in the Court that Mrs. Hutchinson can tell when to speak and when to hold her tongue." She replied: "It is one thing for me to come before a public magistracy and there to speak what they would have me to speak: and another when a man comes to me in a way of friendship, privately. There is a difference in that." When the Governor asked her by what warrant she held her meetings, "She cited in reply the usage she found prevailing in Boston at her coming and the scriptural rule in the second Chapter of Titus, that the elder woman should instruct the younger."

The following conversation then ensued:

GOVERNOR WINTHROP: You know that there is no rule [in the Scriptures] which crosses another; but this rule [in Titus] crosses that in the Corinthians. You must therefore take [the rule in Titus] in this sense, that the elder women must instruct the younger about their business, and to love their husbands, and not to make them to clash.

MRS. HUTCHINSON: I do not conceive but that it is meant also for some public times.

GOVERNOR: Well, have you no more to say but this?

MRS. H.:   I have said sufficient for my practice.

GOVERNOR: Your course is not to be suffered; for, besides that we find such a course as this greatly prejudicial to the State, . . . we see not that any should have authority to set up any other exercises besides what authority hath already set up; and so what hurt comes of this you will be guilty of, and we for suffering you.

MRS. H.:   Sir, I do not believe that to be so.

GOVERNOR: Well, we see how it is. We must therefore put it away from you; or restrain you from maintaining this course.

MRS. H.:   If you have a rule for it from God's Word, you may.

GOVERNOR: We are your judges, and not you ours. And we must compel you to it.

MRS. H.:   If it please you by authority to put it down, will freely let you. For I am subject to your authority.

After this admission the Court could find no fault in her. By thus submitting to authority, she was about to go free when "her own mouth delivered her into the power of the

112

Court." For she began "to speak her mind and to tell of the manner of God's dealing with her, and how He revealed Himself to her and made her know what she had to do . . ." her speech was to this effect:

"When I was in old England I was much troubled at the constitution of the churches there, so far troubled that I had liked to turn Separatist. Whereupon I set apart a day of solemn humiliation by myself, that I might ponder of the thing and see direction from God. And on that day God discovered unto me the unfaithfulness of the churches, and the dangers of them. . . . The Lord bade me not to fear. Therefore take heed what ye go about to do unto me. You have power over my body, but the Lord Jesus has power over my body and soul; neither can you do me any harm, for I am in the hands of the eternal Jehovah, my Saviour."

I am at his appointment, for the bounds of my habitation are cast in Heaven, and no further do I esteem of any mortal man than creatures of his hand. I fear none but the great Jehovah, which hath foretold me of these things, and I do verily believe that he will deliver me out of your hands. Therefore take heed how you proceed against me; for I know that for this you go about to do me, God will ruin you and your posterity, and this whole State.

MR. NOWELL: How do you know that it was God that did reveal these things to you, and not Satan?

MRS. HUTCHINSON: How did Abraham know that it was God that bid him offer his son, being a breach of the sixth commandment?

DEPUTY-GOVERNOR DUDLEY: By an immediate voice.

MRS. HUTCHINSON: So to me by an immediate revelation.

DEPUTY-GOVERNOR: How! an immediate revelation?

MRS. HUTCHINSON: By the voice of his own spirit to my soul.

GOVERNOR WINTHROP: Daniel was delivered by miracle; do you think to be delivered so too?

MRS. HUTCHINSON: I do here speak it before the Court. I look that the Lord should deliver me by his providence.[1]

Such statements condemned her, and there was nothing her friends in the Court, Coddington and the cowardly John Cotton, could do.

So the General Court now heard Governor Winthrop sum up the case against Anne: "The Court has already declared themselves satisfied concerning . . . the troublesomeness of her spirit, and the danger of her course amongst us, which is not to be suffered. Therefore if it be the mind of the Court that Mrs. Hutchinson . . . is unfit for our society, and if it be the mind of the Court that she shall be banished out of our liberties, and imprisoned till she be sent away. Let them hold up their hands."

All but three held up their hands.

Those that are contrary minded hold up yours.

Mr. Coddington and Mr. Colburn only.

MR. JENNISON: I cannot hold up my hand one way or the other, and I shall give my reason if the Court require it.

GOVERNOR WINTHROP: Mrs. Hutchinson, you hear the sentence of the Court. It is that you are banished from out our jurisdiction as being a woman not fit for our society. And you are to be imprisoned till the Court send you away.

MRS. HUTCHINSON: I desire to know wherefore I am banished.

GOVERNOR WINTHROP: Say no more. The Court knows wherefore, and is satisfied.

In the Colony Records of Massachusetss the sentenance reads as follows:—

"Mrs. Hutchinson, (the wife of Mr. William Hutchinson,) being convented for traducing the ministers, and their ministry in this country, shee declared voluntarily her revelations for her ground, and that shee should bee delivred, and the Court ruined, with their posterity; and thereupon was banished, and the mean while was committed to Mr. Joseph Weld until the Court shall dispose of her."

Anne, delivered into the care of her worst enemy and having been cast out of the community, was then cast out of the church by excommunication. The congregation, headed by her enemy the Reverend Wilson, debated from January 15 to January 22, 1638, when Wilson pronounced the excommunication in the following terms: "In the name of the Lord Jesus Christ and in the name of the church I do not only pronounce you worthy to be cast out but I cast you out, and in the name of Christ I do deliver you up to Satan . . . I do account you from this time forth to be a Heathen and a Publican, therefore I command you in the name of Christ Jesus and of this church as a Leper to withdraw yourself out of this congregation." John Cotton had deserted her; Vane had left; Anne walked alone through the throng. But one rose and joined her proudly; her disciple and devoted friend, Mary Dyer, whom Governor Winthrop called "a very proper and fair woman."

Previously, Mary Dyer had given birth to a "monster." Anne, subsequently, had a miscarriage. And this, for their traducers, was proof positive that "God himself brought in his own vote and suffrage from heaven." When a poor barber, acting out of kindness as dentist, was found frozen to death in a ditch after doing his neighborly work, this too was gloated over because he had been a disciple of Anne's.

Meanwhile Anne Hutchinson left Boston for her husband's farm at nearby Mount Wollaston. But her husband, Coddington, and a few others had bought land at Aquidneck, Rhode Island and had gone there, and they were joined by

Anne on March 7, 1638. William Coddington was chosen a Judge, and on April 28, 1639 William Hutchinson was chosen Governor of Providence instead of Coddington, who withdrew to Newport. In the spring of 1640, a delegation came from the Boston Church to Aquidneck, pursuing Anne. But they wrote that "Mr. Hutchinson told us he was more nearly tied to his wife than to the church; he thought her to be a dear saint and servant of God. We came then to Mrs. Hutchinson, and told her that we had a message to do to her from the Lord and for our church. She answered: "There are lords many and gods many, but I acknowledge but one Lord. Which Lord do you mean?' We answered we came in the name of but one Lord and that is God. Then she said, that so far we agreed, and where we do agree let it be set down. Then we told her we had a message to her from the church of Christ in Boston. She replied 'she knew no church but one.' We told her in the Scripture, the Holy Ghost calls them churches. She said 'Christ had but one spouse.' We told her, 'He had in some sorts as many spouses as saints.' But for our church, she would not acknowledge it any church of Christ. At this point John Cotton said, 'Time being far spent it will not be seasonable to speak much.' " And they all left.

Anne's husband died in 1642, and one of her daughters married a young minister, Collins, who came to New England from St. Kitts in the Barbados, where he had been persecuted as a Non-Conformist. He "espoused Mrs. Hutchinson's cause with Warmth" and wrote to Boston "charging our churches and our ministers to be anti-Christian." With his brother-in-law, Francis Hutchinson, he visited Boston in the summer of 1641. They were both imprisoned and fined 150 pounds, but refused to pay. "But after, because the winter drew on and the prison was inconvenient," they were dismissed, but warned if they returned they would be put to death. "Nevertheless, they found some sympathy in the church, and even the constable who had the charge of them was fined for his favor to them."

Soon after her husband's death, Anne with all her children, except for a daughter married to one Thomas Savage, and a son, Edward, who had remained at Boston, moved to

Long Island, a Dutch settlement. It is not certain where she and her family settled, but it is thought to have been near Hell's Gate. In the summer of 1643, in a battle between the Mohegans and the Narragansetts, fifteen Dutchmen had been slain. In August, 1643, a party of Indians fell upon Anne, the Reverend Collins, and all of the party, numbering sixteen, were massacred by the Indians, except for a girl of eight, who was captured. They were "confined to their dwellings and burned, as were their cattle." This was, of course, hailed with delight by the Reverend John Wilson as still further proof that the Lord was on his side. Peter Bulkeley drew the obvious moral: "Let her damned heresies she fell into . . . and the just vengeance of God, by which she perished, terrifie all her seduced followers from having any more to doe with her leaven." Hutchinson River and its Parkway in New York are named after Anne.

Wampage, the Indian chief who had massacred Anne and her family, added her name to his: Annehook, and called his daughter Anne. This daughter married the son of the English colonist John Pell, Thomas Pell. Thomas Pell's granddaughter Sarah married William Bayley, uncle to St. Elizabeth Seton.

John Wheelwright grovelled before Governor Winthrop "Humbly craving pardon for using unsafe and obscure expressions: falling from me as a man dazzled by the buffetings of Satan." He returned to England in 1647, "where he was intimate with Oliver Cromwell" and remained there until after the Restoration, when he returned to New England and settled in Salisbury as a minister. He again denied Anne in a tract: "In spiritual indeed she gave her understanding over into the power of suggestion and immediate dictates, by reason of which she had many strange fancies and erroneous tenets which possessed her."

John Cotton was more truthful, writing that "he could discover no heresy in her," but that she had three spiritual failings. "That her faith was not begotten, nor much strengthened, by public mininstrations, but by private meditions or revelations; that she had a clear discernment of her justification, but little or none of her sanctification, and that she was more sharply censorious of other men's spiritual estates and hearts, than the servants of God are wont to be, who are more taken up with judging of themselves before the Lord than of others."

Mary Dyer, Anne's only courageous disciple, remained in Rhode Island, where she became a Quaker. But in 1659, hearing of the persecution of the Quakers in Massachusetts, she "felt a call to persecution" and came to Boston. Here she was speedily arrested and brought before the General Court:

. . . company with three others. She simply said in her own defence that she came from Rhode Island to visit the Quakers, that she was of their religion, and that the light within her was the rule. They were banished, under pain of death if they returned. Mary Dyer and one other "found freedom to depart;" but within a month they were back again, in company with another woman, who brought some linen for the examination of Governor Endicott, intended to be used as the grave-clothes of that magistrate's victims. They were at once all thrown into prison, and then brought again before the Court, which now sentenced them to death. Mary Dyer's son at this time filled the important office of secretary of the province of Rhode Island, and at his earnest solicitation the death-penalty was remitted in the case of his mother, on condition that she should leave Massachusetts within forty-eight hours. Her companions, William Robinson and Marmaduke Stephenson, were left for execution. When the day fixed for their hanging came, the town had to be put under guard, so great was the sympathy felt for the condemned. Surrounded by a heavy escort, the three prisoners walked together from the jail in Cornhill to the gallows, which had been erected on the Common, Mary Dyer going between the two others and holding a hand of each. She must then have been a woman of middle life, but Edward Nicholson, the marshal, asked her if she was not "ashamed to walk hand in hand, between two young men?" "It is, she answered, "an hour of the greatest joy I can enjoy in this world. No eye can see, no ear can hear, no tongue can speak, no heart can understand, the sweet incomes and refreshings of the Spirit of the Lord which now I enjoy.

When her companions were hanged, she sat beneath the gallows with the halter about her neck, calmly looking at the multitude of horrified spectators, whom a hundred armed men of the train-band kept back from the scaffolding; for so great was the throng upon the Common that day, that the draw-bridge over the canal, which then separated the North End from the town, broke down under the weight of those returning home.

The Reverend John Wilson cursed the Quakers. "The curse of God or Jesus go with you," he said and railed at them at the foot of the gallows.

When her companions were dead Mary Dyer was taken back to prison, and there she first learned of the circumstances of her reprieve. She at once wrote to the governor, repudiating her son's action, and offering her life as a sacrifice. It was necessary to use force to get her out of the jurisdiction. She was at last taken back to Newport, where for a time she seems to have been kept under restraint; but in the following spring she succeeded in eluding those having her in charge, and, journeying "secretly and speedily," found her way back to Boston. She was again thrown in prison; and again her family piteously interceded for her. She was sentenced once more to be hanged, but at the gallows her life was offered her if she would keep away from Massachusetts. Her reply was:—"In obedience to the will of the Lord I came; and in his will I abide faithful to the death."

She was hanged and is buried on Boston Common in an unmarked grave.

12

SOR JUANA INES DE LA CRUZ
(1648–1695)

A Spanish captain born in Vergara, Pedro Manuel de Asbaje y Vargas Machuca, had three children by a young creole woman born in Moreles, Mexico. Of these Juana Inés was the second. This girl, who was to become Mexico's most famous woman poet and to be known, even in her lifetime, as the Mexican Phoenix, and the Tenth Muse, was born and spent the first two years of her life in Nepantla, at the foot of the great volcanoes Popocatepetl and Iztaccihuatl. Nepantla is about eighty kilometers from Mexico City on the Cuautla road. There is ample water, and it is fertile country. Juana's mother, Dõna Isabel, was deserted by Pedro when Juana was two. She withdrew to the hacienda, called Panahoya, administered by her father Pedro Ramirez. Dõna Isabel never learned to read or write, but in her will she declared she had another three "natural" children by one Don Diego de Ruiz Lozano.

Before Juana was three years old, as she relates her story, her sister was having reading lessons in Amecameca, a small nearby town. "Seeing the person who gave my sister lessons, I told her that my mother wished me also to have lessons, and, though she didn't believe me, she taught me. I knew how to read in such a short time, that I could already do it by the time my mother learned from my teacher of my request." Juana then also refused to eat cheese, because she had heard it said that it made people stupid, and "I wanted much more to learn than to eat." When she was about six, and could already read and write, as well as "being able to do those things that women learn," she heard that there was a university and schools where sciences were taught in Mexico City. She pestered her mother to send her there, and not unnaturally, her mother refused, whereupon Juana had to content herself with reading her grandfather's many books. When eight she wrote a *Loa* (a poem) to get a book as a prize. In 1659 she got her wish when she was not quite eleven and went to Mexico City to stay in the house of her maternal aunt, Maria Ramirez de Santillana, who was married to Don Juan de Mata, a gentleman with a "good social and economic position." Her aunt employed Martin de Olivas, a bachelor, to teach the precocious child Latin. She mastered the language in twenty lessons and desciplined herself by cutting her hair. If she hadn't memorized her lessons by the time her hair grew, she cut it again. "It grew fast," she wrote, "and I learned slowly. But I thought it unreasonable to have a head clothed in hair that was so naked of knowledge which to me was a more desirable adornment."

By the time she was thirteen she was indeed educated. She was writing many poems in Spanish, and noted:

If that's bad, I don't know it
I was born such a poet
That, like Ovid, when whipped
Into metre I slipped

She could also write Latin correctly, knew *nahuatl* (the local Indian Language), Potuguese and Basque, her grandfather and father's native tongue. She was also enchantingly pretty, as she herself admits ingenuously:

"I must tell you I was born beautiful
I presume I may be excused for this."

She had huge, dark eyes, a perfectly shaped nose, a small, well-formed mouth, and a charming figure and manner. She lived for five years with her aunt and uncle, and it was probably her confessor, the stern Jesuit Antonio Nuñez de Miranda, who brought her to the Palace of the Viceroys, the Marquis and Marchioness of Mancera, whose confessor he also was. He was proud of the lovely girl, but thought she would be safer in the care of the Vicereine than anywhere else. So he presented his remarkable penitent to their Excellencies. Don Antonio Sebastian de Toledo Molino y Salazar, then Viceroy of Mexico, came there in 1664. He was a well-educated man, and had spent his youth in Peru, before being Ambassador of Spain to Italy and then Germany. His wife, Doña Maria Leonor de Carrete, was a very cultivated women, and liked to surround herself with literary folk.

The Viceroy was enchanted with the "virgin from the mountains," and collected a jury of forty doctors from the University to examine the girl, who answered their questions. They put her through a mock trial: she was questioned by theologians, lawyers, mathematicians, historians, poets, philosophers and humanists. She acquitted herself, the Viceroy declared, like "a royal galleon assailed by small craft." The successful outcome of her trial made her an instant celebrity. The Viceroy was, for his time, very enlightened socially. He fought to mitigate the force of the local laws relating to the liberty of the native (Indian) peoples, and was opposed to the slave trade in Negroes. He also established the feast of the Apparition of Our Lady of Guadalupe as Mexican national day; Our Lady of Guadalupe is black, and her apparition did much to reconcile the natives with the Spanish conquest and religion.

Juana, given the position of lady-in-waiting to the Vicereine, lived for three years with the Viceroy and his wife in the royal palace, a beautiful renaissance building erected in 1564.

During those three years it would seem that the lovely girl fell in love twice, both times unhappily. Silvio, the first object of her affection, obviously hurt, and even insulted her.

She wrote him several stinging poems, among which the following:

> When I consider, Silvio, my error
> And I perceive your vileness
> How grave is the sin's malice of my mistaken love!
> How violent the force of a desire!
>
> I would have wished, indeed, when I came to see you
> Seeing my infamous love, to be able to deny it.
> But then just reason warns me
> That the only remedy would be to publish it.
> Since, for the great crime of loving you
> The only sufficient punishment is to confess it.

Later she fell in love with one whom she called Fabio, and to whom she wrote verses as passionate and as perfect as the English seventeenth century poets wrote. This also ended badly—Fabio was unresponsive, perhaps because it would have been impossible for him to have married a girl, however beautiful and gifted, of illegitimate birth, and without a dowry.

Juana takes leave of him in words which Sir Philip Sidney would have approved (he wrote "Leave me, o love, that reaches but to dust"):

> Finally, I beg your pardon
> For the many injuries I've done you
> By having loved you
> Which injuries are
> That, in your vexation
> You are, reasonably offended at my treatment
> And I, by loving you, have made you disagreeable.

Others, whom she did not love, may well have loved her, as the following verses suggest:

Him who thankless leaves me I seek loving
Him who lovingly seeks me I thankless leave.
Constantly I adore him who maltreats my love:
I maltreat him who constant seeks my love.
In him whom I love I find a diamond
And I am a diamond for him who loves me.
I wish to see him triumph who kills me
And I kill him who wills to see me triumph.

At the end of three years as a very young lady-in-waiting to the Vicereine, Juana decided to enter a convent. She chose the strictest order there was, the Discalced Carmelites. She entered on August 14, 1667, when she was barely eithteen. The Viceroy and his wife attended the novitiate festivities. Juana, who fell ill immediately, remained there only three months, coming out on November 18. "I thought I went of myself," she wrote. But the distance from the foot of the volcanoes to the peak of letters, and thence to the poorest and strictest imaginable convent life, had proved too great.

Yet though she now remained in "the world" another two years, she was disillusioned with it. She was the most famous poet in Mexico, a national treasure, the pet of the Viceroy and of his court, yet she wrote:

World, why do you pursue me? What interest have I
for you?
How have I offended you when my only intent
Is to apply beauty to my understanding
And not my understanding to beauty?

She was obviously torn by an internal struggle, when she wrote:

Into two parts divided
My soul is in confusion:
One part a slave to passion,
The other ruled by reason.

A civil war is burning
Raging persistent in my breast:
Each part seeks to overcome,
Between such various fates
Will die both vexing states
But triumph neither one.

Her confessor was, no doubt, urging her to make up her mind. She decided to enter the Convent of Santa Paula, in the Mexico City suburb of San Jeronimo. Here were Augustinian nuns who required a large dowry of every postlant. Juana's confessor, delighted by her choice, asked Don Pedro Velazquez de Cadena, a gentleman "of limpid lineage and distinguished family" to be Juana's "godfather"; he paid the three thousand pesos of dowry, and she made her will "in order to dispose of my legitimate goods which belong to me according to the provisions of the Holy Council of Trent." She named her mother universal legatee and, should her mother predecease her, Juana's sisters, Josefa and Maria, were to be heirs. These mundane matters taken care of, Juana put on the conventual habit on February 24, 1669, and wrote in the convent's book of profession her vow to "live and die for the time and space of my life in obedience, poverty, without home of my own, in chastity and perpetual enclosure." In his delight, Father Nuñez paid for all the bills incurred upon Juana's taking the veil, and himself had prepared a feast to which he invited the nobility and gentry of Mexico City as well as "all the most brilliant ecclesiastics and the intellectual members of the laity." A day later, February 25, Juana received a visit from her mother, who made her a present of a mulatto slave to take care of her in the convent.

Sor Juana lived in her monastery for another twenty-seven years. At that time it was a big building at the city's edge, with a girl's school on the east side of it. It had several patios, and a big and beautiful garden surrounded with open galeries on pillars, according to tradition. Sor Juana's cell was to the southwest, with a splendid view over Mexico City and the mountains. The convents in Mexico were the centers of civic and social life. Coming and going to Mass and to Vespers, the flower of Mexican society and all the intellectuals delighted in visiting Sor Juana. Everyone asked her to make verses for them, as this was her very special gift. She accepted the waste of time these visits entailed because she had no way of avoiding the people who came to see her. Added to the waste of her time was the fact that not only did her visitors require her to write "occasional poems" for them, but they also borrowed her books. Of these she amassed her own private collection of "4,000 friends," finding time also to study philosophy and theology. She also made a collection of musical and scientific instruments, wrote on harmony and on architecture, made astronomical observations, worked on geometrical and physical problems, had quite an astonishing knowledge of mythology and rhetoric, and knew Greek, Latin, Spanish, Italian, French, Portugese and even Hebrew literature well.

In November, 1673 a new Viceroy arrived in Mexico. He was a descendant of Christopher Columbus, Don Pedro Nuño de Portugal y Castro, Duke of Veraguas. After his arrival the Manceras remained in Mexico a few months longer before setting off on their return to Spain. When they reached Tepeaca, in the State of Puebla, the Marchioness Mancera died and was buried there in the Franciscan church. Sor Juana wrote three funeral sonnets for the Vicereine, her friend and employer, and also for the Duke of Veraguas, who only a few months after he arrived died at almost the same time.

The next Viceroy was the Marquis de la Laguna. He was Don Tomas Antonio de la Cerda y Enrique; his wife Countess of Paredes, was the daughter of the Prince of Guastala of the house of Mantua. The Countess became, for Sor Juana, the "Divine Lisi" to whom she wrote many of her most famous and successful poems. These new Viceroys arrived in Mexico City on November 30, 1680, and Sor Juana was ordered by the Cathedral chapter to write, in honor of their arrival, her elaborate "Allegorical Nepture," a mixture of erudition and mythology.

Sor Juana was having trouble inside her convent. Her superior was "a religious, very holy and very outspoken, who thought that to study was something to be investigated by the Inquisition." One day Sor Juana told her Superior that she "must admit you are a fool." Indignant, the Superior applied to the Archbishop, who replied "Let the Mother Superior prove the contrary, and justice will be done her." On another occasion her Superior forbade Sor Juana to read, and for three months, obediently, she did not open a book. Yet she could not stop her superb mind from working, and describes how: "It happened to me several times, to notice, as I stood at the head of our dormitory, whose sides were parallel and whose roof was flat, that the perspective bent the two lines towards each other, so that the roof was lower in the distance than close up, from which I inferred that sight lines run straight but not parallel: they form pyramids. And I wondered if this could be the reason the Ancients doubted the world was round, for although it seems so, this could will be a '*trompe l'oeil*,' suggesting curvatures where perhaps there were none." Children, playing with a trumpet, led her to speculations on the nature of spiral motion; other children, playing in the courtyard and grouped by chance into a triangle, reminded her of Solomon's seal. And she found so many secrets of physics while cooking that she wrote: "Aristotle would have written more books had he prepared more dinners." But keeping her from her books had such a bad effect on her health that her doctor ordered her to go back to reading. "All I wanted," she wrote, "was to read, and read more; my only master a dumb book, my fellow student and insensible inkhorn." Her special virtue was charity," her confessor wrote; "she was always bringing her sisters food, or looking after them when they were sick."

In 1676 she began writing "Villanelles" and continued to write some two a year, for the major feasts of the Church, until 1691. These were sung by choruses in church, and the combination of her poetry and the music was exquisite. These *Villanelles* were commissioned by the Bishop of Puebla and by the Archbishop of Mexico, and were sung in the two cathedrals of their cities, recently built by the same architect, Claudio de Arciniegas. Meanwhile, the widowed Marquis of Mancera was making Sor Juana famous throughout Europe, and his successor, the Marquis de la Laguna, when he returned to Spain in 1688 (two years after his viceroyalty ended, he was succeeded by the Count of Monclova) helped to get Sor Juana's first book of poems printed in Madrid by Juan Barcia Infazon. This book of poems by the "unique poetess, the tenth Muse, Sor Juana Inés de la Cruz" was dedicated to the Marquis of Laguna's wife, the Countess of Paredes.

Sor Juana not only wrote verses, sonnets, *loas, villanelles* and allegories, but also plays. The first of these to be performed was given on October 4, 1683, in a private house in Mexico City, in honor of the Viceroy de la Laguna and his wife. It was called *The Obligations of One House.* Later Sor Juana wrote a comedy in three acts, *Love is a Labyrinth.* This was performed in 1689 in the Viceregal Palace, for the Count of Galve and his wife Elvira, who had succeeded Count Monclova as Viceroy.

Musical and theatrical evenings continued to be given in Sor Juana's convent, and unfortunately for her, at one of these Sor Juana was given as a gift the works of a Portuguese Jesuit, Antonio Vieyra, who had been a missionary in Brazil, from which he had been deported for having been too much in favor of the natives and the Negroes. Accussed before the Inquisition, he had been forbidden to teach, write or preach, but in the end he triumphed over all his enemies. In a famous Holy Week sermon, he attacked St. Augustine, St. Thomas and St. John Chrysostom. Sor Juana was annoyed at this attack, for her convent was dedicated to St. Augustine. Someone "whom I dared not disobey" asked her to write a criticism of Vieyra's book. She wrote a letter, clearly setting out the opinions of Vieyra and defending those of the three saints. The letter passed from hand to hand until it reached the Bishop of Puebla, Don Manuel de Santa Cruz y Sahagun, a friend of Sor Juana's for many years. Her little work, *Crisis of a Sermon*, received as a reply a letter, written November 25, 1690, by the Bishop, in which he exhorted Sor Juana to abandon profane studies, and told her "You have wasted much time in the study of philosophers and poets; now is the time to perfect your means and improve your occupation." The Bishop signed the letter "Sor Filotea de la Cruz."

Sor Juana took three months to reply to the Bishop's letter, and her reply was sent on March 1, 1691. This reply is one of the glories of early Latin-American literature, and one of the most remarkable pieces of writing ever produced by a woman. This reply to Filotea is an autobiography, a defense of women's right to education, and a passionate defense of the liberty of thought. Sor Juana wrote: "From the first ray of the light of reason that reached me, my inclination to letters was so strong, that no censure from others, of which I had plenty, nor any personal outside repressions, nor any considerations of my own, were enough to prevent my following the natural impulse God put into me. . . . I took orders because although I knew there were many things in this life that repelled me, . . . the one consideration to which all the minor impertinences of my character deferred, was: to live alone, to refuse any occupation that interferred with the liberty of my studies, or household noises that troubled the silence of my books . . . in what did I wrong, if I never even wrote—though that is allowed to women—except when I was bidden to?" She also insists: "Am I not as free to dissent from Vieyra's opinion as he is to dissent from mine? Is my understanding any less free than his? Is it a tenet of our holy Faith that we must believe with our eyes shut?" Yet she meekly concludes, "I have received into my soul, your holy admonition to study the books of Holy Writ."

Sor Juana was very upset when her long time confessor, the Jesuit father Antonio Nuñez de Miranda declared himself in agreement with the Bishop's admonitions, even though another Jesuit, Dr. Juan Maria Castorena, rushed to Sor Juana's defense in writing. (But he was young, only twenty-four.) Sor Juana seems to have gone through some sort of religious crisis as a result of the Bishop's letter and of her reply, for she sold her whole library, all her scientific and musical instruments, and distributed all the money she thus obtained to the poor. The only writing she did after 1691 was a declaration that she would defend the mystery of the Immaculate Conception, which she signed with her blood in her convent on February 8, 1693.

There were grave troubles in Mexico in 1692 when, after a year of bad harvests and much hunger, on June 8 the Royal Palace was set on fire, and the Viceroy took refuge with his family in the convent of St. Francis. There followed a cruel repression. But Sor Juana, whose confessor had returned to her side, "did not run but flew to virtue" and now lived only for prayer and penitence.

In 1695 an epidemic of typhoid swept through Mexico City, and reached the convent of San Jeronimo. Sor Juana nursed her Sisters with the utmost devotion, and as a result herself became sick. "With confidence and great tenderness" she received the Viaticum on March 17, 1695 and "returned her soul to the Source of all Poetry." She was forty-seven years old.

After her death the young Jesuit who had defended her became Bishop of Oaxaca and had all her works recopied. When he went to Spain in 1697 to get the degree of Doctor in Theology from the University of Avila, he took all Sor Juana's manuscripts to Madrid and there edited a third volume of her works (*The Carta Atenagorica* and the *Reply to Filotea* had already been published), which appeared in 1700 under the title *Fame and Posthumous Works of the Phoenix of Mexico.* Several of her poems follow here in English, but translations can give no idea of the quality of the originals: she is unique in her own language, a phoenix indeed, not of Mexico only but among all women everywhere.

Dirge

My divine Lord
If at the time when I depart
My loving heart breathes out complaints
Listen to my sorrow, regard my ills
Ease my pain, if you can feel my sorrow,

At the prospect of losing you
My heart breathes out
Weepings to the earth, grievings to the air.
I do not even want the sun to remove me
From your eyes
Since my sudden fall gives in clear indications
Vengeance to the fire, name to the seas.
Just when your favors
Were about to crown me
More blissful than all
Happier than any
Then the pleasures were grief,
No doubt to be happy
Is the gravest of all faults
Because my ill fortune
Requires that I pay
With my eyes from which your lights are withdrawn,
Ah, hard law of absence
Who can abolish it?
If you take me to where I would not be
Without taking me together with my dead soul
Shall I then live as a corpse?
Could it be, that of your favors
Only the heart's prison
Will still be the silence
If I want to keep them
I, worthless custodian, fragile vessel?
And, as I am about to leave
I promise you
With my spent love and with my constant faith
Always to love you, never to forget you.

Villanelle

Today is the beloved Incarnation
Of the Divine Love

Such a costly perfection
Providing all others with courage.
Although the first good of all who were born
Was to have been made
What use was it to have been created
Without the possibility of being redeemed?
Not even the power of enjoying being
Could have been a pleasure:
For what use was there in being
If being was for suffering?
The mysteries are linked
And what is a medium of the Redemption
For our salvation
Is for Creation a crown.
What has not his beloved Incarnation
Given to the world
If even the fault was fortunate
Since it caused it to happen?
Nor was the primal fault the only cause
Because, for the fault to be repaired
Only Mary was sufficient.
I won't accept any contradiction to this,
Because to me what is strange
Is that the power which was more than her beauty
Was the remedy for a crime
And that even that crime brought consolation
To a world drenched in tears.
How much more worth is she than all the world
Who is worth more than heaven?
Even to become incarnate
May have had a double motive:
For all mankind, compassion,
For Mary, love.
And so the descent to earth this day
Was in various modes:
It was for all our guilt
It was for Mary's grace.

Romance

My divine Lisa
Forgive me, if I dare
Call you thus
Though even were I yours, I would not merit the
name
Because I would not dare to call you so
Since you have an excess of rays
Which were they in me would be insolent.
It is an error of speech
To call the owner of a domain, an empire
Though what appears, are possessions to a serf
My king, says the vassal;
My jail, says the prisoner
And the humblest slave
Without offending, calls his master his own.
So when I call you mine
I do not pretend that they will think you mine
But only that I want to be yours
And even if others are more worthy
Because of their closeness to heaven
The humblest valley is at the same distance
As the proudest mountain.
Anyway, I confess to the crime of adoring you
If you wish, punish me:
This very punishment will be my reward.

Dirge

In the event, my Fabian
That after much sorrow
There remain complaints
Breathing in your soul
In the event, that from among the ashes

Of my dead hope
A tiny branch, because of its insignificance
Sets itself free
Wherewithal, with its limited strength
Can be nourished, by the gentle life-giving breeze,
The moment when you listen to me?
In the event, that from the mortal shears
That threaten me
Inexorable Fate
Grants me a brief truce
Then listen to the sad dirges,
The delicate melodies
That serve as tender elegies
For the dying swan.

Contradiction

I can't hold you and I can't leave you,
and sorting the reasons to leave you or hold you,
I find an intangible one to love you,
and many tangible ones to forgo you.

As you won't change, nor let me forgo you,
I shall give my heart a defense against you,
so that half shall always be armed to abhor you,
though the other half be ready to adore you.

Then if our love, by loving flourish
let it not in endless feuding perish;
let us speak no more in jealousy and suspicion.

He offers not part who would all receive—
so know that when it is your intention,
mine shall be to make believe.

(translated by Judith Thurman)

from "A Satirical Romance"

Ignorant men, who disclaim
women with no reason,
you do not see you are the reason
for what you blame.

Importuning her disdain
with such pressing desires,
why is it goodness you then require,
who have caused her shame?

What humor can be so rare
that carelessly will blur
a mirror, and then aver
that it's not clear?

Critics: in your sight
no woman can win:
keep you out, and she's too tight;
she's too loose if you get in.

(translated by Judith Thurman)

13

GLUCKEL OF HAMELN
(1646–1724)

Glückel Pinkerle was born in Hamburg in 1646, two years before the end of the Thirty Years War, which devastated Germany, following the financial depression of the late sixteenth century, which ruined such great merchants as the Fuggers. Glückel's father, expelled as were all Jews from Hamburg in 1649, moved to Altona. He was allowed to return to Hamburg in 1657, though only "at the mercy and favor of the Town Council," which was the situation of almost all Jews at that time. They then "dealt in small loans, second-hand jewellery . . . and sundry Dutch & English wares, as ribbons, pottery, hardware and cutlery." Glückel tells that, in Altona, the Jews had a synogogue and a cemetary, but all their business was in Hamburg, and they needed a pass, renewable every four weeks for one ducat, to enter the city. There were only forty Jewish families in Altona of which Glückel's father was the second richest; "if it hadn't been for the gout he would have further incresed his fortune" she wrote of him in her memoir. Everyone of the Altona Jews seems to have gone daily to the synagogue, and then "in the early dawn" to Hamburg to trade.

Glückel was betrothed at twelve, married at fourteen, and had fourteen children. She was still a child "alone with strangers in a strange world," as Glückel wrote, but her "new parents" (her in-laws) made her life a joy, in spite of living in a "back country town" (Hameln) where they were the only two Jews. Glückel's husband was her in-laws ninth child, and after a year, the young couple left Hameln to join Glückel's parents in Hamburg. Glückel's husband studied, worshipped and toiled. "Truly the whole day he ran about upon his business, still he never failed to set aside a fixed time to study his daily 'portion,' of the Torah. He fasted, too, a great part of every day the Torah was read forth in the synagogue . . . in short, he was the perfect pattern of a pious Jew as were his father and brothers. Even among the great rabbis, I knew but few who prayed with his fervor. If he were praying, in his room, and some one came to fetch him forth where something could be bought up cheap, neither I nor any servant in my whole house would have the heart to go to him and speak of it. Indeed, he once missed a bargain in this way, to the loss of several hundred thalers." Glückel's mother and she each had a daughter, eight days apart, and Glückel's mother once suckled her granddaughter by mistake, to the amusement of the whole household!

Glückel began to write only after her beloved husband's death, after thirty happy years of married life. She was now forty-four, and still had eight unmarried children to provide for. She opened her own store and ran a stocking factory; she paid off 20,000 thalers of debts and married off all but one of the children with proper doweries. In 1700, she married again, to Cerf Levy, the formost banker in Lorraine, and hoped to spend her last years with him in Metz. But in 1702 Cerf Levy became bankrupt, and died in 1712; Glückel then had to accept the bread of her children. Her son, Rabbi Moses Hameln, and her grandson, Chayim Hameln, preserved her manuscript. (Among her descendants was Heinrich Heine.) Glückel wrote in Yiddish, and her memoirs were first published in the original tongue in 1896; the English translation, by Marvin Lowenthal, was published by Harper & Brothers in New York in 1932.

The following extracts from Glückel's straightforward chronicle illustrates a life suffused with traditional piety and common sense:

The best thing for you, my children, is to serve God from your heart, without falsehood or sham, not

137

giving out to people that you are one thing while, God forbid, in your heart you are another. Say your prayers with awe and devotion. During the time for prayers, do not stand about and talk of other things. While prayers are being offered to the Creator of the world, hold it a great sin to engage another man in talk about an entirely different matter—shall God Almighty be kept waiting until you have finished your business?

Moreover, put aside a fixed time for the study of the Torah, as best you know how. Then diligently go about your business, for providing your wife and children a decent livelihood is likewise a *mitzvah*—the command of God and the duty of man. We should, I say, put ouselves to great pains for our children, for on this the world is built, yet we must understand that if children did as much for their parents, the children would quickly tire of it.

Thou knowest well, Almighty God, how I pass my days in trouble and affliction of heart. I was long a woman who stood high in the esteem of her pious husband, who was like the apple of his eye. But with his passing, passed away my treasure and my honour, which all my days and years I now lament and bemoan.

I know that this complaining and mourning is a weakness of mine and a grievous fault. Far better it would be if every day I fell upon my knees and thanked the Lord for the tender mercies He has bestowed on my unworthy self. I sit to this day and date at my own table, eat what I relish, stretch myself at night in my own bed, and have even a shilling to waste, so long as the good God pleases. I have my beloved children, and while things do not always go as well, now with one or the other, as they should, still we are all alive and ackowledge our Creator. How many prople there are in this world, finer, better, juster and truer than I, such as I know myself for patterns of piety, who have not bread to put into their mouths! How, then, can I thank and praise my Creator enough for all the goodness He has lavished on us without requital!

If only we poor sinners would acknowledge the everlasting mercy of our God who from the dust of the ground formed us into men, and that we may serve our Creator with all our heart, gave us to know His great and terrible and holy Name!

Behold, my children, all a man will do to gain the favour of a king, flesh and blood that he is, here today and tomorrow in his grave, no one knowing how long may live he who asks or he who gives. And behold the gifts he receives from the transient hand of a king. Honours the king can grant him and put him too in the way of wealth; yet honours and money are but for a space and not for eternity. A man may hoard his honours and his gold until the very last, and then comes bitter Death to make all forgotten; and his honours and his gold are of no avail. Every man, he knows this well and yet he strives loyally to serve a mortal king to gain the passing reward.

How much more, then, should we strive day and night, when we come to serve in duty bound the King of kings who lives and rules forever! For He it is whence come the favours we receive from human kings, and He it is who gives these kings their all and who puts it in their heart to honour whomsoever His holy will decrees, for "the king's heart is in the hand of the Lord." And the gifts of a human monarch stand as naught against the gift of the God of Glory upon those whom He delights to honour: eternity without stain, measure or term.

So, dear children of my heart, be comforted and patient in your sorrows and serve the Almighty God with all your hearts, in your evil days as in your good; for although we often feel we must sink beneath our heavy burdens, our great Lord and Master, we must know, never lays upon His servants more than they can bear. Happy the man who accepts in patience all that God ordains for him or for his children.

Wherefore I, too, beg my Creator give me strength to bear without fret the contrarieties of the world, all of them, be it said, of our own making. "Man is bound to give thanks for the evil as for the good."

Thus we must ever keep a measure in our grief when, God help us! the evil days are come, and knowing that His judgment is just, glorify the true and righteous Judge.

All of us suffer bitter losses, but far from helping us, grief and mourning only harm our body and weaken our soul. And no one depressed in body can worship God as he should. When the prophets of old invited the spirit of the Lord to come on them, they played the tabret, pipe and harp to rejoice their limbs, for the spirit of the Lord is slow to come on the sick in body.

Glückel only ceased writing when she was seventy-three; she died six years later on September 19, 1724.

14

ANNE LEE
(February, 1736–September 8, 1784)

Ann Lee was born in Toad Lane, an industrial slum of Manchester, England. Her father was a blacksmith, as was also her brother William. All her life Ann was illeterate. She was "rather short, thickset, but straight and well proportioned . . . her complexion was light and fair, her eyes were blue, but keen and penetrating. Her natural constitution was sound, strong and healthy. By many of the world, who saw her without prejudice, she was called beautiful." As a girl, she had not wished to marry, and her mother sympathized with her in this, but her father married her to another blacksmith, Abraham Stanley, by whom she had four children, who all died young. These deaths made her melancholy, for she thought they were a punishment for sin, and she used to spend whole nights "in laboring and crying to God for deliverance from sin."

When she was twenty-three, Ann met a couple called Wardley, belonging to a sect of French Huguenots, *Camisards*, who had fled from France after the Revocation of the Edict of Nantes and who made many converts, as they preached that the Second Coming of Christ was imminent. Ann asked continually, in prayer, "Why did men sin?" and came to the conclusion that it was because of sex. So she gave it up. Together with the Wardleys, she proposed as the four principles of Shakerism (as their sect came to be called): confession of sins, community of goods, celibacy and withdrawal from the world. Ann took nine years elaborating these doctrines, and then she had a vision of "more than earthly beauty" in which she was shown Adam and Eve sinning, and was then herself anointed as the successor to Jesus Christ, and appointed "Mother Incarnation of the Word, the Second Coming of Christ." The Wardleys believed in her, and together they preached in Toad Lane, and indulged in "frenzied dancing." This brought the authorities down upon them, and Ann was accused of Sabbath breaking and of blasphemy. At one point she was seized and confined in a stone cell not big enough to lie down in and was kept fourteen days without food and water. James Whittaker, a devoted follower, managed to pass a pipe through a keyhole and fed Ann at night with milk and wine. Her enemies were confounded when the cell was opened and she "walked out as she went in."

Brought before a tribunal of four clergymen, all Anglicans, by her enemies who demanded her tongue be bored through with a hot iron, "these men, being desirous to hear her own testimony, gave her liberty to speak for herself. Accordingly she spoke, and manifested such evident power of God, that they thought proper to dismiss her and admonished her accusers to let her alone, and not abuse her." However, her persecutors took the law into their own hands and tried to stone her to death. Four of her Shaker brethren, one being her brother William Lee, were taken out of town to a valley where their enemies could stone them from the side of a hill. In spite of repeated attempts, with sufficient quantities of stone, suitable for their purpose, the men on the hillside failed to hit anyone but Daniel Whitaker, whom they wounded slightly on the temple. He was the only one of the four who later reverted. Mother Ann declared that "while they were thus throwing their stones, I felt myself surrounded with the presence of God, and my soul was filled with love. I knew they could not kill me, because my work was not yet done, therefore I felt joyful and comfortable, while my enemies felt distress and confusion." The enemies at last got tired, and for her last two years in England Ann and her followers enjoyed their faith in peace.

Ann received a "special revelation" to repair to America, and at the same time received a divine promise that the work of God would greatly increase there, and that the Milennial Church would be established in that country.

On May 19, 1774, Ann Lee, her husband and six companions sailed from Liverpool in the *Mariah*, whose Captain Smith was from New York. The Wardleys were left behind. Money had been provided for the journey by John Townley, a well-to-do bricklayer, and John Hocknell, both of whom accompanied Ann. On board, the eight "went forth in obedience to their inward feelings to praise God in songs and dances," but the Captain said he'd throw them overboard if they didn't behave themselves. When a severe storm sprang up, the ship sprang a leak, and Captain and crew were in despair. But Ann told the Captain: "Be of good cheer; there shall not a hair of our heads perish; we shall arrive safe to America. I just saw two bright angels of God standing by the mast, through whom I received this promise." The ship was saved, and the Captain was so pleased he allowed the Shakers to worship as they pleased for the rest of the trip, and honorably declared he owed his life to them when he put into port in New York, where they arrived on August 6, 1774.

Ann and her husband stayed with Mr. Smith, a blacksmith. Ann did the washing and ironing for the family. Then Abraham Stanley fell ill, and Ann had to nurse him. "Her only shelter from the inclemency of the weather was a small uncomfortable room without bed or bedding, no furniture but a cold stone for a seat, and a cruse of vinegar for all their food and drink." Ann sat down on the stone, drank her vinegar, and wept. Abraham recovered, but wanted sex; when Ann wouldn't oblige, he left her and returned with a prostitute, whom he threatened to marry if his wife still refused him. She did, and he left her, never to return.

The little group, minus Abraham, then went up to Niskayuna, a piece of land they purchased eight miles north of Albany. Here they lived, worked and worshipped in peace for three years, but made no new converts.

Then, in 1779, at New Lebanon, New York, there were a number of revivalist meetings. It was the middle of the American Revolution, but this revival lasted all summer. At summer's end, the ardor cooled, but a few people who had heard of the strange group in the wilderness of Niskayuna, travelled there to find that, indeed, here were like-minded people. All went well until the Shakers started missionary activities. New Lebanon folk resented it when one Baptist, Joseph Reimer, and a Presbyterian, Samuel Johnson, were converted to Shakerism.

Political troubles also followed. The Shakers, having arrived recently from England, were suspected of being in the pay of the British Army. David Darrow, driving sheep down the road towards the Niskayuna community, was seized and put in jail because he would not swear. Ann and the others were also then put into jail in Albany. But even while she was in prison, Ann mananged to attract and to hold a large crowd of listeners. She preached through the prison gates to large assemblies and made many converts. She was transferred to Poughkeepsie, but released in December by Governor Clinton.

In may, 1781, the Shakers set out on a missionary journey, and reached Harvard in June. In December they arrived at Petersham, where the crowd attacked them, dragging Ann feet first out of the house where she was staying, and "throwing her into a cart with as little ceremony as they would have the dead carcase of a beast, committing at the same time acts of inhumanity which even savages would be ashamed of." The Shakers went on to Enfield, Connecticut in March 1782.

By August they were back in Harvard, and on August 19 they again received brutal treatment from the mob, who dragged the believers out by their hair, collars and throats. Clubbed, lashed, shaken, pounded, dismissed with threats and turned out of Harvard, the Shakers insisted on praying for their assailants. "Such marks of Christianity were too much for the seed of Cain to endure," and only made matters worse.

Ann went to Shirley, but persecution followed her there too. The Shakers tried Harvard again, but left for good in 1783. They were mobbed at Petersham too, where Elder Johnson read aloud the articles from the Bill of Rights declaring freedom of conscience and worship. The hostile crowd molested him, and in Richmond the Shakers were fined $20 for disturbing the peace, and were ordered out of the state. They paid the fine, but remained in Massachusetts. Some were imprisoned in Barrington jail, where Mother Ann visited them. They finally returned to New Lebanon, but were mobbed even there. They crossed the Hudson in a ferry, and were met by the Indians crying out in joy: "The good woman is come! The good woman is come back!" On September 4, 1783, they returned to Niskayuna, having been absent two years and four months. They had taken no part in the Revolution, but had well and duly founded the Shaker society in the newborn U.S.A.

A group of Shakers in New York chartered a boat on August 28, 1784 to make the trip to Niskayuna. But the *Shark* ran into rough seas. The frightened travellers saw Mother Ann appear. She "breathed peace into the troubled sea." When they reached Portland safely it was to find Mother Ann had died six hours before their vision of her.

Her death marked the end of the first phase of the Shaker adventure. She seems to have had almost constant mystical experiences. "She stood erect on the floor for the space of an hour," writes one contemporary, "her countenance was angelic, and she seemed to notice nothing of the things in the world. She sang chiefly in unknown tongues, though sometimes she uttered expressions in her own language." Another Shaker, Joseph Main, wrote: "I was passing through a room where Mother Ann was. I saw her sitting in a chair and singing very melodiously, with her hands in motion, and her whole soul and body seemed to be in exercise. I felt as it were a stream of divine power and love flow into my soul, and was convinced it was from heaven." Another account, by Sister Blanchard: "She never saw Mother under any violent usurpation of the power of God. She seemed to possess within herself an inexhaustible fountain of that power which she would often communicate to a whole assembly by singing (not in a loud voice) gently motioning with her hand or speaking a few words. . . . She was the supporter of all the Shaker gifts and the centre of their influence."

She insisted that everyone work. "Hands to work, heart to God," she would say, and the Shakers became famous for the excellence of their crafts.

15

ST. ELIZABETH SETON
(August 28, 1774–January 4, 1821)

The first American-born United States citizen to be canonized was born two years before the Declaration of Independence, beautified on March 17, 1963, and canonized September 12, 1965. Her ancestors on both sides had long been established in the New World. Jacques Lasty, her father Richard Bayley's maternal progenitor, arrived at the end of the seventeenth century, while another ancestor, William le Conte, obliged as a convinced Protestant to leave France after the Revocation of the Edict of Nantes, became in 1690 one of the founders of New Rochelle. On Elizabeth Seton's father's side, her grandfather, William Bayley, left England in 1726 to settle in New York, where he married Suzanne le Conte. Their son Richard Bayley became one of the best-known surgeons of New York, and married the daughter of the Rev. Richard Charlton, Episcopal minister of St. Andrew's parish on Staten Island. Richard Charlton's son John was, like Richard Bayley, a surgeon, who practiced at the court of George III. After Richard Bayley married his friend John Charlton's sister Catherine in 1769, he left the same year for London to study anatomy under the great William Hunter. Richard Bayley's first child, Mary Magdalen, was born while her father was in England, and was more than a year old before he returned, to work with his brother-in-law, John Charlton.

In 1774, on August 28, a second daughter, Elizabeth, was born to Richard Bayley and Catherine Charlton; a year later, in 1775, he set off again for London, to return on a ship as military surgeon under the command of Admiral Howe. Landing in New York on July 12, 1776, he was back on his ship the night New York went up in flames. Mrs. Bayley with her two small daughters escaped to her parents' home in Newtown, where on May 8, 1777, Catherine Bayley died giving birth to a third daughter, Catherine. Thirteen months later Richard Bayley married again, Charlotte Barclay, aged 19, whose mother was Helen Roosevelt. In October 1778 Catherine died, and Elizabeth, now aged 4, remembered watching the clouds go by while her baby sister lay in her coffin.

In the following ten years, Elizabeth was to have seven half-brothers and sisters. Another of her early memories was lifting her little half-sister Emma to the window, to show her the sunset, and telling her God lived there and children who were good would go to Him up there. She also taught her to pray. It was probably after the end of the War of Independence that Dr. Bayley decided to send his two motherless daughters as boarders to a select educational establishment, that of Mama Pompelion, where they were taught excellent French and music. Elizabeth remembered her father passing by with her uncle: she would run to the window when she heard their carriage. When permitted, she would run down to be hugged by her father. On the holidays, the two girls would stay with their paternal uncle, William Bayley, who had married Sarah Pell. Sarah Pell was the granddaughter of the Indian chief Wampage, who had in 1637 massacred Anne Hutchinson and all her family except one daughter.

At Shore Road, the William Bayleys' home in New Rochelle, Elizabeth Seton loved to watch the clouds, thinking of her dead mother and little sister Catherine, and would sit by the sea alone, or wander for hours along the shore, collecting shells and singing. As she wrote in her *Dear Remembrances*, her greatest joy was in learning about religion. Aged eight, she cried when her little cousins stole birds' eggs and killed the baby birds in the nests. Aged 12, back in her father's house, she loved to read prayers, and to take care of her young step-siblings.

In April, 1788, when she was 14, she notes she spent a

night of terror, reciting the Lord's Prayer. Her father had been giving his anatomy course as usual, when a student, for a prank, waved an arm he was dissecting out of the window and cried, "Here is your mother's arm, which often smacked you." One of the boys playing outside the hospital windows in the street had just lost his mother. Horrified, he ran home, repeated the words he had heard, and, furious at not finding Richard Bayley, collected a group of grown-up sympathizers who forced the doors of the hospital and destroyed everything they found. The insurrection continued next day, and even one of the heroes of Independence, Sir John Jay, was hurt. The mayor of New York, Duane, gave the police orders to fire: five persons were left dead and many wounded.

Obliged to leave New York, Dr. Richard Bayley left his two motherless girls once more with his brother William, and departed again for London. Not a word came from him for more that a year, but Mary and Elizabeth were happy at Shore Road, where William Bayley, his business ruined by the Declaration of Independence, lived the peaceful life of a country squire, devoted to his own children and to his two nieces. Elizabeth felt the absence of her father more than did her elder sister, already in love with Wright Post, whom she married in 1790. But Elizabeth consoled herself with her joy in God, who was her father—"my father was far away, perhaps dead, but God was my father." She wrote, aged 15, that she had a remarkable mystical experience, which she vividly recalled and described while she was sitting beside her dying husband in the Lazaretto of Leghorn:

> In the year 1789, when my father was in England, one morning in May, with the lightness of a cheerful heart, I jumped in the wagon that was driving to the woods for brush, about a mile from home. The boy who drove it began to cut and I set off in the woods; soon found an outlet in a meadow, and a chestnut tree with several young ones growing around it attracted my attention as a seat. But when I came to it, found rich moss under it and a warm sun. Here,

then, was a sweet bed. The air still, a clear blue vault above, the numberless sounds of spring melody and joy, the sweet clovers and wild flowers I had got by the way, and a heart as innocent as a human heart could be, filled with even enthusiastic love of God and admiration of His works. Still I can feel every sensation that passed through my soul. I thought at that time my father did not care for me. Well, God was my Father, my all. I prayed, sang hymns and laughed, talking to myself of how far He could place me above all sorrow. Then I lay still to enjoy the heavenly peace that came over my soul, and I am sure in the two hours so enjoyed grew ten years in my spiritual life. Told cousin Joe to go home with his wood, not to mind me. Walked a mile, made another hearty prayer, then sang all the way home. Had a good appetite for the lamb fat and fat pork."

Dr. Bayley finally returned to the United States in January, 1790, in time for Mary's wedding. But her beloved father's return did not bring Elizabeth the happiness she expected; there were family rows, which she could not understand: Why, when she spoke nicely to her relatives, did they not reply? She could not understand how anyone could be an enemy to anyone else. She was comforted by her female friends: Julia Scott, Eliza Craig, and Catherine Dupleix, who often with Elizabeth visited the sick. These remained her friends for all of Elizabeth's life.

At eighteen she was pretty and popular, but already longed for a little country house where she could gather together all the local children and teach them their prayers, where people could shut themselves away from the world and pray, and "be always good." That same year, 1792, her father was appointed professor of anatomy at Columbia University. Elizabeth, feeling herself very much alone, thought of taking laudanum with the intention of committing suicide, "in most audacious presumption." She was forever properly grateful to God for having prevented her from accomplishing this horrible action and made Him "a thousand promises of eternal gratitude."

A year later, Elizabeth became engaged to William Magee Seton. It was an excellent match. William's father, aged 45, was one of the twelve directors of the Bank of New York, founded in 1786. William Seton had arrived in London from Scotland in 1763. He was descended from Mary Seton, one of Queen Mary Stuart's "four Maries." He married Rebecca Curson in New York in 1767, and their eldest child was born at sea, in 1768. Aged ten, William and his younger brother James returned to London to school where they remained for six years. After returning to the United States, aged 16, William Magee started to work for his father in the Bank of New York at 18. Soon he left again for a long trip to Europe, where he visited Spain, Italy and England. In Italy he made great friends with Filippo Filicchi, a businessman for whom he worked and who had married Mary Cowper of Boston. After returning to New York for a family reunion on July 16, 1791, at which William Seton had his second (sister of the first, who had died of tuberculosis) wife and his twelve children around him, William Magee again returned to Leghorn to work with two of his brothers in the Filicchi's commercial establishment.

Elizabeth was very much in love with William: "don't come too late," she wrote him while they were courting, when telling him at whose party he would find her. They were married on Sunday, January 25, 1794. The young couple lived at first with William Magee's family, and her in-laws doted on Elizabeth, her father-in-law even showing her family papers and letters before any of his own children had seen them. "You will be pleased to find, in all these," he told her, "how profound is the paternal affection I have always felt for my dear William, your husband." Yet, happy though she was to be so loved and cherished, Elizabeth was even happier, as she wrote in her *Dear Remembrances*, when she was "20 years old, with my very own home." This "home" was a little rented house on Wall Street.

William had brought back from Cremona a Stradivarius

violin, and Elizabeth would accompany him on the piano. On May 2, 1795, while writing to her friend, Julia Scott, Elizabeth went into labor, and next morning gave birth to her first child, a girl, Anna Maria, baptized in Trinity Church (Episcopal) on June 4. The godparents were Elizabeth's father, Dr. Richard Bayley, and William's sister Rebecca.

Even before the birth of her second child, a boy, William, born in November, 1796, William Magee's health was causing Elizabeth anxiety. She wrote to her friend Eliza Sadler in Paris on August 11: "I have learnt to commune with my own heart and I try to govern it by reflection and yet that heart grows every day more tender. This I attribute to the state of my William's health. Oh! That health on which my every hope of happiness depends, and which either continues me in the most perfect human felicity or sinks me in the lowest depths of sorrow. That health does not mend, and although it is my fixed principle, both as a Christian and a reasonable being, not to dwell on thoughts and future events which do not depend on myself, yet I never view the setting sun or take a solitary walk but melancholy tries to seize me." In February 1796 she wrote again to Eliza Sadler: "Your description of the people awakens what formerly was a reigning passion in my breast, a curiosity to see the world and Europeans in particular. But all that is long ago laid aside. A half dozen form my world." And Elizabeth goes on to describe her little Anna Maria and relates that her "grandfather Bayley" will tell you that he sees more sense, intelligence and inquiry in that little face than in any other in the world, and that "he can converse more with her that with any woman in NY."

Elizabeth herself adored her father, who must have been a very exceptional man. Once, when a surgeon came to ask him to come and see a sick patient, Dr. Bayley refused, pleading fatigue, and the distance Staten Island was from New York. The surgeon commented that this refusal would sadly grieve the "needy family of the patient, so unfortunate and so poor." "They are poor?" Dr. Bayley got up and said, "Why didn't you tell me? Let us go to them immediately." Elizabeth had the highest opinion of Dr. Bayley: "Your spirit," she wrote him, "surrounds your child, and guards against the least word you might condemn. It asserts itself, making everything she does merit your approval."

Dr. Bayley was made Health Officer for the Port of New York in 1795, and, though not yet aware that the mosquitoes breeding in the swamps in and around the city were the cause of yellow fever, he realized that the epidemics which occured annually in the summer were somehow connected to these swamps. At that time no vaccine against yellow fever had been found, and the immigrants pouring into the United States brought with them not only yellow fever but many other contagious diseases. Dr. Bayley, in 1799, moved the quarantine station to Staten Island, near Tomkinsville. Here he lived, and here Elizabeth Seton spent her summers, with her father and her children, her husband spending there at least three nights a week. Here younger son Richard was born in 1798, and she nursed him as she did all her children. In 1799 he was able to stand up and lay his head on her bosom, yet "I cannot find courage to wean him yet." In 1800 Elizabeth's second daughter, Catherine, was born, and nearly cost her mother her life. Catherine was to live until 1891, and to become a nun after her fortieth birthday.

In a letter Elizabeth wrote at this time she declared she could not help feeling "extremely uneasy" about her own father. Her beloved father-in-law, William Seton, had died as the result of a fall on the ice in 1798. This left William Magee, barely 30, in charge of his twelve siblings, while Elizabeth, just 24, had to take over the big house on Stone Street and the Seton's little summer house at Cragdon, where 18 people could barely find room to eat and sleep. It was at this time of stress and sorrow that Elizabeth discovered the true value of her sister-in-law, Rebecca, who was the first friend with whom she could share her feelings for the Almighty. For neither her father, her father-in-law, or her beloved William were more than marginally intersted in religion. Unfortunately, Rebecca, like William, had tuberculosis like their mother. Dr. William Bayley went daily into down town New York, exposed to the terrible contagion of the epidemic of yellow fever.

Owing to the war between England and Napoleon, the affairs of William Seton and his brother-in-law, James Maitland, went from bad to worse. The young United States had decided on neutrality, which meant U.S. ships were raided and pillaged on the highseas, or blocked in the continental ports by the British fleet. From London and from Hamburg, nothing but disastrous news, and to American ports none of the Seton ships returned. "If hearts shipwrecked at the same time as do fortunes," Elizabeth wrote, "things would be in a bad way for us." Maitland suspended payments in London, and "We are obliged to do the same here. It is a cruel situation for William." Early in 1800 yet another Seton ship, loaded with valuable cargo, was lost outside of Antwerp. Day and night, Sundays and weekdays, William worked, while Elizabeth, acting as his secretary, expected another baby. Seton, Maitland & Co. were forced to declare themselves bankrupt before the end of 1800. The Setons were obliged to give up the family house on Stone Street, and in May, 1801, Elizabeth, William and their four children moved to a three story house on the Battery. Williams' sisters, Cecilia and Rebecca, moved in with them.

That summer of 1801 Elizabeth was more than ever aware of the horrors of the epidemic: "Rebecca, I can no longer sleep. The dead and dying obsess my mind. Babes perishing in the empty breasts of their expiring mothers. This does not proceed from my imagination, it is the very scene that lies about me. My father says no one has ever seen the like of it. . . . O, God, Merciful Father, how gladly would I give to each of these poor little creatures a part of the inheritance of my own child, if it only depended upon me." Dr. Bayley had to dissuade Elizabeth from weaning her own child to feed some of the unfortunate. In August, 1801, he had given orders that the baggage and passengers of an Irish ship should be taken to the quarantine established for yellow fever patients. Next morning when he returned to the hospital he learned his orders had not been carried out. He rushed into the room where baggage and passengers were, and instantly was attacked by severe pains in the head and stomack. Taken home, Elizabeth nursed him, but she wrote to Rebecca, "The chance of saving him is so slim." A month later, on September 5, 1801 she described his death: "No remedy could give him a moment's relief, nor could he ever lie still without holding my hand. 'All the horrors are coming, my child, I feel them all' . . . he said. He was in extreme pain until about half-past two Monday afternoon, the seventeenth (of August) when he was perfectly easy, put his hand in mine and breathed the last of life." Burying him was a problem: "Neither the sexton nor any of the people dared approach because of the contagion, so his faithful boatman took him in his barge to within half a mile of the graveyard, and himself buried him."

Elizabeth's fifth and last child, a daughter called Rebecca after her sister-in-law, was born on August 19, 1802.

Eliza Sadler had brought back from France as a present for Elizabeth Seton the complete works of Jean-Jacques Rousseau. The latter enjoyed them tremendously, and constantly quotes her "dear J.J." And she wrote Eliza: "Every half-hour I take down the three volumes of *Emile*. They gave me much pleasure." Later, as Mother Seton, she confessed that she had experienced the "fatal influence of Rousseau, and there was a time when they were for me my Sunday reading." A more orthodox employment of Sunday came from attending the Rev. Henry Hobart's church. Rev. Hobart was the new curate at Trinity Church, and Elizabeth and Rebecca undertook not to accept any profane distractions on Communion Sundays. They became such devotees of the Anglican sacrament that they would stay behind to persuade the sacristan to give them what remained of the bread and wine, and also they would go from church to church in order to "'receive as often as they could." Once home, they would sigh, "nothing more until next Sunday."

In 1803 William, to his wife's great joy, came with her to church and took the Sacrament, but Elizabeth was now in no doubt that his days were numbered. To Eliza Sadler she wrote on September 28: "My husband has had new and severe suffering since I saw you. All say that it is presumption and next to madness to undertake such a voyage, but we reason differently. Saturday is now the day. Everything is ready and on board. We will, dear Eliza, rest upon Him, our only strength." The young Setons had decided to travel to Italy, to the Filicchis, who had been so good to William ten years before. They took Anna Maria, aged 8, with them, leaving the other four children with their aunts Harriet and Rebecca, and baby Rebecca, only 14 months old, with Elizabeth's sister, Mary Post. Writing at sea, Elizabeth described how "my dear little Anne shed many tears on her prayer book over the 92nd psalm, in consequence of my telling her that we offended God every day. Our conversation began by her asking me if God put down our bad actions in his book, as will as our good ones. She said she wondered how anyone could be sorry to see a dear baby die. She thought there was more cause to cry when they were born."

Elizabeth kept a journal on board from which the following is extracted:

At Sea, November 14

Considering the infirmity and corrupt nature which would overpower the spirit of grace, and the enormity of the offense to which the least indulgence of them would lead me, in the anguish of my soul, shuddering to offend my adored Lord, I have this day solemnly engaged that, through the strength of His Holy Spirit, I will not again expose that corrupt and infirm nature to the smallest temptation I can avoid. Therefore, if my Heavenly Father will once more reunite us all I will make a daily sacrifice of every wish, even the most innocent, lest they should betray me to deviation from the solemn and sacred vow I have now made.

O my God! Imprint it on my soul with the strength of the Holy Spirit that, by His grace supported and defended, I may never more forget that Thou art my all, and that I cannot be received in Thy heavenly kingdom without a pure and faithful heart supremely devoted to Thy holy will. Oh, keep me for the sake of Jesus Christ!

November 16

A heavy storm of thunder and lightning at midnight. My soul, assured and strong in its Almighty Protector, encouraged itself in Him, while the knees trembled as they bent to Him; the worms of the dust writhing at the terrors of its Almighty Judge, a helpless child clinging to the mercy of its tender Father, a redeemed soul strong in the strength of its adored Savior!

After reading a great deal, and long and earnest prayer, went to bed, but could not rest. A little voice (my own Anna, who I thought was asleep) in a soft whisper said, "Come hither, all ye weary souls." I changed my place to her arms. The rocking of the vessel and breaking of the waves were forgotten, the heavy sighs and restless pains were lost in a sweet refreshing sleep. Adored Redeemer! It was Thy refreshing sleep. Adored Redeemer! It was Thy word, by the voice of one of Thy little ones, who promises indeed to be one of Thy angels.

After seven weeks at sea, on November 18, the *Shepherdess* docked at Leghorn at the time of the Angelus. But the passengers were immediately informed they must spend four weeks in quarantine, imprisoned in the Lazarette. Elizabeth wrote in her journal the following day:

When I heard in the morning a boat was alongside our ship, I flew on deck and would have thrown myself into the arms of dear Carlton, but he retired from me and a guard whom I saw for the first time said, "Don't touch." It was now explained that our ship was the first to bring the news of yellow fever in New York, which our want of a bill of health discovered; that the pilot who brought us in the mole must lose his head. Our ship must go out in the roads and my poor William, being ill, must go with his baggage to the Lazaretto. At this moment the band of music that welcomes strangers came under our cabin windows and played "Hail Columbia" and all those little

156

tunes that set the darlings singing and dancing at home. Mr. O'Brien and the rest were half wild with joy, but I was glad to hide in my berth the full heart of sorrow, which seemed as if it must break. Do not judge me. You can never have an idea of the looks and tears of my poor William, who seemed as if he would not live over the day. Presently appeared a boat with fourteen oars. We hurried into another, with only one change of clothes, as they promised we should have the rest on Monday. The Lazaretto being some miles out of the town, we were towed out to sea again, and, after an hour's ride over the waves, the chains which are across the entrance of the canal which leads to this place were let down at the signal of several successive bells. After another rowing between walls as high as our second-story windows and amidst the quarreling and the hallooing of the waterman where we should be landed, the boat stopped.

Another succession of bells brought down one guard after another, and in about an hour Monsieur le Capitaine, after much consultation and whispering with his Lieutenant, said we might come out, upon which everyone retreated, and a guard pointed with his bayonette the way we were to go. An order from the Commandant was sent from our boat to the Capitano, which was received on the end of a stick, and they were obliged to light a fire to smoke it before it could be read. My books always go with me, and they were carefully put up, but must all be looked over and papers in the little secretary examined.[3]

She goes on to describe:

My husband, on the cold bricks without a fire, shivering and goaning, lifting his chin and sorrowful eyes with a fixed gaze on my face, while his tears ran on his pillow, without one word! Ann rubbed one hand, I the other, till his fever came on.

The Capitano brought us news that our time was lessened five days—told me to be satisfied with the dispensations of God. He was answered by such a succession of sobs that he soon departed. Mr. Filicchi now came to comfort my William and when he went away we said as much of our blessed service as William could go through with. I then was obliged to lay my head down. Dinner was sent from town and a servant to stay with us during our quarantine—Louis, and old man, very little, gray hair, and blue eyes which changed their expression from joy to sorrow, as if they would console and still enliven. My face was covered with a handkerchief when he came in, and tired with the sight of men with cocked hats, cockades, and bayonets, I did not look up. Poor Louis, how long shall I remember his voice of sorrow and tenderness when I refused the dinner. With lifted-up hands he prayed that God would comfort me. And truly I was comforted, when I did not look at my poor William; but to see him as he then was was worse than to see him dead. And now the bolts of another door were hammered open, and Louis, who was become an object of equal terror, having entered our room and touched what we had touched, had an apartment allotted him. How many times did the poor dear man run up and down the nearly perpendicular twenty steps to get things necessary for our comfort next morning!

My William, wearied out, was soon asleep. Ann amid tears said her prayers, and soon forgot her sorrows. It seemed as if opening my prayer book and bending my knees was the signal for my soul to find rest. It was nine o'clock with us; three o'clock at home.

A week later Elizabeth wrote to William's sister Rebecca:

December 12, 1803
A week has passed, my dear sister, without even one little memorandum of the pen. The first day of it,

Sunday, that dear day in which I always find my blessing, was passed in interrupted prayers, anxiety, and watching.

Was early awakened to-day by my poor William in great suffering. Sent for Dr. Tutilli, who as soon as he saw him told me he was not wanted, but I must send for him who would minister to his soul. In this moment I stood alone as to this world. My William looked in silent agony at me, and I at him, each fearing to weaken the other's strength. At the moment he drew himself toward me and said, "I breathe out my soul with you." The exertion he made assisted nature's remaining strength, and he threw a quantity from his lungs, which had threatened to stop their motion, and so doing, experienced so great a revolution that in a few hours afterward he seemed nearly the same as when first we entered Lazaretto. Oh, that day! It was spent close by his bedside on my little mat. He slumbered the most of every hour, and did I not pray and did I not praise? No inquiring visitor disturbed the solemn silence. No breakfast or dinner to interrupt the rest. And then came our Capitano with so much offered kindness. He was shocked at the tranquillity of my poor William.[4]

On December 19, the Setons were finally allowed to leave the Lazaretto. William was carried by two men to Filicchi's coach. He supported the fifteen miles of heavy roads better than expected, and found the apartment taken for him by the Filicchis charming. William insisted the following day on going for a drive, as again two days later on the following Friday, but on Christmas Eve Elizabeth wrote:

> Christmas Eve, 1803
> Constant suffering and for the first time confined to his bed. The disorder of the bowels so violent that he said he could not last till morning. Talked with cheerfulness about his darlings, thanked God with great earnestness that He had given him so much time

to reflect, and such consolation in His Word and prayers. With the help of a small portion of laudanum rested until midnight. He then awoke, and observed I had not lain down. I said, "No, love, for the sweetest reflections kept me awake. Christmas day is begun. The day of our dear Redeemer's birth is the day that opened to us the door of everlasting life."

"Yes, he said, "and now I wish we could have the sacrament." "Well, we must do all we can" and putting a little wine in a glass I said different parts of Psalms and prayers which I had marked, hoping for a happy moment, and we took the cup of thanksgiving, setting aside the sorrow of time in the views of eternity. Oh, so happy to find its joys were strongly painted on him! On Sunday, O'Brien came and my William gave me in his charge to take me home, with a composure and solemnity that made us cold. Did not pass a mouthful through my lips that day, which was spent on my knees by his bedside, every moment I could look off my William. He anxiously prayed to be released that day and followed me in prayer whenever he had the least cessation from extreme suffering.

December 26 and 27, 1803

Was so impatient to be gone that I could scarcely persuade him to wet his lips, but continued calling his Redeemer to pardon and release him. As he always would have his door shut, I had no interruption. Carlton kept Anna out of the way, and every promise in the Scriptures and prayer I could remember I continually repeated to him, which seemed to be his only relief. When I stopped to give him anything: "Why do you do it? What do I want? I want to be in heaven. Pray, pray for my soul!" He said he felt so comfortable an assurance that his Redeemer would receive him that he saw his dear little Rebecca smiling before him, and told Ann, "Oh, if your father could take you with him!"

At midnight when the cold sweat came on he would reach out both his arms and say repeatedly, "You promised me you would go; come, come, fly." At four the hard struggle of nature ceased into a settled sob: "My dear wife and little ones," and "My Christ Jesus, have mercy and receive me," was all I could distinguish. He again repeated "My Christ Jesus," until a quarter past seven, when the dear soul took its flight to the blessed exchange it so much longed for.

I often asked him when he could not speak: "You feel, my love, that you are going to your Redeemer?" and he motioned "yes" with a look of peace. At a quarter past seven on Tuesday morning, December 27, his soul was released, and mine, from a struggle next to death. And how will my dear sister understand except you could conceive the scene of suffering my poor William passed through, that I took my little Ann in my arms and made her kneel again with me by the dear body and thank our heavenly Father for relieving him from his misery.[5]

William Magee Seton was not quite thirty-five when he died. Elizabeth was obliged to lay him out herself, with the aid of a "poor woman who had washed for him." According to local law he had to be buried within twenty-four hours, and the American consul and clergyman came to the funeral. The latter's first words to the twenty-nine-year-old widow were: "Whether the tree falls to the south or to the north, and in whatever place it falleth, there shall it lie." The Filicchis—the two brothers, Filippo and Antonio, and their two wives—were endlessly kind to the pretty widow and her little girl. The two Filicchi ladies took Elizabeth and Ann to spend some days in Florence, and Elizabeth wrote in her diary:

"I had a good fire in my room, locked the door, and with my Ann, books and pen passed a happy evening for this world. When we had said our dear service together, she burst into tears as she has always done, since we say it alone. She says: 'My dear papa is praising God in Heaven, and I ought not to cry for him. But I believe it is human nature, is it not, Mama? I think of what David said, "I shall go to him, he cannot return to me.'" Her conversation is dearer to me and preferable to any I can have this side of the grave. It is one of the greatest mercies that I was permitted to bring her, for many reasons."[6]

The Filicchis, noting Elizabeth's piety, talked with her of religion, and took her on a pilgrimage to Monte Nero, where the Vallombrosian monks had hidden Filippo during the French occupation of Leghorn. Mass was said in the chapel, and Elizabeth asked to be allowed to attend. At the elevation of the Sacred Host, a young Englishman approached her and said in a subdued but sarcastic tone, "There is what they consider their Real Presence."

> My very heart [she says] trembled with pain and sorrow for his unfeeling interruption of their sacred adoration; for all around was dead silence, and many were prostrated. Involuntarily I bent from him to the pavement, and thought secretly on the words of St. Paul, with starting tears, "They discern not the Lord's body": and the next thought was, how should they eat and drink their own damnation for not discerning it, if indeed it is not there? And how did He breathe my soul into me? And how, and how a hundred other things I know nothing about? I am a mother; so the mother's thought came also. How was my God a little babe in the first stage of His mortal existence in Mary? But I lost these thoughts in my babes at home, which I daily long for, more and more.[7]

In April, 1804 she embarked for New York with Anna, again on the *Shepherdess* and with Antonio Filicchi, whom his brother sent as Elizabeth's escort, since "many things might happen on the voyage from the danger of pirates and hostile cruisers." But in the night the *Shepherdess* collided during a storm with another ship and was seriously damaged. Little

Anna, the next day, had a high fever; the doctor diagnosed scarlet fever. Three more weeks before they could sail, but no sooner was Anna well, than Elizabeth came down with the same illness. The Filicchis improved upon the occasion to encourage Elizabeth's devotion to the Blessed Sacrament.

"The other day, in a moment of extreme distress," she wrote, "I fell on my knees as the Blessed Sacrament passed and, as though in agony, cried to God to bless me, if He were there, since my soul only longed only for Him."

In *Dear Remembrances* she recalls her anguish, whenever the Blessed Sacrament passed in the street: was she the only one He did not bless? Antonio taught her to make the sign of the Cross one evening when she was standing by a window in full moonlight, which shone on Antonio's face, standing beside her. Lent began, and Elizabeth was impressed by the fact that Mrs. Filicchi never ate a mouthful before 3 p.m., telling Elizabeth she offered her fatigue and the discomfort of the fast for her sins, in union with the sufferings of her Saviour. But even more impressive was the fact that all four Filicchis went daily to Mass.

The Filicchis also gave her books: Bossuet, and St. Francis de Sales, and they wrote on her behalf to Monsignor John Carroll, the first Catholic bishop in the U.S.A. who had become Bishop of Baltimore in 1789.

Finally, on April 8, an Italian ship, the *Flamingo* with Elizabeth, Antonio and Anna on board, left Leghorn, Filippo Filicchi's last words to Elizabeth were: "I will see you again on Judgment Day." The journey took fifty-six days, and later Elizabeth wrote: "Very dear Antonio, a thousand times dearer to me because of your soul's struggles." On June 4 the *Flamingo* docked in New York. On the quay were Elizabeth's four children, also her sister Mary, her brother-in-law Wright Post, her sisters-in-law Harriet and Cecilia. But Rebecca Seton was not there. She, like her brother William, was dying of consumption. Elizabeth spent all the time she could with the dying girl; on July 8 Elizabeth wrote: "this is my Rebecca's birthday in heaven." "No home anymore," Elizabeth noted trenchantly in *Dear Remembrances*. "Husband, husband's sister, home all gone; nothing left but poverty and sorrow."[11]

And persecution. For when Elizabeth declared her intention of becoming a Catholic, her friends, one and all, first tried to dissuade her, then, finding they could not, abandoned her or tried to hurt her.

Elizabeth wrote to Filippo Filicchi's wife on July 19, 1804:

The children are all asleep. This is my time of many thoughts. I had a most affectionate note from Mr. Hobart today, asking me how I could ever think of leaving the church in which I was baptized. But though whatever he says to me has the weight of my partiality for him, as well as the respect, it seem to me, I could scarcely have for anyone else, yet that question made me smile, for it is like saying that wherever a child is born, and wherever its parents place it, it will find the truth. And he does not hear the droll invitations made me every day since I am in my little new home and old friends come to see me. For it has already happened that one of the most excellent women I ever knew, who is of the Church of Scotland, finding me unsettled about the great object of a true faith, said to me, "Oh! do, dear soul, come and hear our J. Mason, and I am sure you will join us."

A little after came one whom I loved for the purest and most innocent manners, and belonging to the Society of Friends, to which I have always been attached. She, too, coaxed me with artless persuasion: "Betsy, I tell thee, thou had best come with us."

Then my faithful old friend, Mrs. T. of the Anabaptist meeting, says, with tears in her eyes, "Oh! could you be regenerated, could you know our experiences and enjoy with us our heavenly banquet."

And my good servant Mary, the Methodist, groans and "contemplates," as she expresses it, "my soul so misled, because I have yet no convictions."

But, O my God! all this will not do for me! Your

word is truth and without contradiction wherever it is!
One faith, one hope, one baptism, I look for wherever
it is, and I often think of my sins, my miseries, hide
the light. Yet will I cling to my God to the last, begging for that light, and never change until I find it.[8]

Elizabeth was to find true an old-fashioned, snobbish
American definition of denominations which declares: "A
Methodist is a Baptist who has gone to High School; a Presbyterian is a Methodist who has gone to college; an Episcopalian is a Presbyterian who has gotten into society; a Papist
is an Episcopalian who has gotten religion." It was the *social*
status of Catholics which made Elizabeth Seton's relatives
totally unable to understand her Roman leanings. More than a
century later, one of Elizabeth's great-nieces, Catholic by
birth, was asked at her school: "How can you belong to that
Church of cooks?" This surprised Katherine Seton Henry not
a little, as, raised in France, she had found her co-religionists
there to be oftener duchesses than cooks.

Mr. Hobart suggested Elizabeth read Thomas Newton, a
Protestant divine; the pastor of St. Peter's Catholic church
offered Manning's *Conversion of England*. Elizabeth, per-
plexed and torn, finally sent Filippo Filicchi's letter to Monsignor Carroll. She received his reply on August 22, 1804.
This letter has disappeared, but her anguished letters to Antonio remain, and show how unsure she was. Only on the
Feast of the Epiphany, 1805, did she resolve her doubts:
reading a sermon of Bourdaloue's for that day, she decided
that her quest for the "true church of Christ" must be pur-
sued, even though Mr. Hobart had told her that she was
exposing herself to temptation in undertaking such a search.
On Ash Wednesday, 1805, she became a Catholic and made
on the Feast of the Annunciation (March 25) her first communion in the Catholic church. As she wrote to Filippo's wife,
"At last God is mine, and I am His."

Financially, Elizabeth was in desperate straits. William
Magee had left his wife and five children practically destitute.
Elizabeth refused to return to the Filicchis, who offered to

receive them all in Leghorn. Now that she could go to Mass daily in the United States, why should she leave her country? A couple called White suggested they open a school together, for both boys and girls. Elizabeth had to leave the house she had rented, and went to live with her sister Mary in Greenwich, in the country. No Mass, and Mary overtly despized Elizabeth's church: "Catholics are dirty, they spit on the floor of their churches" she said.

Elizabeth was nonetheless called to the dying: her step-mother and step-sister. But assisting the dying was not a way to earn her daily bread, and Elizabeth found herself in worse and worse penury. Antonio Filicchi, who had been travelling in Canada, proposed that Elizabeth should go there to open a school, or at least that she should send William and Richard to school in Montreal. She refused. Matters worsened when Cecilia, William Magee's sister, now aged fifteen, walked out of the house, where she had been locked up lest Elizabeth contaminate her, and became a Catholic on June 20, 1806. Now all hell broke out: the Rev. Hobart warned his parishoners against Elizabeth, Eliza Sadler and Catherine Dupleix disowned her, and her maternal uncle Dr. John Charlton and her godmother, Mrs. Startin, cut her out from their wills. (They had made her sole heir, and were both immensely rich.) On Christmas Day, 1806, there were anti-Catholic riots around St. Peter's church; one man was killed, several were wounded. Elizabeth was in New York. She realized she must move. Monsignor Carroll suggested to Elizabeth that she come to Baltimore and open a school. Elizabeth agreed, and arrived there in June, 1808.

On June 19 she took the coach for Washington, to collect her two sons from Georgetown for the summer. (She had sent them to Georgetown, a Jesuit college founded by Monsignor Carroll.) In the coach she sat next to Father Hurley, who was accompanied by a new Catholic convert, Samuel Sutherland Cooper. He was 39, Elizabeth 33. They instantly were attracted to each other and might, indeed, have married, both being quite free. But both had already felt another call, that of life devoted exclusively to God. Cooper was very rich; he could easily have raised Elizabeth's children and taken every care of her and of them. But it was not to be. Elizabeth gave him her rosary, and he entered the seminary. She, after opening a school for seven girls in Paca St., Baltimore (she accepted only Catholic girls), decided to move to Emmitsburg, in Frederick County, fifty miles from Baltimore. Here, with money provided by Mr. Cooper, on a site two miles from the new Sulpician foundation of Mount St. Mary, a small farm with a stone house was bought.

Elizabeth Seton, with three other aspirants to the religious state, was blessed by Bishop Carroll, who was the first to call her "Mother Seton," the name she bore for the rest of her life, and beyond it. She pronounced her vows to him in private, and she and her four companions took the name of "Sisters of St. Joseph." Their habit closely resembled her widow's garb: a long black robe with a cape and a hood, and a small bonnet of white starched muslin with a ruche surrounding the face. Mother Seton and four other Sisters assumed this habit on June 1, 1809 (the Feast of Corpus Christi) in Baltimore.

On June 21 the five new Sisters, plus Cecilia and Harriet Seton, who had joined Elizabeth, made the move to Emmitsburg. It was a two-day journey, and "we were obliged to walk the horses all the way, and have walked ourselved, all except Cecilia, nearly half the way; this morning four miles and a half before breakfast . . . the dogs and pigs came out to meet us, and the geese stretched their necks in mute demand to know if we were any of their sort, to which we gave assent."

Cecilia, who, like her brother and sister Rebecca, had tuberculosis, at first improved quickly in the mountain air of Emmitsburg. She was able, in that glorious June weather, to take long walks, accompanied by Harriet and Elizabeth. Already, in the first days of July, two new sisters joined the little group, and on July 31, 1809, community life began in the Stone House. There were 20 living there, and already the house was too small. The Sulpician father who directed the community, Father Dubourg, bade them grow carrots as quickly as they could, as "carrot coffee" would be their daily drink, salt pork their food. The dream Elizabeth Seton had at 18, of a little country house where "she could collect the local children and teach them their prayers, to keep clean and be good" had become reality.

The new community was modelled on St. Vincent de Paul's Sisters of Charity. Elizabeth Seton wrote to Antonio Filicchi in December, 1809 that "you will laugh when I tell you that your wicked little sister is placed at the head of a community of saints, ten of the most pious souls you could wish, considering that some of them are young and all are under thirty. Six more postulants are waiting till we move into a large place to receive them, and we might be a very large family if I received half who desired to come."

Elizabeth Seton's eldest son William now fell very ill and was expected to die. He recovered, but his aunt Harriet, who had been sewing his shroud, fell ill instead of a "brain fever" and died on December 22. The following February 22 the Sisters opened their school for the village children. Cecilia, meanwhile, was dying, in perfect resignation, as the following letter she wrote testifies:

March 5
I cannot express to my soul's father my longing for the Holy Communion. I receive as often as the Sisters, but I seem to desire still more; and days that I do not receive Him I am not the same creature. I have much more comfort in my Communions than formerly. According to our necessities He gives. Death and eternity ever before me! Why is it so? Because Thou, dearest Lord, givest me some pain, some bodily uneasiness, to remind me of the slightness of that thread which holds my existence. Was it always so? Once you saw my weakness, and pitied it. You have made me see, dear Lord, the vanity of all human things. I now truly feel this life a weary pilgrimage, and long for the hour when my mortal part shall be dissolved, and I shall be at rest. Cut and crucify this sinful body here; here let it pay the penalty that is

due; but oh, my Jesus, spare me hereafter! At the hour of death, comfort and receive me!

Mother Seton wrote to Mrs. Eliza Sadler at the same time:

March, 1810
Soon I expect my dear, dear, a thousand times dear, Cecilia will take her flight. Oh, Eliza, how many strings draw up as well as downward! Yet my heart faints when I think of this separation. No one can conceive what she is to me—but—but—fiat! Cecilia will very soon follow Harriet, I think in a few months, more probably weeks. What can I say? They are both far dearer to me than myself;—we part, nature groans, for me it is an anguish that threatens to solution. Not in convulsive sobs, but the soul is aghast, petrified; after a short while it returns to its usual state, and all goes on as if nothing had happened. This same effect has followed the death of all so dear. Why, Faith lifts the soul, Hope supports it, Experience says it must, and Love says—let it be.[9]

Cecilia died on April 29, 1810. On May 3, Anna Maria was fifteen and had a beau, Charles Dupavillon, almost 18 at her Catholic College in Baltimore. He was born into an excellent Catholic family, and had been sent from his native Guadeloupe to Baltimore. Elizabeth, leaving Anna Maria alone for the first time in her life in order to be with Cecilia at Emmitsburg, insisted all her letters must be read by Mrs. Barry, with whom Anna was staying, and that under no circumstances must Anna ever be alone for a moment with Charles. Charles left Baltimore for the summer, having told Anna Maria—"Anina"—that he would return in the fall, and officially ask for her hand. Anina had refused him a farewell kiss . . . he wrote her two heartbroken letters, then forgot her and married another.

At the end of May, 1810 Mother Seton wrote: "We have

had uninterrupted sickness in our house throughout the entire winter. . . . I have a large school to supervise, together with furnishing religious instruction to all the country around. Everyone has recourse to the Sisters of Charity, who are devoted day and night to the sick and the ignorant. Our holy Bishop intends to transfer some of us to Baltimore in order that we may render the same services there. . . . Our dear Bishop is so much in love with our community that he regards us as the most cherished portion of his flock. This is my consolation in every difficulty and obstacle. . . . We can hope that which we have begun here is the seed of a great future good."

Anina returned in the summer to Emmitsburg. There she remained for the following two years. In the summer of 1811 she learned that Charles Dupabillon was engaged to a Guadeloupan girl. Her mother wrote to her friend Julia Scott that all was thus for the best, and that she was thankful to have Anina stay quietly with her at Emmitsburg. In October, Mother Seton wrote Julia that Anina was as quiet as a cat in its corner. At 16, Anina decided she had a religious vocation. She ate as little as the professed sisters; she carried water with them from the river, and wrote to her Baltimore schoolmates that she did not despair of seeing them rejoin their little *nun*. In October influenza (not yet known by that name) attacked the Emmitsburg community. William and Anina took it badly. Exhausted by their fever, both children recovered, though Anina had a tiresome cough, and by December could no longer leave her room. Running on the ice, little Rebecca, aged nine, fell and was never out of pain after the fall. "Everyone will say," Anina remarked one day, "that the reason for her illness was that she had been jilted by her Charles. That," Anina said, "was a mortification, but my Lord knows how much I have thanked him." When a painful surgical thread was introduced into her side to drain the mucous, she said that would be her penance for having tightened her stays to try and have a tiny waist, like her friends. On January 30 she received the last sacraments "with *my* feelings towards them," her mother noted in her diary. She lived on until March 12, when she died while her mother was in the chapel.

The conflicting demands of a mother's life and that of a professed nun have always torn those who attempted both. Saint Jeanne Chantal actually stepped over the body of her eldest son, who did not want her to enter a convent. After Marie Martin-Guyard entered the Ursulines at Tours, her son Claude, aged twelve, threw stones at the convent windows crying: "Give me back my mother." Later, as Dom Claude Martin, a Benedictine, he wrote his mother's life and declared that her vocation had engendered his. Louise de Marillac, another Founder, had a son, Michael, who entered the seminary only to leave it and marry.

It was in July, 1819, that seventeen Sisters of Charity of St. Joseph made for the first time their annual vows. Already in 1814, the Sisters took over an orphanage in Philadelphia; by January, 1817, when the State of Maryland officially incorporated the institute founded by Mother Seton, there were twenty-eight members of the Association. Meanwhile, her own children continued to give her trouble. William wanted to go to sea; his mother adored him, as she did her tall Richard, at sixteen as big as his eighteen-year-old brother. But, as she wrote to Antonio Filicchi, "they are, so far, children of exemplary conduct . . . but they have no striking talents, no remarkable qualifications, nor are their dispositions even unfolded." Father Bruté de Remur, a French Supician much attached to Mother Seton, was scheduled to leave for Europe to seek for young priests willing to come to the United States. Mother Seton decided to send her son William with him, to be apprenticed to the Filicchis at Leghorn as his father had been. She had not heard from either of the Filicchi brothers for two years; the Napoleonic wars had interrupted correspondence. But she sent William off with a letter to Antonio saying, "poor William was obliged to go on to you without waiting to know your will on the subject." Her farewell letter to William on May 21, 1815 begins, "My own William, Your two dear letters from New York came safe and your last word opposite the battery. Oh, my William, tears will overpower and my soul cries for our eternity. My dear, dear one, if the world should draw you from our God and me! Not meet there! That thought I cannot bear. I will hope, I do hope. My God, who knows a mother's love, sees and will pity . . . dearest, dear, dear William, we are all taking care of one another, that we may live to see you again. . . . Guard well, my dear one, that pure heart which will be the charm of our reunion. Oh, if our God should be forgotten in that heart and it should become . . . No, no never, never let me die and be gone before that insupportable sorrow comes. I pray for you incessantly."

Less than two years later, William returned to the U.S.A. He was hopeless. Antonio Filicchi would not even employ him as his secretary, as his right hand had some kind of shakiness which made him inept at copying. William was now allowed to go into the navy, while his younger brother Richard took his place with Antonio Filicchi. William abandoned his first ship for a frigate, the *Macedonia*, which was to be two years in the Pacific. Meanwhile, at home—in the convent at Emmitsburg—Rebecca died amid intolerable suffering, from a huge tumor on her hip. Rebecca was only thirteen, but she was able to say, on October 17, 1816, that if the doctor were to say to her, "Rebecca, you are going to recover,' I would not want it. Oh, no, no, no, my dear Saviour, I know now the joy of dying young and sinning no more." She died in her mother's arms on November 3rd.

Mother Seton wrote to tell William the news. "My soul's William," she began, and told him his last letter had arrived the day before Rebecca died, while "she was even in her last agony. I told her your tender love, and she raised her eyes to the crucifix . . . 'Tell him only to meet me.' In the arms and on the doting heart of her mother, she gave the last sigh. Nine weeks, night and day, I had her in my arms, even eating my meal with one hand often behind her pillow. Her pains could find no relief or solace but in her own poor mother, so happy to bear them with her that truly it has in no way hurt me." William seems to have been an affectionate son; in April, 1818 his mother wrote him: "My soul's own beloved. Now do tell me what a mother can say to so bad a child? You love me, but not one word will you ever say about my idol, yourself . . .

my soul's dear one, pity my anxiety. I can no more hinder it than I can stop my desires for our eternal reunion."

In 1819, on March 13, William wrote from Valparaiso: "Oh, my dearest mother! May God grant us the blessing to meet again and find you well. Don't be tired of life before I can see you once more."

Mother Seton confided some of her most private thoughts at this time to paper: "Alone on a rock this afternoon, surrounded by the most beautiful scenery, and adoring and praising Him for His magnificence and glory, the heavy eye could find no delight the soul cried out: 'O God, O God, give yourself. What is all the rest?' A silent voice of love answered: 'I am yours.' Then dearest Lord, keep me as I am, while I live, for this is true content, to hope for nothing, to desire nothing, expect nothing, fear nothing. Death, Eternity."

Another time when she was sitting writing at a table looking at the door of the chapel, she asked herself whether this was not a daily martyrdom! She loved and she lived in an indescribable state of being torn. Her being and her existence, she realized, were real enough, since she meditated, she prayed, she took communion, she directed her community and did it all with regularity, abandonment to God's will and simplicity. Yet it was not she who did all; it all proceeded from a sort of automatism, no doubt approved by the all merciful Father, but proceeding from another source than that from which arises the momentum to our acts. In meditation, in prayer, in communion, she declared she found herself without a soul; in the tabernacle, she knew He was present, but she neither saw nor felt Him. A thousand threats of death would not make her deny His presence there for a single instant . . . yet to her it seemed He was not there for her.

Father Bruté de Remur had, she wrote him, made her realize the "grace of the present moment" so luminously that perhaps "it is to that I shall owe my salvation, because this light has made me able to avoid faults and sins." And she was aware of, and grateful, both to God and to Antonio Filicchi, that "the little grain of mustard seed" which Antonio, by

God's hand, had planted in the U.S.A., had grown and spread so widely, in sixteen short years. "So many orphans fed and clothed," she wrote, and added that "the orphan asylums in Philadelphia and New York promise more than we could have hoped."

From 1819 on, Mother Seton had been failing. No pain, only increasing weakness and fatigue. In August, 1820, she was very ill but rallied when she learnt that William would be returning to "the Mountain," as he called Emmitsburg, in January to see her. Later that fall, however, she learned that Richard, whom she thought safely in Italy with the Filicchis, had proved to be as total a failure as William had been, and was actually back in the U.S.A., held for debts in Norfolk, Virginia. Eternity grew daily nearer, and on January 1, 1821 she said, "One communion more and then Eternity." She died, very peacefully, at about two a.m. on the morning of January 4, 1821, with her remaining daughter Catherine and her Sisters praying beside her. She was 47 years old.

NOTES CHAPTER 15

1. Madame de Barbarey, *Elizabeth Seton* (Emmitsburg: Guild Press, 1957), p. 58.

2. *Ibid.*, p. 43.

3. *Ibid.*, p. 45.

4. *Ibid.*, p. 63.

5. *Ibid.*, p. 69.

6. *Ibid.*, p. 81.

7. *Ibid.*, p. 86.

8. *Ibid.*, p. 110.

16

MARY BAKER EDDY
(1821–1910)

Perhaps the most remarkable woman ever to be born on the American continent, and the only female founder of a world religion, was a total failure until she was over sixty. Yet in less than thirty years—she died aged 89—she established a Church which had nearly half a million adherents in the U.S., in 1936 and 3200 branches world wide as of 1975, with devotees around the globe. *The Christian Science Monitor*, founded by Mrs. Eddy in 1908, is one of the most influential journals in the world, and Mary Baker Eddy, who was almost penniless until 1875 (she was then unable to pay $1.50 a week for board and lodging) died worth over $3,000,000 personally. She herself believed that her book, *Science and Health with Key to the Scriptures* was not "of human origin" and also believed herself to be a "scribe echoing harmonies of heaven in divine metaphysics." When 88 she wrote to her only son, George Glover, "Although it is duly estimated by business characters that I am obeyed by 300,000 people at this date . . . . Hoke Smith says I am the most illustrious woman on the continent. What is all this? I am not made the least proud of it or a particle happier for it. I am working for a higher purpose."

Mary Baker, whom Mark Twain called "the most daring and masculine and masterful woman that has appeared on earth in centuries," was born on 16 July 1821, the youngest of the six children of Mark and Abigail Baker. Her father farmed five hundred acres in the township of Bower in New Hampshire. Mark Baker was "a tiger for temper and always in a row" as a neighbor characterized him, whereas Mary's mother, Abigail Ambrose, was a gentle person, of whom her daughter later wrote:

> "O sweet that home where *Mother* smiled
> It paid a father's frown."

Mary claimed six generations of Bakers behind her, the first coming from East Anglia to Charlestown, Mass. in 1654. Mary also claimed a former British Ambassador to Persia, the Right Honorable Sir John MacNeil, G.C.B. among her ancestors, taking as hers his coat of arms, and his motto, *Vincere aut mori* (win or die). His relatives denied her right, and requested "biographers to refrain from connecting her" with Sir John. Mary Baker, however, continued to use Sir John's arms, crests and mottoes, and retained the paragraph in her *Introspection and Retrospection* in which she asserted her relationship to him.

Mary's father declared that his youngest child had ten devils to Mary Magdalen's seven: she had constant fits of hysteria which he called tantrums. She would sometimes have convulsions, sometimes fall into a cataleptic state in which she would lie motionless on the floor. Her first childhood religious experience before she was ten, according to her own account, was hearing a voice call "Mary" many times. Once Mary's cousin Mehitabel heard the voice too, so Mary's mother bade Mary answer in the words of Samuel "Speak Lord, for thy servant heareth." She did so, and the voice neither replied nor ever was heard again. Mary has given a moving account of the effect the Calvinist doctrine of predestination had on her also at an early age. She was "so perturbed by the thoughts aroused by this erroneous doctrine" that she fell ill with a fever. Her mother bathed her burning temples, and bade her "lean on God's love, which would give me rest if I went to him in prayer, as I was wont to do, seeking his guidance. I prayed. I felt a soft glow of ineffable joy come over me. The fever was gone. The physician marvelled, and the 'horrible decree,' as

John Calvin rightly called his own tenet, forever lost its power over me." (*Retrospection and Introspection*, by Mary Baker Eddy, p.13). At the examination for candidates for admission to the Tilton Congregational Church, (which Mary said occurred when she was 12, but which the official church records show did not occur until she was seventeen) Mary refused to be united in communion with the said church if she had to assent to the doctrine of predestination. Her denial was so eloquent that "even the oldest church members wept" (according to Mary) and she was admitted to chuch membership in spite of her heresy.

Mary was always enchantingly pretty. As a child she had curly reddish-brown hair and large, deep eyes of changing color, "steady gray or angry black or seraphic blue, according as mood, costume, or sky affected them." (*Mary Baker Eddy*, by Ernest Sutherland Bates, Alfred A. Knopf, N.Y. 1932 p.16) She had small hands and feet and was alway slender. In 1832 her eldest brother married Eliza Glover, and George Washington Glover, Eliza's brother, took pretty Mary on his knees and promised to return in five years and marry her. Mary's other two brothers left home to better themselves, and Mary's letters to them, although mispelled and ungrammatical, are nevertheless delightful, full of warmth and spirit.

In 1836 Mary's father sold his farm and moved to Sanborton Bridge, and fifteen year old Mary, who had rarely attended school at Bow, now went to the district school, where she studied long division. She remained however only three or four weeks, then left because of illness. In 1842 she was sufficiently recovered to attend Sanborton Academy. She may have attended Shaker meetings at this time, and her first poems were published in the *Belknap Gazette*.

George Washington Glover reappeared in 1843, and he and Mary were married on December 12, by Dr. Enoch Corser, ths pastor of the Congregational Church who had long admired Mary's interest in "deep subjects." Glover was a Royal Arch Mason from Charleston. He belonged to the State Militia and was on the Governor's staff. Mary Baker referred to him as "Colonel Glover" and, when someone questioned his rank, explained "I called my late husband Colonel, because he was connected with the militia and I had got mixed on his rank." He and Mary took a ship for Charleston and later moved to Wilmington, where Glover's plans for a Haitian cathedral went awry. He died of a bilious ailment after nine days of fever, on 27 June 1844. "Maj. Geo. W. Glover" was buried by his brother Masons, and his indigent widow, seven months pregnant, was escorted by one of them home to her parents. Her only child was born on Sept. 11, 1844, six weeks after her return. Too ill to nurse her baby, George Washington Glover was given to a wet-nurse, and later to the Bakers faithful maid, Mahala Sanborn; Mary, according to her own father "acts like an old ewe that won't own its own lamb." When Mahala married one Russell Cheney of North Groton, she took the six-year old boy with Mary's approval, and he remained with her until he was a grown man, never seeing his mother again until he was 34 and married.

The young widow now "welcomed the attentions" of a Methodist minister, the Rev. Richard Rust, who was principal of a school called the New Hampshire Conference Seminary, where Mary acted as a substitute teacher. She also at this time contributed to a magazine called *The Covenant*, in which she published stories and poems. Later she also published in the *New Hampshire Patriot*. A serious suitor, John H. Bartlett then appeared, and he and Mary became engaged, but he died three weeks after Mary's mother, in November 1849. Mark Baker married again in a few months, and Mary went to live with her married sister, Abigail Tilton. It was not a success. In 1852 Mary had her teeth fixed by a travelling dentist, Daniel Patterson, who in March, 1853, asked for her hand. She was still ailing, and had been taking morphine; as a neighbor, Mrs. H.L. Philbrook of Sanborton Bridge wrote in the New York World on October 30, 1906: "the morphine made her crazy." On April 29, 1853, Mary herself wrote Daniel Patterson she had "neuralgia in spine and stomach, my only relief is to take *morphine*." When Mary Baker Glover and Daniel Patterson were married on 21 June 1853, Patterson carried his bride, too ill to walk, downstairs for the ceremony, and upstairs after it.

Mary's health did not improve with marriage, and when her husband was away she was left in the care of a blind girl. She loved to be rocked. The Pattersons removed to North Groton, but Mary's sisters foreclosed on a mortgage they held of the Patterson's house, and moved their invalid sister to a boarding house, where her husband joined her. In 1861, Mary learned that her son had enlisted in the Northern army, and that Daniel Patterson "with perhaps vague ideas of becoming an army physician" on a trip south blundered into the Confederate lines and was taken prisoner, not getting home until July 1862. He found his wife had gone to Portland, Maine, where she had been cured, completely, she declared, of all her ills, by Phineas Parkhurst Quimby, a mental healer, of whom Mary now talked constantly.

In 1907 Georgine Milmine published the story of Mary's cure by Phineas Parkhurst Quimby in *McClure's Magazine*. Later she published her articles as a book entitled *Life of Mary G. Eddy and History of Christian Science*, in 1909, during Mary's lifetime.

The Christian Science Directors brought so much influence to bear on Georgine Milmine's publishers that the book was withdrawn and the plates destroyed; it is now a collector's item. But no substantive denial was made, either during Mary Baker Eddy's lifetime nor since her death, of the facts and affidavits, given both in the *McClure Magazine* articles and in the book.

Pertinent passages from the suppressed volume follow.

"According to George A. Quimby, Quimby's son and secretary, Mrs. Patterson's first stay in Portland lasted about three weeks. As far as her health was concerned the visit seemed a complete success. Under Quimby's treatment the spinal trouble disappeared and Mrs. Patterson left his office a well woman. But this hardly-achieved visit to Portland meant much more to her than that. For the first time in her life she felt an absorbing interest. Her contact with Quimby and her inquiry into philosophy seem to have been her first great experience, the first powerful stimulus in a life of unrestraint, disappointment, and failure. Her girlhood had been a fruitless, hysterical revolt against order and discipline. The dulness and meagreness of her life had driven her to strange extravagances in conduct. Neither of her marriages had been happy. Maternity had not softened her nor brought her consolations. Up to this time her masterful will and great force of personality had served to no happy end. Her mind was turned in upon itself; she had been absorbed in ills which seem to have been largely the result of her own violent nature —lacking any adequate outlet, and, like disordered machinery, beating itself to pieces.

"Quimby's idea gave her her opportunity, and the vehemence with which she seized upon it attests the emptiness and hunger of her earlier years. All during her stay in Portland she haunted the old man's rooms, asking questions, reading manuscripts, observing his treatment of his patients. Quimby at first took a decided liking to her. "She's a devilish bright woman," he frequently said. Always delighted to explain his theories, in Mrs. Patterson he found a most appreciative listener. Both on this and subsequent visits he permitted her to copy certain of his manuscripts. Undoubtedly he saw in Mrs. Patterson, in her capacity as an "authoress," a woman who could assist him in the matter dearest to his heart,—the popularisation of his doctrines.

"Her devotion to her teacher was that of a long-imprisoned nature toward its delivered. Her greatest desire seems to have been to teach Quimby's philosophy and to exalt him in the eyes of men. Soon after her recovery she wrote the following letter to the Portland *Courier*:

> When our Shakespeare decided that "there were more things in this world than were dreamed of in your philosophy," I cannot say of a verity that he had a foreknowledge of P. P. Quimby. And when the school Platonic anatomised the soul and divided it into halves to be reunited by elementary attractions, and heathen philosophers averred that old Chaos in sullen silence brooded o'er the earth until her inimitable form was hatched from the egg of night, I would not at present decide whether the fallacy was found in their premises

or conclusions, never having dated my existence before the flood. When the startled alchemist discovered, as he supposed, an universal solvent, or the philosopher's stone, and the more daring Archimedes invented a lever wherewithal to pry up the universe, I cannot say that in either the principle obtained in nature or in art, or that it worked well, having never tried it. But, when by a falling apple, an immutable law was discovered, we gave it the crown of science, which is incontrovertible and capable of demonstration; hence that was wisdom and truth. When from the evidence of the sense, my reason takes cognizance of truth, although it may appear in quite a miraculous view, I must acknowledge that as science which is truth univestigated. Hence the following demonstration:—

Three weeks since I quitted my nurse and sick room *en route* for Portland. The belief of my recovery had died out of the hearts of those who were most anxious for it. With this mental and physical depression I first visited P.P. Quimby; and in less than one week from that time I ascended by a stairway of one hundred and eighty-two steps to the dome of the City Hall, and am improving *ad infinitum*. To the most subtle reasoning, such a proof, coupled too, as it is with numberless similar ones, demonstrates his power to heal. Now for a brief analysis of this power.

Is it spiritualism? Listen to the words of wisdom. "Believe in God, believe also in me; or believe me for the very work's sake." Now, then, his works are but the result of superior wisdom, which can demonstrate a science not understood; hence it were a doubtful proceeding not to believe him for the work's sake. Well, then, he denies that his power to heal the sick is borrowed from the spirits of this or another world; and let us take the Scriptures for proof. "A kingdom divided against itself cannot stand." How, then, can he receive the friendly aid of the disenthralled spirit, while he rejects the faith of the solemn mystic who crosses the threshold of the dark unknown to conjure up from the vastly deep the awestruck spirit of some invisible squaw?

Again, is it by animal magnetism that he heals the sick? Let us examine. I have employed electro-magnetism and animal magnetism, and for a brief interval have felt relief, from the equilibrium which I fancied was restored to an exhausted system or by a diffusion of concentrated action. But in no instance did I get rid of a return of all my ailments, because I had not been helped out of the error in which opinions involved us. My operator believed in disease, inde-pendent of the mind; hence I could not be wiser than my master. But now I can see dimly at first, and only as trees walking, the great principle which underlies Dr. Quimby's faith and works; and just in proportion to my right perception of truth is my recovery. This truth which he opposes to the error of giving intelli-gence to matter and placing pain where it never placed itself, if received understandingly, changes the currents of the system to their normal action; and the mechanism of the body goes on undisturbed. That this is a science capable of demonstration, becomes clear to the minds of those patients who reason upon the process of their cure. The truth which he establishes in the patient cures him (although he may be wholly unconscious thereof); and the body, which is full of light, is no longer in disease. At present I am too much in error to elucidate the truth, and can touch only the keynote for the master hand to wake the harmony. May it be in essays, instead of notes! say I. After all, this is a very spiritual doctrine; but the eter-nal years of God are with it, and it must stand firm as the rock of ages. And to many a poor sufferer may it be found, as by me, "the shadow of a great rock in a weary land."

"Her extravagance brought general ridicule upon Quimby and herself. "P. P. Quimby compared to Jesus Christ?" exclaimed the Portland *Advertiser*, in commenting on her letter, "What next?" Mrs. Patterson again took up the cudgels. She wrote in the Portland *Courier*:

Noticing a paragraph in the *Advertiser*, commenting upon some sentences of mine clipped from the *Courier*, relative to the science of P. P. Quimby, concluding, "What next?" we would reply in due deference to the courtesy with which they define their position. P. P. Quimby stands upon the plane of wisdom with his truth. Christ healed the sick, but not by jugglery or with drugs. As the former speaks as never man before spake, and heals as never man healed since Christ, is he not identified with truth? And is not this the Christ which is in him? We know that in wisdom is life, "and the life was the light of man." P. P. Quimby rolls away the stone from the sepulchre of error, and health is the resurrection. But we also know that "light shineth in darkness and the darkness comprehendeth it not."

"Mrs. Patterson expressed her admiration of Quimby in verse also:

SONNET

Suggested by Reading the Remarkable Cure of Captain J. W. Deering

To Dr. P. P. Quimby

'Mid light of science sits the sage profound,
Awing with classics and his starry lore,
Climbing to Venus, chasing Saturn round,
Turning his mystic pages o'er and o'er
Till, from empyrean space, his wearied sight

Turns to the oasis on which to gaze,
More bright than glitters on the brow of night
The self-taught man walking in wisdom's ways.
Then paused the captive gaze with peace entwined,
And sight was satisfied with thee to dwell;
But not in classics could the book-worm find
That law of excellence whence came the spell
Potent o'er all,—the captive to unbind,
To heal the sick and faint, the halt and blind.

Mary M. Patterson

For the *Courier*.

"Mrs. Patterson returned in good health, as she thought, to Sanbornton Bridge. Quimby became the great possession of her life. She talked incessantly of him to all her friends, and sought to persuade the sick to visit him. In 1863 she wrote many times to Quimby. Her letters, now in the possession of George A. Quimby, describe, in the most reverential terms, her indebtedness.

"The following extracts illustrate the tone of these communications:

> Sanbornton Bridge, January 12, 1863.
> . . . I am to all who see me a living wonder, and a living monument of your power . . . I eat, drink, and am merry, have no laws to fetter my spirit. Am as much an escaped prisoner, as my dear husband was . . . My explanation of your *curative principle* surprises people, especially those whose minds are all matter . . . I mean not again to look mournfully into the past, but wisely to improve the present.

"In a letter dated Sanbornton Bridge, January 31, 1863, she asks for "absent treatment." "Please come to me and remove this pain." In this letter she says that her sister, Mrs. Tilton, and her son, Albert Tilton, are going to visit Mr. Quimby. She says that Albert smokes and drinks to excess, and begs Quimby to treat him for these habits, "even when

Albert is not there." She explains that she herself has treated Albert to help him overcome the habit of smoking and, while doing so, felt "a constant desire to smoke!" She asks Quimby to treat her for this desire. In other letters Mrs. Patterson repeatedly asks for absent treatements, and occasionally incloses a dollar to pay for them.

"In a letter from Saco, Me., September 14, 1863, Mrs. Patterson says that Quimby's "Angel Visits" (absent treatments) are helping her. "I would like to have you in your omnipresence visit me at eight o'clock this evening." On this occasion she speicifies that she wishes to be treated for "small beliefs," namely, "stomach trouble, backache, and constipation."

"In the early part of 1964, Mrs. Patterson again spent two or three months in Portland. She found congenial companions in one Mrs. Sarah Crosby, who was likewise a patient of Quimby's, and Miss Anna Mary Jarvis, who had brought her consumptive sister to Quimby for treatment. Mrs. Crosby and Mrs. Patterson became warm friends. They occupied adjoining rooms in the same boarding-house and spent much time together. Mrs. Patterson told Mrs. Crosby that she intended to assist Quimby in his work. The latter, says Mrs. Crosby, frequently expressed his pleasure at Mrs. Patterson's enthusiasm. "He told me many times," she adds, "that I was not so quick to perceive the Truth as Mrs. Patterson." Quimby now gave Mrs. Patterson much of his time. He was practising then mainly in the morning, and allowed Mrs. Patterson to spend nearly every afternoon at his office. "She would work with Dr. Quimby all afternoon," says Mrs. Crosby, "and then she would come home and sit up late at night writing down what she had learned during the day."

"This second visit to Quimby seems to have been more stimulating to Mrs. Patterson than the first. She gave all her time and strength to the study of this esoteric theory. It was during this visit that she first manifested a desire to become herself an active force in the teaching and practising of his "Science." The desire became actually a purpose, perhaps an ambition—the only definite one she had ever known. She was groping for a vocation. She must even then have seen before her new possibilities; an opportunity for personal growth and personal achievement very different from the petty occupations of her old life. In one of her letters to Quimby, written some months after she left Portland, there is this new note of aspiration and resolve:

> Who is wise but you? . . . Doctor, I have a strong feeling of late that I ought to be perfect after the command of science . . . I can love only a good, honourable, and brave career; no other can suit me.

"Upon leaving Portland, after this second visit, Mrs. Patterson went to Warren, Me., to visit Miss Jarvis. Here she seems to have tried Quimby's treatment upon Miss Jarvis, putting into practice what she learned from Quimby himself during the last three months. "At the mere mention of my going," writes Mrs. Patterson, "Miss Jarvis has a relapse and is in despair."

"She confidently believes that she has benefited the sick woman. Once, after receiving an "absent treatment" from Quimby, she successfully transmitted its blessings to Miss Jarvis. She became so "cheerful and uplifted" that Miss Jarvis "was gay and not at all sad." She also writes that she feels herself not yet ready, being still in her "pupilage."

"In a letter from Warren, March 31, 1864, she says:

> I wish you would come to my aid and help me to sleep. Dear Doctor what could I do without you?.

"In a letter dated Warren, April 5, 1864:

> I met the former editor of the *Banner of Light*, and he heard for once the truth about you. He thought you a defunct Spiritualist, before I quitted him at Brunswick, he had endorsed your *science* and acknowledged himself as greatly interested in it.

"In another letter from Warren, under date of April 24, 1864, she says:

Jesus taught as man does *not*, who then is wise but you? Posted at the public marts of this city is this notice, Mrs. M. M. Patterson will lecture at the Town Hall on P. P. Quimby's Spiritual Science healing disease, as opposed to Deism or Rochester Rapping Spiritualism.

"In a letter dated Warren, May, 1864, she writes that she has been ill, but,

I am up and about to-day, i.e., by the help of the Lord (Quimby).

"Again,

Dear doctor, what could I do without you? . . . I will not bow to wealth for I cannot honour it as I do wisdom . . . May the peace of wisdom which passeth all understanding be and abide with you.—Ever the same in gratitude.

"In one letter she describes the sudden appearance of Quimby's wraith in her room. She spoke to it, she adds, "and then you turned and walked away." "That," she says, "I call dodging the issue." She repeatedly calls his treatment his "Science"; her illnesses, her "beliefs" or "errors"; and her recoveries, her "restorations."

"Mr. Quimby died January 16, 1866. As in the case of many mental healers, his own experience apparently belied his doctrines. He had for years suffered from an abdominal tumour. He had never had it treated medically, but asserted that he had always been able, mentally, to prevent it from getting the upper hand. The last few years of his life he worked incessantly. His practice increased enormously, and at last broke him down. In the summer of 1865 he was compelled to stop work. He closed his Portland office and went home to Belfast to devote the rest of his life to revising his manuscripts and preparing them for publication. His physical condition, however, prevented this; he became feebler every day. He now acknowledged his inability to cure himself. As long as he had his usual mental strength, he said, he could stop the disease; but, as he felt this slipping from him, his "error" rapidly made inroads. Finally, Quimby's wife, with his acquiescence, summoned a homoeopathic physician. Quimby consented to this, he said, not because he had the slightest idea that the doctor could help him, but merely to comfort his family. His wife had never accepted the "theory"; his children, for the most part, had no enthusiasm for it. They all, however, loved the old man dearly and could not patiently witness his suffering without seeking all means to allay it. Quimby followed implicitly all the doctor's instructions. His son, George A. Quimby, says:

> An hour before he breathed his last, he said to the writer: "I am more than ever convinced of the truth of my theory. I am perfectly willing for the change myself, but I know you will all feel badly; but I know that I shall be right here with you, just the same as I have always been. I do not dread the change any more than if I were going on a trip to Philadelphia."
>
> His death occurred January 16, 1866, at his residence in Belfast, at the age of sixty-four years, and was the result of too close application to his profession and of overwork. A more fitting epitaph could not be accorded him than in these words:
>
> "Greater love hath no man than this, that a man lay down his life for his friends." For, if ever a man did lay down his life for others, that man was Phineas Parkhurst Quimby.

"Many mourned Quimby's death. No one felt greater grief or expressed it more emphatically and sincerely than

Mary M. Patterson. She wrote at once to Julius Dresser, asking him to take up the master's work. Her letter follows:

Lynn, February 14, 1866.

Mr. Dresser:

Sir: I enclose some lines of mine in memory of our much-loved friend, which perhaps *you* will not think overwrought in meaning: others *must* of course.

I am constantly wishing that *you* would step forward into the place he has vacated. I believe you would do a vast amount of good, and are more capable of occupying his place than any other I know of.

Two weeks ago I fell on the sidewalk, and struck my back on the ice, and was taken up for dead, came to consciousness amid a storm of vapours from cologne, chloroform, ether, camphor, etc., but to find myself the helpless cripple I was before I saw Dr. Quimby.

The physician attending said I had taken the last step I ever should, but in two days I got out of my bed *alone* and *will* walk; but yet I confess I am frightened, and out of that nervous heat my friends are forming, spite of me, the terrible spinal affection from which I have suffered so long and hopelessly . . . Now can't *you* help me? I believe you can. I write this with this feeling: I think that I could help another in my condition if they had not placed their intelligence in matter. This I have not done, and yet I am slowly failing. Won't you write me if you will undertake for me if I can get to you?.

Respectfully, Mary M. Patterson

"The verses referred to had already been published in a Lynn newspaper.

Lines on the Death of Dr. P. P. Quimby, Who Healed with the Truth that Christ Taught in Contradistinction to All Isms.

Did sackcloth clothe the sun and day grow night,
All matter mourn the hour with dewy eyes,
When Truth, receding from our mortal sight,
Had paid to error her last sacrifice?

Can we forget the power that gave us life?
Shall we forget the wisdom of its way?
Then ask me not amid this mortal strife—
This keenest pang of animated clay—

To mourn him less; to mourn him more were just
If to his memory 'twere a tribute given
For every solemn, sacred, earnest trust
Delivered to us ere he rose to heaven.

Heaven but the happiness of that calm soul.
Growing in stature to the throne of God;
Rest should reward him who hath made us whole,
Seeking, though tremblers, where his footsteps trod.

Mary M. Patterson[1]

Lynn, January 22, 1866.

Julius Dresser, newly married, working as a journalist in Portland, replied to Mary's plea for help: "You say you have not, in your troubles, placed your intelligence in matter, and yet you are slowly failing. If you believe you are failing, then your intelligence is placed in matter. But if you can really place your intelligence outside of matter then do so, and let the Devil take the hindmost . . . be assured he can't get *you*, nor any part of you. Keep your intelligence, which is yourself, out of your matter, and the devil or death won't get you, for he is in matter and that's what's the matter."

[1]*Letter by Mrs. M. M. Patterson (now Mrs. Mary Baker G. Eddy)* in the Portland *Courier*, November 7, 1862.

On February 1, 1866, after her fall, Mary had been taken to the residence of Samuel Bubier, a shoe manufacturer. Here, Dr. Alvin M. Cushing, called upon "to attend said Mrs. Patterson, who had fallen upon the icy sidewalk and had injured her head by the fall" found her "very nervous, partly unconscious, semi-hysterical, complaining by word and action of severe pain in the back of her head and neck . . . I gave her medicines every fifteen minutes till she was more quiet." The next day, Dr. Cushing found her "quite rational." He accompanied her while two men carried her to her home, and visited her "twice on 1 February, twice on 2nd, once on 3rd & once on 5th and 13 my bill was paid" by Mary's husband, Daniel Patterson. Six months later, on August 10, 1866, Dr. Cushing again attended her, on Summer St. in Lynn. She was then suffering from a bad cold. Dr. Cushing made three more professional calls on her at that time, but never met her again after August 31, 1866. To prove these facts Dr. Cushing in 1904 produced his records, and made an affidavit before a notary public. Mary's version of the "fall on the ice" is that on Sunday February 4, 1866—the third day after her fall and eleven days before she wrote to Mr. Dresser—was the day she "discovered" Christian Science. She declared she sent everyone out of her room, opened the New Testament and therein read of the man healed of palsy. At that moment she felt "the lost chord of Truth healing as of old." She rose dressed and walked into the parlor, cured.

Mrs. Milmine comments: "Mrs. Eddy herself says that it was in 1866 she named her discovery Christian Science. Quimby, however, called his theory Christian Science at least as early as 1863. In a manuscript written in that year, entitled "Aristocracy and Democracy," he used these identical words. In the main, however, Quimby called his theory the "Science of Health and Happiness," the "Science of Christ," and many times simply "Science."

What is extraordinary is Mary Baker Glover Patterson's single-mindedness. As Mrs. Milmine points out:[2]

Everything depended upon her getting a hearing. In the first place, her doctrine was her only congenial means of making a living. In the second, it was the one thing about which she know more than the people around her, and it gave her that distinction which was necessary to her. Above all, she had a natural aptitude for the subject and absorbed it until it literally became a part of her. Mercenary motives were always strong with Mrs. Glover, but no mercenary motive seems adequately to explain her devotion to this idea. After Quimby's death in '66, his other pupils were silent; but Mrs. Glover, wandering about with no capital but her enthusiasm, was preaching still. Her fellow students in Portland were people of wider experience than she, and had more than one interest; but only one idea had ever come very close to Mrs. Glover, and neither things present nor things to come could separate her from it. But Mrs. Glover had not the temperament of the dreamer and devotee. There was one thing in her stronger even than her monomania, and that was her masterfulness. Others of his pupils lost themselves in Quimby's philosophy, but Mrs. Glover lost Quimby in herself.

After her last visit to Quimby, Mary wrote she found her husband had "eloped" with a married woman. But records show that she lived with her husband for over a year after this date. After he left her in 1866, Patterson sent his wife an allowance of two hundred dollars annually for some years. In 1873 Mary Patterson obtained a divorce for desertion. Patterson died in the poorhouse in 1896 and was buried in the potters field.

During the first four years after her husband's desertion, Mary Patterson moved nine times, being poor and homeless. Her family would not help her; the friends who took her in soon wearied of her. During those four years Mary Patterson was faithful to Quimby's memory, and still proclaimed herself his disciple.

It was Quimby who gave her a structured system, which she made into a religion. He gave her the name, Christian

Science, and the idea of the feminine principle in the Deity, which she elaborated into the "Father-Mother-God" invoked by her followers. Georgine Milmine wrote:[3]

It is difficult to ascertain definitely just when Mrs. Eddy arrived at the conclusion that mortal mind, not matter, causes sin, sickness, and death, as her own recollection of her initial revelation seems to be somewhat blurred. "As long ago as 1844," she writes in the *Christian Science Journal*, in June, 1887, "I was convinced that mortal mind produced all disease, and that the various medical systems were, in no proper sense, scientific. In 1862, when I first visited Mr. Quimby, I was proclaiming—to druggists, Spiritualists, and mesmerists—that science must govern all healing.

To her discovery of the principle of mental healing, she has assigned no less than three different dates:

In a letter to the Boston *Post*, March 7, 1883, she says:

We made our first experiments in mental healing about 1853, when we were convinced that mind had a science, which, if understood, would heal all disease.

Again, in the first edition of *Science and Health* (1875), she says:

We made our first discovery that science mentally applied would heal the sick, in 1864, and since then have tested it on ourselves and hundreds of others and never found it failed to prove the statement herein made of it.

In *Retrospection and Introspection*, she says:

It was in Massachusetts, in February, 1866, . . . that I discovered the Science of Divine Metaphysical Healing, which I afterwards named Christian Science.

Having found, experientially, that "Mind is All-in-All, and that the only realities are the divine mind and idea" Mary started lecturing. She needed a practicing partner and found one in a young factory worker of twenty-one, Richard Kennedy. Having failed miserably in small towns, she now moved to Lynn, a city then of thirty thousand. Here she signed up students for one hundred dollars for twelve lectures by her. She was also to receive half of Richard Kennedy's earnings as a healer. This agreement was drawn up legally. After a few weeks she raised her tuition fee to 300 dollars, "for tuition lasting barely three weeks. This amount troubled me greatly," she wrote, (*Retrospection and Introspection*, p. 50) "I shank from asking it, but was finally led by a strange providence to accept this fee." In only eighteen months her share of the partnership with Kennedy was almost six thousand dollars.

Mary believed that Christ's second coming was Christian Science: "the second appearing of Jesus is unquestionably the spiritual advent of the advancing idea of God as in Christian Science" she wrote in *Retrospection and Introspection* (pp. 95-96). Quoting Rev.XII.1: "And there appeared a great wonder in Heaven, a woman clothed with the sun, and the moon under her feet upon her head a crown of twelve stars," Mary said "Christ, God's idea, will eventually rule all nations and peoples—imperatively, absolutely, finally—with Divine science. This immaculate idea, represented first by man and last by woman, will baptize with fire" (*Science and Health*, 1898, p. 557). Of herself she wrote in *Science and Health*, 1898, pp. 1-4: "In the year 1866, I discovered the Science of Metaphysical Healing, and named it Christian Science. God had been graciously fitting me, during many years, for the reception of a final revelation of the absolute Principle of Scientific Mind-healing. . . . No human pen or tongue taught me the Science contained in this book . . . and neither tongue nor pen can ever overthrow it."

Although the Christian Science Church was not chartered until 1879, in 1875 Mary's students asked to conduct services of public worship in Lynn, and in June formed a society to be known as the "Christian Scientists." To this society Mary spoke on five successive Sundays in the Templars Hall, receiving five dollars for each address. On December 30, 1876, Mary wrote to her student, Dr. Spofford, "It is mesmerism that I feel and is killing me. It is mortal mind that only can make me suffer." The next day Mary decided to marry, and wrote Dr. Spofford: "For reasons best know to myself I have changed my views in respect to marrying and ask you to hand this note to the Unitarian clergyman and please wait for his answer." It was however another student, Gilbert Eddy, whom she married on New Years day 1877, not Dr. Spofford. The latter noticed that the age of both bride and groom was given as 40 years. Dr. Spofford knew Mary was in her fifty-sixth year, and remarked on the inaccuracy, but the new Mrs. Eddy explained that the statement of age was mere formality, and a few years more or less was of no consequence.

Dr. Spofford had been very helpful in advertising Mary's book *Science and Health*, which was finally published in 1875, and paid for by two students, Elizabeth Newhall and George Barry. The first edition of 1000 copies, which cost $2,200, was peddled personally by Dr. Spofford. Between 1875 and its author's death the book went into over five hundred editions.

The most theologically interesting of the many editions was the third, published in the spring of 1881, upon which Mary and her husband, Gilbert Eddy, worked together. It contains the chapter on *Demonology* which discusses Mary's "enemies"—all erstwhile pupils—and declares them motivated by Malicious Animal Magnetism (M.A.M.), mentioning them by their initials: Richard Kennedy, her first assistant; Barry, who financed the first edition of her book; and D.S.—Daniel Spofford, who so valiantly had peddled it. In this, and her many lawsuits, Mary tried to prove her "enemies" used witchcraft against her and thus admits to a gnosticism entirely absent from Quimby's teaching, though she never knew the meaning of the word. "What," she asked the Rev. James Henry Wiggin, "is the difference between Agnosticism and Gnosticism?" How to account for death, evil, sickness, death? Mary's answer was Malicious Animal Magnetism.

The *Key to the Scriptures*, added to "my book" by Mary Baker Eddy in 1884 contains a glossary, giving new meaning to Biblical words: "Death" is "an illusion"; "Mother" should read "God." In the chapter *Apocalypse*, added in 1886, Mary Baker Eddy suggests she is the "feminine principle of deity" referred to by St. John. She believed she suffered from the fears she removed from others: three months after her marriage to Mr. Eddy, she wrote to a student: "Direct your thoughts and everybody else's that you can away from me . . ."

It was in 1885 that Mary Baker Eddy first met the Rev. Wiggin, whom she hired to "rewrite" the third edition of *Science and Health*. To his surprise, she "acceded to my terms of recompense." It was he who persuaded her to leave out much of the *Demonology* chapter as being libellous. Miss Milmine describes the collaboration: "On the whole Mrs. Eddy seems to have got along amicably with Mr. Wiggin. She liked him, greatly respected his scholarship, and was pleased to make use of his versatile talents. He, on the other hand, assisted her with good nature, advised her, and defended her with a sort of playful gallantry that went with his generous make of mind and body."[4]

The Rev. James Henry Wiggin, an ordained Protestant minister, was theologically sound. His account of Christian Science and of its founder's ideas follows:

> Christian Science, on its theological side, is an ignorant revival of one form of ancient gnosticism, that Jesus is to be distinguished from the Christ, and that his earthly appearance was phantasmal, not real and fleshly.
>
> On its moral side, it involves what must follow from the doctrine that reality is a dream, and that if a thing is right in thought, why right it is, and that sin is non-existent, because God can *behold* no evil. Not that Christian Science believers generally see this, or practice evil, but the virus is within.
>
> Religiously, Christian Science is a revolt from orthodoxy, but unphilosophically conducted, endeavouring to ride two horses.

Physically it leads people to trust all to nature, the great healer, and so does some good. Great virtue in imagination! . . . Where there is disease which time will not reach, Christian Science is useless.

As for the High Priestess of it, . . . she is—well I could *tell* you, but not write. An awfully (I use the word advisedly) smart woman, acute, shrewd, but not well read, nor in any way learned. What she has, as documents clearly show, she got from P.P. Quimby of Portland, Maine, whom she eulogised after death as the great leader and her special teacher . . . She tried to answer the charge of the adoption of Quimby's ideas, and called me in to counsel her about it; but her only answer (in print!) was that if she said such things twenty years ago, she must have been under the influence of *animal magnetism,* which is *her* devil. No church can long get on without a devil, you know. Much more I could say if you were here . . .

One of Mrs. Eddy's followers went so far as to say that if she *saw* Mrs. Eddy commit a crime she should believe her own sight at fault, *not* Mrs. Eddy's conduct. An intelligent man told me in reference to lies he *knew* about, that the wrong was in *us*. "Was not Jesus accused of wrong-doing, yet guiltless?"

Only experience can teach these fanatics, *i.e.*, the real believers, not the charlatans who go into it for money. . . . As for the book, if you have any edition since December, 1885, it had my supervision. Though now she is getting out an entirely new edition, with which I had nothing to do, and occasionally she has made changes whereof I did not know. The chapter B—told you of is rather fanciful, though, to us Mrs. Eddy's language in her last note, her "friends think it a gem." It is the one called "Wayside Hints," and was added after the work was not only in type, but cast, because she wished to take out some twenty pages of diatribe on her dissenters. . . . I do not think it will greatly edify you, the chapter. As for clearness, many

Christian Science people thought her early editions much better, because they sounded more *like* Mrs. Eddy. The truth is, she does not care to have her paragraphs clear, and delights in so expressing herself that her words may have various readings and meanings. Really that is one of the tricks of the trade. You know sibyls have always been thus oracular, to "keep the word of promise to the ear, and break it to the hope."

There is nothing really to understand in "Science and Health" except that *God is all*, and yet there is no God in matter! What they fail to explain is, the origin of the *idea* of matter, or sin. They say it comes from *mortal mind*, and that mortal mind is not divinely created, in fact, has no existence; in fact, that nothing comes of nothing, and that matter and disease are like dreams, having no existence. Quimby had definite ideas, but Mrs. Eddy has not understood them.[5]

On June 3, 1882, Gilbert Eddy died. According to the doctor who attended him, his death was due to organic heart disease. Mary Baker Eddy, however, told the *Boston Post* (interview published on June 5, 1882) that "circumstances debarred me from taking hold of my husband's case . . . I was so entirely absorbed in business that . . . when I had awakened to the danger it was too late. I have cured worse cases." She added, "My husband's death was caused by malicious mesmerism. . . . I know it was poison that killed him, not material poison but mesmeric poison."

It was only after Gilbert Eddy's death, when she was sixty, that Mary Baker Eddy's real triumphs began. She moved often, from Lynn to Boston to Chicago, and was involved in many lawsuits, most of them against former students or relatives. But her Church grew and more editions of her book were published. Since every Christian Scientist had to buy a copy of the most recent edition, the book continued to sell. Her "Nexters" as she called them (Next Friends) who included her son and his family, also brought suits against her, but still Mary Baker Eddy won over or outlived them all.

When she died, at 10:45 p.m. on December 3, 1910, of pneumonia, she was in her ninetieth year. On Dec. 1, she had written in pencil on a pad: "God is my life."

Mary Baker Eddy had asked Adam Dickey, a member of the Board of Directors of the Mother Church, to write a description of how she had been "mentally murdered rather than "died". This was published as a book of 147 pages in 1927, but was suppressed by the other Directors, because Dickey had published his book when he had been authorized "merely to write it." His book, like that of Mrs. Milmine, was thereafter destroyed by the faithful Christian Scientists, but the copywright copies in the Library of Congress, and one in the New York public library remain. *Scripta manent.*

But what do Mary Baker Eddy's many lawsuits, her peccadiloes or failures matter now? Her writings remain, and only they (and the Bible) are read in her churches (no sermons or comments are allowed) and they are permanently copywrighted. Above all her Church remains, the most astonishing artifact ever produced by any woman. It does not matter whether she stole the original ideas from Quimby; what matters is that she so absorbed and propagated these ideas, that it is she who is rightly revered as the Foundress of Christian Science, to which she left the bulk of her immense fortune. Mary Baker Eddy's combination of astonishing financial acumen, perseverance, and final success, coming so late in her life and continuing for more than a century after the formation of the Christian Scientists, make her an outstanding example of a woman's way to God in the United States.

NOTES CHAPTER 16

1. Georgine Milmine, *Life of Mary Baker G. Eddy and History of Christian Science* (1907), pp. 57–70.

2. Op. cit., p. 133.

3. Op. cit., p. 38.

4. Op. cit., p. 336.

5. Op. cit., p. 336–37.

17

RAISSA MARITAIN
(September 12, 1883–November 4, 1960)

In all literary history there has surely never been such a perfect union as that of Jacques Maritain and Raïssa Oumançoff, for all of its 54 years. As Jacques put it in the preface to his *Carnet de Notes*:[1]

"The help and inspiration of my beloved Raïssa have penetrated all my life and work. If there is any good in what I have done, it is to her, after God, that I owe it." This was written in 1954, when, as Jacques put it, "the word happiness still had meaning for me." Elsewhere he noted that, after her death "Now I live only a sort of ghost's life."

Raïssa's parents had decided to emigrate from Russia because of the Tsarist pogroms (they both were Jewish). Even before they arrived in Paris Raïssa, aged ten, had acquired a good knowledge of Russian literature. By the time she was seventeen, she was a student at the Sorbonne, where she and Jacques first met. He had her name on a list of students he was going to ask to join a committee to protest the ill-treatment suffered by Russian socialist students in Tsarist Russia.

Jacques Maritain (1882–1973) was the son of Paul Maritain, a lawyer in Jules Favre's law office, who married his boss's daughter, Genevieve, but only briefly. After their divorce, she took back her maiden name, and her two children, Jacques and his sister Jeanne, grew up on the fourth floor of their mother's apartment, where Genevieve Favre's Thursday luncheons were justly famous for the brilliant literary stars who gathered there. Jacques used to escape his mother's friends by taking refuge with the family cook, Angéle, and her husband, François Baton. At sixteen Jacques wrote to Baton: "I will be a socialist and I will live for the revolution . . . Do not think that I am not ashamed that at my age the children of the proletariat work somtimes 11 hours a day (only yesterday it was 12, 13, and 14 hours) and that it is thanks to their work, not paid for at its worth, that I, idle, without doing a thing, without creating anything, without sweating, nourish myself, tepidly satisfied with daily bread and with the bread of science."

Jacques Maritain had indeed decided to devote himself to science, and it was on leaving a plant physiology class that Raïssa first saw him, with his shock of blond hair and his slight stoop. Jacque's greatest friend was Ernest Renan's grandson, Ernest Psichari, and Henri Massis, a contemporary, remembers the two young men, in velvet trousers tight at the ankles, wearing red belts "to make them look like workmen," reading Baudelaire and Verlaine at the Union Prolétaire of the LXX arrondissement. "The problem was to save oneself from interior guilt," they declared.

Jacques and Raïssa's engagement took place "in the simplest way, without any proposal. We were alone in my parents' living room. Jacques was sitting on the rug, close to my chair; it suddenly seemed to me that we had always been near each other, and that we would always be so. Without thinking, I put out my hand and stroked his hair. He looked at me, and all was clear to us. The feeling flowed through me that always—for my happiness and my salvation—that always my life would be bound up with Jacques. It was one of those tender and peaceful feelings which are like a gift flowing from a region higher than ourselves, illuminating the future and deepening the present. From that moment our understanding was perfect and unchangeable."[2] After three years at the Sorbonne, Raïssa and Jacques, one sunny day when they were at the Paris zoo, made a pact. If the meaning of life did not reveal itself "the solution would be suicide."

From this solution, Jacques and Raïssa were saved by

Bergson. Henri Bergson (1859–1941), a small, dry man, with a large forehead, thin chin, and huge, high-bridged nose, wearing a high collar and black tie, lectured on Fridays at 5 P.M. at the Collège de France. His lectures had such a vogue that servants came ahead of time to keep places for high society ladies; students endured a dull lecture on economics which took place before Bergson's, just to be sure of having seats; the crowd of carriages made a traffic jam. Bergson spoke with absolutely no gestures, without notes, his hands folded in front of him.

Like Heraclitus, Bergson believed change is the basis of all reality, that time is a continuous flow in which past and present are inseperable to the consciousness and the memory. His courses were crowded with poets, artists, rich old maids and Russian exiles. It has been said of him that he opened a door to a concept of physics locked since Descartes. For the first time, to postulate the existence of two separate realms of being, only one of which is marked by awareness, as Descartes did, came under suspicion as possibly a treacherous, and worse, an unreal dualism. Indeed, there might, Bergson suggested, be a single realm of continuous and mainly unconscious mental processes. But Bergson proceeded too slowly for these impatient young people. Bergson had said to Henri Massis, "Truth is arriving. It had already appeared in physics. Later . . ." But for Jacques Maritain, Raïssa Oumançoff, and Ernest Psichari, "later" was too late, and philosophy not enough. It was indeed enough to think about, but not, as Massis put it, "to live and die for." Yet the solution was to come through Bergson, though he himself was not to be immediately aware of it. Once a week Jacques and Raïssa attended a course Bergson gave on Greek texts. The year they were studying with him, Bergson was commenting on Plotinus. One day, reading the Enneads alone in her room, Raïssa suddenly experienced the God of Whom they speak. The book fell fom her knees, and she onto them. Later, after she and Jacques had been baptized, Bergson asked her one day, "If *it* began with Plotinus?"—"it" being the way to the Church. The answer for her, as it was later to be for Bergson himself, was in the affirmative. But Bergson never publicly proclaimed his conversion, out of a feeling of solidarity for his suffering people. When World War II and the Germans came to Paris he did not flee. With immense courage, he returned all his honors and medals to the French Government (of Pétain), but he asked to be buried, when he died, according to the rites of the Catholic Church and was. On June 11, 1906 Jacques, Raïssa and her sister Vera were baptized into the Catholic Church in Montmartre. Léon Bloy was their godfather.

The Maritains' baptism was the beginning of an ever increasingly devout life. From August 1906 through June 1908, they were in Heidelberg. Jacques had obtained a fellowship to study experimental embryology under Hans Driesch. Jacques was very interested in the embryogenetic theory of neo-vitalism, which had led Driesch to "re-introduce into biology concepts of entelechy." But though they personally liked Driesch, the Maritains did not care for what Raïssa called "the coarse and saber-scarred university," and their daily life hardly echoed its rhythm. They rose at 6. Mass and communion at 7:15. Breakfast. Work until 10:30. 10:45-11:30, prayer. 12:30, lunch. After a bief rest, darning for the two ladies, a few psalms, more work: Latin, German . . . 5 P.M., visit to the Blessed Sacrament. 7 P.M., supper. Preparation for the next day. Compline. Rosary. Raïssa and Vera were in bed by 8 P.M. Jacques worked on until 11.

On December 11, 1906, Vera, chaperoned by Madame Oumançoff, arrived in Heidelberg. She remained with Raïssa and Jacques for the rest of her life (she died in Princeton, New Jersey on December 31, 1959) and looked after them completely, regarding her "Marthadom" as a religious state. Her health was not good enough for her to become a nurse, so she thought of her life with Jacques and Raïssa as her vocation, thanking God for having given her a "sheep and a lamb" to cherish.

Jacques Maritain had written that he did not think there had ever been "between three human beings a closer or deeper union than that which existed between us . . . each one was extraordinarily sensitive to the other two, and prepared to leave all for them. It was as if a single respiration kept us alive."

In January, 1907 Raïssa fell ill, and on January 17 she received the last sacraments, immediately, to the suprise of the local German doctor, taking a turn for the better. Was it at this time that she had a miscarriage, and she and Jacques decided to live thereafter as brother and sister? Jacques told their great friend, Marston Morse, that this had happened, but did not say when. In March Jacques went from Heidelberg to Paris, because Raïssa's parents were said to be in despair at their conversion to Catholicism (Jacques had been baptized and raised a Protestant, which his mother had become after her father's second marriage). "I was able, not without difficulty, to calm them by making them understand their children had found happiness. I had less luck with my mother," wrote Jacques.[3] In June, 1907 they left Heidelberg and went to live in Paris for the summer with Raïssa's parents, then back to Heidelberg for another year.

Jacques's sister Jeanne now returned to the Church, and her daughter Eveline was baptized. When the Maritains returned to Paris, in May 1908, they found the Léon Bloys down to their last three francs. They themselves were poor, too: Jacques notes "the microscope I took to the pawnbrokers only brought in twenty fancs. I had hoped for fifty." Bloy doted on both the Maritains and touchingly wrote in his diary, "It's not natural to have such friends when one has worked hard for thirty years to make enemies." Jacques and Raïssa somehow paid for a new edition of Bloy's *Salut par les Juifs*, which was dedicated to Raïssa.

In 1909 the Maritains moved to the ground floor of an old and noble house, 16 rue de L'Orangerie, at Versailles. Here Massis brought Ernest Psichari, to a "vast room empty and polished with high white panelling on which a picture of Pope Pius X stood out. In this monastic simplicity Jacques advanced towards us with his two hands stretched out, slightly bent, behind him his wife and sister-in-law. From these beings inhabited by grace emanated a luminous tenderness. They did not argue; they simply wove a web of love around us," Massis wrote of this visit. For three years after their return to France, Jacques worked on a Dictionary of Practical Life. He detested the work. "The dictionarry suffocates me. I am furious I have no time for theology," he wrote in 1910. And in 1911 again, "Profoundly discouraged by my work on the Dictionary . . . Revolting food for the intellect, that one is continually obliged to regurgitate . . ." In 1910 Jacques's first aricle, on "Modern Science and Reason," after being refused by the *Correspondant*, was accepted in June by the *Revue de Philosophie*. It was the first of literally countless articles, and more than fifty books. In 1912 Maritain began his lectures at the Collège Stanislas and in 1913 at the Institut Catholque, where he became professor in 1914. At this time Ernest Psichari was received into the Church. On August 22, 1914, Psichari was killed in battle; on September 5 of the same year, Charles Péguy.

In April, 1917 Jacques had gotten a letter from an unknown soldier, Pierre Villard, who had left the Church when young, but who continued to "retire into the cell of my self-knowledge." He and Jacques became friends briefly; he was killed in June, 1918 at the front. He left half his fortune to Jacques, who was thus able to give 50,000 francs to the *Revue Universelle*, which had a double function: to promulgate the ideas of *Action Francaise* in the political, and Thomist ideas in the philosophical, sphere. Jacques was also able, with this legacy, to open, with Raïssa and Vera, a center for Thomistic studies, in October 1919. In 1921, the monthly meetings became regular, and annual retreats of three weeks were started, to which some 250-300 people came regularly. Jacques and Raïssa were also able to buy the house they lived in at Meudon with Villard's legacy.

In the notebooks, later edited and published (after her death) by Jacques, Raïssa wrote from 1906 on, without showing them even to Jacques (except once, in 1934, when she showed him some loose pages), of her way to God. She was very practical: "31 August, 1916: Not to see in my neighbour anything but the love with which God loves him."[4] "24 July 1917: Offered to God my heart preyed on by sorrow . . . If we had nothing to immolate, what should we have to offer? . . . .

25 August, 1917. Sacrifice is an absolutely universal law for the perfecting of the creature. Everything which passes from a lower to a higher nature has to pass through self-sacrifice, mortification, and death. The mineral assimilated by the plant becomes living matter. The vegetable which is consumed is transformed in the animal into sensible living matter. The man who yields up his whole soul to God through the obedience of faith finds it again in glory. . . . 1918, 9th February. The benefits of temptation; it maintains the vigour of the soul and its vitality. Sustained virtue is a proof of will-power, not of poverty of nature and insensitiveness."

For Holy Week, 1918, Jacques and Raïssa went to Rome. They had a private audience with Benedict XV, who does not seem to have impressed either of them very favorably; they also seem to have been unimpressed by Rome.

In May, 1918 Raïssa wrote, "Two years already of this prayer of passive absorption. How slow the soul is in being transformed. How the Saviour delays in increasing my love. But already his mercy towards me is such that it can only be measured by the infinite. All my heart and all my life are his."[5]

On May 12 she notes: "There have to be souls occupied solely with drinking this heavenly spring (of contemplation). Through them, afterwards, the living water of love and its divine taste reach those whose vocation comprises more activity. Contemplation is like a waterwheel which draws up the water and makes it flow into channels. If contemplation ceased entirely hearts would soon be dried up."

She was humanly afraid of the divine exigencies. In September, 1918 she wrote:[6] "I do not want to weary of asking God that his will should be accomplished. Thy will be done. With that I shall have all the rest, even courage, even generosity, even that ecstasy of love in which one no longer lives by one's own will. But the peace which will result from this will perhaps be that peace which 'surpassing all understanding' leaves our nature in sorrow, travail, darkness, almost disquiet.

"And it is of that I am frightened."

"It seems to me that I no longer know what God wants of

me and I am frightened of what he wants. All I can do is moan and implore and expect everything from a mercy that is infinite. I am truly too poor, suspended between heaven and earth by the mediocrity of my desires."[7]

At this time also she wrote the following about women: "Women possess keenness of intellectual vision, but not *active* power of mind; . . . they lack the self-control, the patience, the wisdom, to order, and the co-ordination to draw all the conclusions. But they assimilate the great abstract truths extremely well. Woman's realism delights in the knowledge of ultimate reality."

Woman's sense of order ("she would tidy up God himself," Peguy had written) "is satisfied by being able to order her whole being in the light of intelligence."[8] "It is not because you do not love God that he does not love you," she wrote a hesitating friend.

Meanwhile, Jacques became philosophical editor of the *Revue Universelle* and "more and more people flock to Jacques: how can I keep my time of silent prayer . . .? What is God's will? If I could live like a recluse among my family? But is it not my duty to be at Jacques' side?"

It was on June 5, 1923, thanks to Pierre Villard's legacy, that they moved to 10 rue du Parc, Meudon, where they had a chapel with the Blessed Sacrament reserved and where Raïssa had a study which gave access to the chapel, with only a small glazed window in the door between. Raïssa wrote: "God is too good . . . here is a house where I can live like a hermit."

Some hermit. For here came young people and old, students and professors, lay men and women, priests and seminarians, philosophers and doctors, poets, musicians, politicians, learned and ignorant folk, and all were the guests of Raïssa, for they came to a home, not an institution. As Raïssa said, "God and souls, there is no other interest in life." For all three, Jacques, Raïssa and Vera, the years at Meudon—they lived there from 1923 to 1938—were the happiest of their lives. They entertained a great deal, as examples from Raïssa's notebook show:

"1 Nov 1931 Yves Simon, Willard Hill, George Izard, the Severinis, the Pichets and Arthur Louries." "22 Nov.

Psichari's eldest sister, Willard Hill and Pearson, Eveline, Roland-Manuel, Francois Mauriac, Perre van de Meer . . . the Fumets." "15 Dec To Salle Faveau for the concert conducted by Desormières . . . everyone there: Stravinsky, Louriés, Nabokov, Markevitch, Jean Cocteau, Julien Green, Max Jacob. We see Stravinsky after."[9]

In 1938 the trio sailed for New York on October 1. They stayed first in Chicago with friends, then at the University of Notre Dame. Raïssa and Vera returned in November to France. Jacques followed a month later and they were together again at Meudon for Christmas. The following Easter Jacques and Raïssa stayed at Kolbsheim with their godchildren the Grunelius, and on Low Sunday Raïssa at Mass offered her life for peace.

In October, 1939 Jacques was invited to lecture in Toronto, and to go on to the U.S.A. All three sailed from Marseilles in January, 1940 and became, as Jacques wrote, "uprooted people. We were leaving forever everything that had constituted the nourishing soil of our life, our affections, our work." After the fall of France the Cultural Relations Ministry in Paris cabled Jacques, in reply to his request for instructions, that he should remain in the United States. There they stayed until November, 1944, when Jacques flew to Paris in an American military plane, returning in January, 1945: General de Gaulle had nominated him French Ambassador to the Vatican. Jacques left on April 1 again in an American military plane, this time for Rome, and Raïssa and Vera followed him on the *Mariposa*, sailing from Boston on July 30. Raïssa had to buy everything that was needed for the French Embassy and send it all by sea—Italy was out of stock of everything.

Arriving in Rome, she found the life distasteful: "4 March 1946: I wake up in a state of profound sadness—my heart full of tears. But I have not time to weep. Day after day, I wait to be able to begin to work. Since I wait in vain, I decide to abandon the thought of writing altogether. In my misery, curiously enough, I found no help at all, either from Jacques or Vera. I have been very much alone. God permitted it to be like that."[10]

Jacques resigned his office in 1948, and they sailed from Naples to New York, and in August began living in Princeton. There they remained through Vera's long illness (cancer) and death, until the spring of 1960, when they returned to France. For four "agonizing months" Raïssa was "walled up in herself" by a sudden attack of aphasia, due to a cerebral thrombosis. She died on November 4, 1960, telling Jacques at the end: "It's good to be with God, isn't it?" She is buried at Kolbsheim, where Jacques thereafter spent part of his summers: he became a Little Brother of Jesus, and died in 1973.

Though Jacques is always thought of as the great rediscoverer of St. Thomas Aquinas, he and Raïssa actually came to study him together: Jacques noted in the first months of 1909 that Raïssa had begun reading the *Summa Theologica,* and was "inundated with joy, light and love. Exultation of the intellect in an intuition given once and for all."[11] It was in St. Thomas that both found the certainty that for the Christian the center of life is the Beatific Vision of the three divine persons, and not the perfection of morality: that, indeed, the end of man is not action, but contemplation. And both realized (Raïssa perhaps more even than Jacques) that, as St. Thomas says, *"In finem nostrae cognitionis deum tanquam ignotum cognoscimus"* (at the end of our knowledge we learn that God is the unknown). "For us," Raïssa wrote, "God is, at first, Truth and then Love. But he is only that love which is but one with the sovereign and eternally living truth. In Himself, God is Love as He is truth."[12] And "love in itself is not guilty and can never be: since everything is good in the degree that it has being, so everything is worthy of love to the same degree. And to deny the creature is to deny the Creator."

"God, my God," she wrote, "I deceive myself perhaps about the degree of your love for me, but what I know very definitely is that your love is my only treasure . . . For if I have other joys, those that come from the affection and the blessed presence of Jacques—and of Vera and of Mother— I know very well that if one day you definitely made it known to me that your love had never dwelt in my Soul, all joy would be extinguished for me and I should have lost my reason for living."[13]

In 1936, at Meudon, she wrote Jacques: "Go on loving me like this, I need a great deal of love in order to live and I know that *I* have to love 'as not loving' in St. Paul's sense . . . What a terrible vocation. It is for that God has placed your marvellous love at my side."[14]

NOTES CHAPTER 17

1 Jacques Maritain, *Carnet de Notes* (Paris: Desclee de Brower, 1965) p. 11.

2 Raissa Maritain, *We Have Been Friends Together* (New York: Doubleday, Image Books, 1961) pp. 84–85,

3 J. Maritain, *Carnet de Notes*, p. 57.

4 *Raissa's Journal* (Albany, New York: Magi Books, Inc., 1974), pp. 38, 55, 59, 67.

5 *Ibid.*, p. 72.

6 *Ibid.*, p. 73.

7 *Ibid.*, p. 80.

8 *Ibid.*, p. 112.

9 *Ibid.*, pp. 214–15.

10 *Ibid.*, p. 304.

11 J. Maritain, *Carnet de Notes*, p. 74.

12 *Raissa's Journal*, p. 156.

13 *Ibid.*, p. 170.

14 *Ibid.*, p. 255.

18

ANANDAMAYI MA

(April 30, 1896–   )

Anandamayi Ma, one of the most outstanding contemporary upholders of traditional Hinduism, was born Nirmala Devi on April 30, 1896 in the Indian village of Kheora in East Bengal, into an orthodox Brahmin family. Her father was ascetically inclined, and loved to go on *kirtana* parties, leaving his family often for months at a time. Among her mother's paternal relatives there had been a recent case of a widow joyously burning herself (*sati*), and this was a source of family pride.

Anandamayi Ma was thought by her parents to be retarded as a child, for she talked to trees, plants and invisible beings. She attended elementary school for at most two years and never learned to read and write. In later years, when asked to autograph a book, she would sign with a dot. She had four younger brothers and two sisters. At the age of twelve she was married to Ramani Chukravati, known later as Pitaji, who also came from a well-known Brahmin family. According to Anandamayi Ma's biographers (twelve volumes of her life have already appeared), the marriage was never consummated. After her marriage, Anandamayi Ma (later known as Mataji, or Ma) stayed only a few months in her husband's house, and in all her life spent only a total of some six years with him. From the ages of twelve to twenty-seven she travelled constantly, staying with relatives.

Aged seventeen, she began to experience psychic phenomena: her body would stiffen while she chanted, her limbs "spontaneously" formed themselves into various yogic poses, and her relatives, fearing she might be possessed by an evil spirit, had her exorcized, but the exorcists were forced to withdraw in fear and amazement. When, aged about twenty-five, she lived continuously with her husband for fifteen months, she became dumb. She then left him and went to live in Dacca, but still remained dumb for another two years.

It was in Dacca that she met Sri Jyotash Chandra Ray, later known as Bhaiji (elder brother). He was born in 1880 at Chittagong, and was educated there. He had lost his mother as a small boy, and would weep whenever he heard other children calling out "Ma, Ma." His father was a saintly man, and in 1908 Bhaiji was initiated by a family *guru* into *sakti mantra*. His deity thereafter was the Mother Divine, and he longed to find a Living Mother, consulting astrologers to discover whether he would ever have the good fortune to meet such a mother; they all held out high hopes. He had a government job in Calcutta, but was transferred to Dacca in 1918.

In 1924 he learned that Anandamayi Ma had been living for some months in Shah-Bag, a property belonging to the Nawab of Dacca, keeping silence and always seated in some yogic posture. "On some rare occasions," he wrote, "she would draw a line on the floor round her seat and have very short talks with people after reciting some mantras or sacred texts." One morning he went to see her, and was "fortunate to see Mataji through the kind courtesy of her husband Pitaji." It sent a thrill into his heart to "see her serene yogi posture along with all the modesty and grace of a newly married girl," Bhaiji wrote of that first meeting.[1] Many years later, when Arthur Koestler visited Ma, she was sixty-three, but she still "gave the impression of a gypsy beauty in her forties. Her earlier photographs show a dark, slim ravishing girl with the grace of a wildcat and a face to tempt St. Anthony." On that first visit Bhaiji asked her: "Have I any chance of spiritual uplift?" She replied: "Your hunger for the spiritual is not yet strong enough."[2] He felt rebuffed and did not return for a long time, but went daily to a nearby temple where he could see her over the garden wall.

After seven months he brought her to his house, to meet his wife and son, but when he bowed to touch her feet, she withdrew them. He then published a small book on religion, and sent a copy to Anandamayi Ma, who sent for Bhaiji. When he arrived, he learned the silence she had observed for three years was over. He read the whole book to her, and she came and sat near him, and told him, "Due to three years of silence, my vocal cords are not functioning properly, yet words are forcing themselves out of my mouth. Your book is quite good."[3]

After that he went to Shah-bag frequently, and sent his wife with offerings. "At that time Mother used to put on a golden nose ring. My wife took with her one large silver plate, some curd, sandal paste and a diamond nose-ring as presents. Until then, Ananadamayi Ma used to have her food put on the bare ground, and Pitaji, her husband, said to her with great disgust, 'You don't take your food from brass or bell-metal plates. Will you then eat from a silver plate?' She laughed and said, 'Yes, but do not tell anybody this for the next three months, and please do not make any attempt yourself to procure silver plates.' Now before the three months were over, the silver plate was given her."[4]

Ananda said to Bhaiji, "Remember, you really are a Brahmin and there is a very subtle close spiritual link between this body (herself) and yourself." From then on he told his wife they must live as brother and sister. One day he asked Mataji:

"Mother, pray, tell me what are you in reality?" She laughed out loudly and said with all affection: "How could such childish queries arise in your heart? I am what I was and what I shall be; I am whatever you conceive, think or say. But it is a supreme fact that this body has not come into being to reap the fruits of past karma. Why don't you take it that this body is the material embodiment of all your thoughts and ideas. You all have wanted it and you have it now. So play with this doll for some time. Further questions will be

213

fruitless." I said, "These words of yours, Mother, do not satisfy my yearning." Hearing this She spoke with slight vehemence, "Say, say, what more you desire" and immediately a dazzling flood of heavenly light shone forth from Her face. I was struck dumb with awe and wonder. All my doubts were laid at rest.

About fifteen days later, I went to Shah-bag one morning and found the door of Mother's bedroom closed. I sat down in front of it some 25 to 30 cubits away. The door opened all at once. I found to my bewilderment, the figure of a divinely beautiful goddess as genially bright as the sun at dawn, illumining the whole interior of the room. In the twinkling of an eye She withdrew all the radiance within Her body and Mother was there, standing and smiling in Her usual manner . . . I realized at once that Mother had revealed Herself in response to what I had said a few days back. I began to recite a hymn and prayed to Her.

After a little while Mother advanced towards me. She picked up a flower and a few blades of durba grass and placed them on my head, as I fell at Her feet. I was beside myself with joy and rolled on the ground at Her feet. From that moment a deep conviction began to take root in my mind that She was not only my mother but *the Mother* of this universe . . .[5]

Yet Bhaiji felt he had to test her:

On one occasion Mother came to our house. In the course of our talk I said casually—"It appears, Ma, that to you hot and cold are the same. If a piece of burning coal fell on your foot, would you not feel pain?" She replied, "Just test it." I did not press the point further.

After a few days, taking up the thread of our previous conversation, Mother placed a piece of burning coal on Her foot. There was a deep burning sore. For one month it did not heal up. I felt very upset about that silly suggestion of mine. One day I found Her sitting on the veranda with Her legs stretched out and Her gaze fixed on the sky. Some pus had gathered on the sore. I bowed down at Her feet and licked the pus up with my tongue and lips. From the following day the sore began to heal up . . .

"I asked Mother how she felt when the live coal was burning her flesh. She said in reply: 'I was not aware of any pain. It looked like nothing but fun; with great joy I watched what the poor coal was doing on my foot, and I noticed that at first some hair, then the skin began to burn. It smelt of burn, and gradually the coal was put out after doing its work. When later a sore formed, it continued its course but as soon as strong desire arose in you that the wound be healed up soon, it took a rapid turn for the better."[6]

In 1925 some devotees, who had assembled in Shah-Bag for her *darsana* (blessing) asked her to perform *Kali Puja* (puja-worship). An image of Kali[8] was brought. "Then mother started chanting mantras and placing flowers with sandal paste upon her own head instead of the image. A goat was to be sacrificed. It was bathed in water. When it was brought to Mother, she took it on her lap and wept as she stroked its body gently with her hands . . . then she worshipped the scimitar with which the goat was to be sacrificed. She prostrated herself on the ground, placing the knife upon her own neck. Three sounds like the bleating of a goat came from her lips. Afterward when the animal was sacrificed, it neither moved nor uttered a cry, nor was there any trace of blood upon the severed head or body."

Her identification with Kali was so complete, that on one occasion, walking on the beach in Chittagong "she suddenly said with a smile: 'Look at my wrist: is it broken? Isn't it? Just examine it closely. There may be a fracture.' That very night a thief had entered the Kali temple at Ramn (many miles away) and stolen Kali's ornaments, breaking the wrist of the image." In a *festschrift* written for her sixtieth birthday[10] the Principal of the Government Sanskrit College, Benares, the leading Hindu theological college in India, wrote that in 1928 there was a difference of opinion "concerning the precise status of Mother. Some held she was a goddess in human form, Kali according to some . . . some thought she was a human aspirant, who had attained perfection in this life after a series of births during which her spiritual progress had been continued."

From May, 1926 on, Ma ceased eating food from her own hand, saying, "I look upon all hands as mine; actually I always eat with my own hand." She is always surrounded with people, from early morning till late at night. "Some are painting her forehead with vermilion drops, others dressing her hair, yet others offer to give her a bath, or to wash her face and mouth, or to clean her teeth with toothpaste. Some may request her permission to change her sari, others express a desire to put some sweets or a slice of fruit into her mouth." There are over one thousand photographs of Ananadamayi Ma, no two alike.

In 1929 the Dacca ashram was inaugurated. Once the ashram was in existence, Bhaiji, from 1929 until 1931, used to go there very early in the morning in order to see Ananadamayi Ma first. He walked, in spite of Hindu-Muslim strife then violent in the streets in Dacca, and in spite of having tuberculosis. His death came in 1937 when he and another devotee were accompanying Mataji on a pilgrimage to Mount Kailash. On arrival at Lake Mansarovar, Bahiji threw his clothes and sacred thread into the lake and plunged into the icy waters. When Mataji arrived, he accompanied her back to Almora, where he developed a high fever. His last words were: "Listen. We are all one. Ma and I are one. Pitaji and I are one." Then, fixing his eyes on Mataji and pronouncing "Ma, Ma," he died.

Arthur Koestler[11] visited Ananda's ashram overlooking the Ganges, but found she was in her Calcutta ashram. In the Benares ashram were about twenty, mostly elderly, men and women living there in cells, who seemed happy. He found later that the Calcutta ashram was a little cleaner than the

Benares ashram; also it was grander and noisier. Ma was dressed in a white silk sari, and had lovely feet and toes with which she played. She was chewing *pan*; Koestler was told he could ask her any question he liked. He asked: "Does Mother approve of what has been written about her, claiming that she was of divine origin?" She replied, "Everybody sees in me what he likes," then gave him two tangerines out of a basket and dismissed him while continuing to play with her toes.

In a collection of her words compiled by Atmananda and published by the Shree Shree Anandamayee Sangha at Varanasi in 1961, many replies to oral questions are given. "Here," she told one questioner, pointing to herself, "nothing is rejected. Whether it is the state of Enlightenment or Ignorance, everything is all right. The fact is that you are in doubt. But here there is no question of doubt. Whatever you may say, and from whatever level, is He and He and only He." Again, she said: "You want to know whether Grace is without cause or reason. When working, one reaps the fruit of one's actions. If, for instance, you serve your father, and he, being pleased with your service, gives you a present, that would be called the fruit of action. But the eternal relationship that by nature exists between father and son, does surely not depend on any action. The Supreme Father, Mother, and Friend, God, is all of these. Consequently, how can there be a cause or reason for His grace? You are His, and in whatever way He may draw you to Him, it is for the sake of revealing Himself to you. The desire to find Him that awakens in man—who has instilled it into you? . . . You speak of the Absolute as Truth, Knowledge, Infinity . . . When you say 'This indeed is He and that also is He' you have limited yourself by the word 'also' . . . In the One there can be no 'also.' The state of Supreme Oneness cannot be described as 'That,' and also as something other than 'that.' Whatever line you follow represents a particular aspect of the Whole. Each method has its own methods, its beliefs and disbeliefs, to what purpose? To realize Him, your own Self. What or who is this Self? Depending in your orientation, you find Him, who is your own Self, in the relation of a perfect servant to his Master, of a part

to the whole, or simply as the one Self. What is pure existence? The Self, the Supreme spirit, call it what you will. That
which you variously name God, is only He the one. He is
immutable, the non-doer, since He does not act. Since He
himself is present in all causes and effects, how can one speak
of Him as controlliing or not controlling them? Thus, here he
is actionless. You speak of him as the doer or non-doer, trying
to limit Him to the one or the other . . . He is whatever you
take Him to be; you see Him according to your way of thinking; as you portray Him, so He is . . . Man's true nature, call
it by any name, it is the Supreme, I myself."[12]

Mataji met Mahatma Gandhi several times, but they
never mentioned politics. She has declared that "this body
does not as a rule interfere with anyone's natural ways: whatever is meant to come about just happens spontaneously."[13]
She wishes only to direct everyone to God: "every breath with
which we do not remember God is wasted. Birth in a human
body is a rare boon. If you had been born animals or birds,
what significance would your lives have? Human beings alone
are endowed with the capacity to find God."[14]

NOTES CHAPTER 18

1 *Mother As Revealed To Me* (Shree Shree Anandamayee Sangha,
1962), p. 11.

2 *Ibid.*, p. 3.

3 *Ibid.*, p. 6.

4 *Ibid.*, p. 7.

5 *Ibid.*, p. 8–9.

6 Ibid., pp. 21-22.

7 Ibid., p. 40.

8 A Hindu goddess.

9 Javanti, *Souvenir* (Benares: 1956), Mayee ashram.

10 Arthur Koestler, *The Lotus and the Robot* (New YorK: Macmillan and Co., 1961), pp. 82–84.

11 Atmanada, ed., trans., *Words of Sri Anandamayi Ma* (Benares: 1961).

12 Mataji's *Amara Vanino*, III, No. 3, p. 209.

13 Melita Maschmann, "From the diary of a European," *Ananda Varta*, August, 1965, pp. 52–53.

(The Shree Shree Anandamayee Shangha has published a quarterly, *Ananda Varta*, from 1951 on, in Bengali, Hindi and English.)

19

DOROTHY DAY
(November 8, 1897–   )

Dorothy Day's way to God is the most complete possible antithesis from that of Raïssa Maritain. In fact the two women themselves could not be more different. Raïssa was an ailing Russian Jew, transported first to France, then to the U.S.; Dorothy is as American as a malted, the all-American woman, a goddess of the hearth—if there still is an American hearth. She is healthy, outgoing, and as perfectly average as she is absolutely singular. She looks like the great Greek statue of Demeter, the earth mother, in the British Museum, except that Demeter has no arms and Dorothy's are very strong and forceful. She looks like good homebaked bread and feels and smells and *is* like good homebaked bread. She is shapeless, wrinkled, with excellent bones to her face, lovely white hair, and a low, hesitant, gentle, very feminine voice and manner, clear blue eyes, and a glorious sense of humor.

She attracts the most diverse people. Evelyn Waugh, about to be taken down to see her by Clare Luce with whom he was staying, telephoned to ask whether Clare's large limousine should draw up at the door. "Better go by subway," was suggested. Later, when asked by Virgilia Peterson to appear on her television program, *Author Meets the Critic*, he said: "If I do, will you give me $100 for Dorothy Day?" "We don't pay authors," Virgilia replied. "They get the publicity for sole reward." "You get paid, don't you?" Evelyn asked Virgilia. "It's the way I earn my living," she replied. "Couldn't you do something more useful?" Evelyn asked her.

"Great shortage of domestic staff in this country, isn't there?" "I do housework, and cooking," Virgilia replied, "but am paid for neither." "Well, if you won't give me any money for Dorothy Day," Evelyn said, "I won't appear on your program." And he did not. Summoned by her landlord to pay five hundred dollars for violations on her building, Dorothy was standing in court before the judge when Wystan Auden appeared and shoved an envelope into her hand. "Here's two-fifty," he murmured. She thanked him warmly, thinking he was offering her $2.50. It was, of course, $250.

Dorothy Day's life divides into two. For twenty-five years she felt that "sense of insecurity one hears so much about these days." Then, five years after she became a Catholic, she met Peter Maurin, and he was "my master and I was his disciple." He gave her a "way of life and instruction" which grew into the Catholic Worker Movement.

She came of sound stock. Her father was from Cleveland, Tennessee, and his father had been a surgeon who served in the Confederate army. Her mother was from Marlboro, New York, and her father, a chairmaker, had fought on the Northern side, coming home with TB of the larnynx. Her mother's mother had married at fourteen and bore eighteen children, of whom only six lived.

Dorothy was born on November 8, 1897. She had two older brothers and a younger sister. Her parents had a maid, Mary, who was Catholic, and once took Dorothy to Mass. But little Dorothy stood up on the pew, staring around her, and Mary was so embarrassed she never took her again. Dorothy and her family first lived in Brooklyn, where she started school.

She had a happy childhood, playing on the beach, fishing for eels in a creek and playing house in an abandoned shack in a swamp. When she was six, her family moved to California, first to Berkeley, then to Oakland. Her father was a newspaperman: in New York he had worked nights on a morning paper; in San Francisco he lost his job after the earthquake, as the printing plant went up in up in flames. He was sports editor and kept a horse at a stable near their bungalow.

The night before the earthquake, the horses in the stable were restless. The earthquake the next morning lasted two minutes and twenty seconds. There was a deep rumbling, and the "earth became a sea which rocked our house." Dorothy's mother fainted, and her father, having got all the children safely out of the front door, carried his wife back to bed. Their house was damaged—chimneys fallen, the walls cracked from roof to ground. Luckily there was no fire in Oakland. But across the bay the great flames could be seen, and for days the refugees poured over and camped on the racetrack. Dorothy remembers best the "joy of doing good, of sharing whatever they had with others," for all the neighbors joined in serving the homeless. After the earthquake, Dorothy's family moved to Chicago. In Chicago they lived in a dingy, six-room apartment, and had no servant. They lived near a breakwater along the lake, where Dorothy remembers a brother and sister drowned in each other's arms.

Dorothy had begun at eight to be pious. She believed, but did not know in what she believed. She sang hymns and prayed, and went to Sunday School and church with a Methodist family next door, because none of her own family went to church. She was already afraid of God, of death and of eternity. She longed to be a saint, and began to enjoy the housework she did to help her mother, who had been weakened by a series of miscarriages. One day, coming upon a neighbor on her knees, Dorothy "felt a feeling of gratitude and happiness" that warmed her heart. After that, she would plague her little sister by saying long prayers, and soon the two children practiced being saints as a game.

Dorothy's father was a remote figure, as he worked at night and slept in the morning. She never really knew him until after she had graduated from high school at sixteen. She now went to the Episcopal Church, and when her family moved to the North Side, it was in this denomination that she was baptized and confirmed. Her family was poor no longer, as her father had found a good job as a sports editor, and they now had a cozy house with fireplaces and rooms for all. When Dorothy was fourteen there was a new baby, and also a first love: a musician to whom she never spoke. But how she hungered for his look! He led the park band, and Dorothy and her sister never missed a concert that summer. It seemed to her that her two loves, for her baby brother and for her musician, fused. Her heart, first awakening, loved equally a grown man and a baby boy. She describes enchantingly the baby in his crib discovering his toes, discovering the brass knob on his crib, and the singsong creaking of the spring and the peeping of the birds that he imitated, the jingle of the milkman's horse's harness and the metallic sound of bottles being deposited. Dorothy rose at four to feed the baby, then did her homework: Latin and Greek, which she loved; history, which bored her. At this stage she wrote long priggish letters to her school friend Henrietta, a butter-pat with blond curly hair and blue eyes, a frankly sensual girl. Dorothy, at fifteen, would write of "sensual love and the thrill that comes from the meeting of lips," but pronounced it wrong to think so much about mere human love.

It was when she was fifteen, too, that she began to be aware of the labor movement. Her brother got a job on a Scripps-Howard paper that discussed working class conditions. Carl Sandburg wrote for this paper and Dorothy learned from it about Eugene Debs and the Industrial Workers of the World (the IWW, better known as the Wobblies). Dorothy at this time was reading Jack London, Upton Sinclair, and Frank Harris. Her first story, written in high school, was about a Russian revolutionary's martyrdom. After she went up to the University of Illinois on a scholarship, she joined the Socialist party. She was delighted to leave home. Her father's paper had folded, and now she was "on her own, no longer to be cared for by the family." The idea of earning her own living, by her own efforts, appealed far more to her than the idea of an education. How she worked! Dorothy was seventeen. For her board, she worked afternoons and evenings for a Methodist professor of languages, and took on extra jobs washing and ironing clothes and baby sitting. She read everything she could lay hands on by Dostoevski, Gorki, Tolstoi. Soon she moved, in order to gain more time to read and write, to the home of an instructor with five children. Her bare room had no carpet, only a bed, a table, a chair, and a little stove on which Dorothy cooked. She spent only forty cents a day on food: this she earned washing clothes at twenty cents an hour.

Dorothy began writing as well as reading. She wrote at space rates for a local Urbana paper. When she criticized the existing order, her columns were not published; when she criticized the student's working conditions she was published, but her writings led to her being refused jobs by the Y, which controlled the employment bureau. Sometimes Dorothy was hungry, always she was cold, even in bed. And she carrying her full University work load as well. Dorothy's mother sympathized. She had worked in a shirt factory as a girl, and had suffered from working ten hours a day for several years.

In 1916 Dorothy's family moved east to New York, where her father got a job on the *Morning Telegraph*. She decided to move with them, and got a job on *The Call*, a Socialist daily. The first thing she noticed about New York was the smell of poverty, a smell that has never ceased to affront her. A damp ooze coming from the very walls of tenements permeates everything, even clothes, and is a sepulchral stink. She found, however, that however poor she was in New York, she could live cheaply and well: a quick meal of roasted sweet chestnuts and a piece of fruit or a good bean soup and bread and butter with it, in those blissful days, cost but ten cents. And as a reporter she had no fares to pay. She covered protests: those against the conscription act of 1917, as well as streetcorner meetings and appeals. There were also plenty of strikes: transportation strikes, garment factory strikes, strikes in smelting factories. And there were food strikes too. She met Trotsky, but did not become his follower, preferring to join the IWW, as being more indigenously American, more grass-rootsly concerned with poverty. She was at the great meeting at Madison Square Garden, on March 21, 1917, to celebrate the beginning of the Russian Revolution. Dorothy can never forget the enormous sense of a new beginning: of one sixth of the world dismissing the bigoted rulers who jailed students simply because they were students, and condemned such men as Dostoevski to be shot, and by their pogroms showed Hitler what to do and how to do it. When her job on *The Call* folded, Dorothy joined the staff of *The Masses*. After *The Masses* was suppressed, she went again to Washington, to picket the White House as a suffragist. Her description of the thirty days she had to spend in jail for picketing is as graphic today as when she wrote it.

Our spokeswoman got up and began to announce that we were all going on hunger strike unless our demands were met, but before she could get the first words out of her mouth, Whittaker, the matron, had turned to the door and beckoned. Immediately the room was filled with men. There were two guards to every woman, and each of us was seized roughly by the arms and dragged out of the room. It seems impossible to believe, but we were not allowed to walk, were all but lifted from the floor, of the effort the men made to drag, rather than lead us to our place of confinement for the night.

The leaders were taken first. In my effort to get near Peggy I started to cross the room to join her, and was immediately seized by two guards. My instinctive impulse was to pull myself loose, to resist such handling, which only caused the men to tighten their hold on me, even to twist my arms painfully. I have no doubt but that I struggled every step of the way from the administration building to the cell block where we were being taken. It was a struggle to walk by myself, to wrest myself loose from the torture of those rough hands. We were then hurled onto some benches and when I tried to pick myself up and again join Peggy in my blind desire to be near a friend, I was thrown to the floor. . . .

I found myself flung into a cell with one of the leaders, Lucy Byrnes, a tall, red-haired schoolteacher from Brooklyn, with a calm, beautiful face. She was handcuffed to the bars of the cell, and left that way for hours. Every time she called out to the other women who had been placed up and down a corridor in a block of what we found out afterward were punishment cells, Whittaker came cursing outside the bars, threatening her with a straight jacket, a gag, everything but the whipping post and bloodhounds which we had heard were part of the setup at Occoquan . . . It was not until the next day that we were offered food.[1]

Later, when living in Chicago, Dorothy had gone to an IWW rooming house to help a sick friend. The house was raided, and all found there arrested. Dorothy was thus a victim of the Palmer Red Raids, occasioned by the Red hysteria of the time. The Chicago jail was worse even than the Washington jail, and in a few words Dorothy etches the horror unforgettably:

> We were driven first of all through the dark and silent streets of the city to the West Chicago Avenue police station. . . . The next day we were photographed and fingerprinted and brought back to the cell. . . . The room was foul. The beds had mattresses, but no sheets or pillow slips. It was summer so there was no need for blankets. Fortunately, open windows gave enough light and air. On one side was a niche in which there was a toilet, unscreened by any door. There was no wash basin . . .
>
> We were searched for drugs. We were stripped naked. We were given prison clothes and put in cells. The routine was to keep us locked in the cells, then leave us free to roam the corridors in alternate periods of several hours each . . .
>
> This particular experience lasted only a few days. Manny Gomez arranged our release by getting a lawyer, and the case was afterward dismissed.[2]

In 1918 her first novel was published and the movie rights were sold for $5,000. With the money Dorothy bought a little house on the beach on Staten Island and settled down, with a lover, to write. This was for her a time of natural happiness. There was love and later a child, and Dorothy wrote of her maternity so graphically for *The Masses* that when, four years later, in Mexico, she met Diego Rivera, he saluted her as the author of this article. There were friends too: Malcolm Cowley and his wife; Allen Tate and Caroline Gordon; Hart Crane, Kenneth Burke and John Dos Passos. Staten Island in those days was idyllic, with lobster pots, clam bakes, spider crabs, and skunk cabbage, arbutus and dandelion greens. Dorothy found she wanted more and more to pray. Gradually, the strain between herself and her atheist, anarchist lover became too great to bear. He left her repeatedly. Finally, one day when he returned "as he always had," she would not let him into the house. "My heart was breaking," she writes simply "with my own determination to make an end, once and for all, to the torture we were undergoing."

The very next day she was conditionally baptized, made her first confession, received communion. She was lonely and poor, but found work always, one time cooking for some Marist brothers, another time going to Hollywood, where a play of hers had been taken by Metro-Goldwyn-Mayer. But always:

> I was lonely, deadly lonely. And I was to find out then, as I found out so many times, over and over again, that women especially are social beings, who are not content with just husband and family, but must have a community, a group, and exchange with others. . . . Young and old, even in the busiest years of our lives, we women especially are victims of the long loneliness. Men may go away and become desert Fathers, but there were no desert mothers.[3]

She had been three years a Catholic, and felt she had nothing to show for it but a deep spiritual life and a few

227

articles in *Commonweal*, when, in December 1932, when Dorothy was already 35, she returned from a hunger march to Washington and met the man whose "spirit and ideas" would dominate the rest of her life. He very literally walked into her life. He was waiting for her in her tenement flat.

Peter Maurin was then a "short, stocky man in his mid-fifties," ragged and rugged. Although he had already been twenty years in America, he still spoke with a strong French accent, and always looked and behaved like the French peasant he was. I remember him only as a mindless old man, inert, fat, inarticulate, a helpless body treated with a mixture of hospital jollity and filial affection by all the Catholic Worker Group. To Dorothy, he was Tolstoi and Gandhi, Thoreau and Trotsky, rolled into one. "He aroused in you a sense of your own capacities for work, for accomplishment," she wrote of him. He, meanwhile, went about comparing Dorothy to "a St. Catherine of Siena who would move mountains and influence governments." Together they began a paper. The first issue was twenty-five hundred copies of an eight-page tabloid that the Paulist Press printed for $57. This first issue appeared on May 1, 1933 and sold for one cent. There were "articles about labor, strikes, unemployment factual accounts, and half a dozen of Peter Maurin's Easy Essays"—short sentences, broken up to look like verse. Peter liked to think of himself as a "troubadour for Christ" and he wanted "nothing but his own essays to be printed, over and over, and broadcast throughout the country." He thought "everybody's paper is nobody's paper." Yet, within a few months, the *Catholic Worker's* circulation rose to 150,000, then 200,000 and during the first years the streets were "literally lined with papers" on May Day. Young people joined Dorothy and Peter, accepting only their carfare. They formed Champion Committees, and married each other. One seminarian sold the paper on a corner of Times Square, standing next to a comrade touting *The Daily Worker*. The seminarian shouted: "Read the *Catholic Worker* daily!" "Between sales, they conversed," Dorothy wrote happily. In 1933, Dorothy estimates the unemployed numbered thirteen million.

Peter and Dorothy started houses of hospitality, for the people they brought in off the streets. At first, Dorothy herself cooked and cleaned, edited the *Catholic Worker* and sold it. Then a Lithunanian girl turned up, and made vast amounts of mashed potato with mushroom sauce "which filled everyone up nicely." Soon some twenty people of both sexes were sharing the house, and then other houses of hospitality began: within a few years there were thirty-three in the United States, one in England, and one in Australia. With World War II, most of the houses closed, but after the war's end others began. In 1950, there were still twenty houses and farms. When I first knew Dorothy, there were two farms near New York, both as nearly self-supporting as they could be made, one near Newburgh, N.Y. and one on Staten Island. There was another in Michigan. In every house of hospitality, all who come are made welcome, and may stay as long as they desire. But as long as they stay, they are invited to share in the alternation of work and of prayer, of Mass and dishwashing, of Benediction and ditchdigging. Nearly 100 couples, still working in various Catholic Action groups, met each other while working with Dorothy, and have founded *Catholic Worker* families.

Dorothy writes modestly:

It has been said that it was the *Catholic Worker* and its stories of poverty and exploitation that aroused the priests to start labor schools, to go out on picket lines, to take sides in strikes with the workers.

"It is good that we live in a country where we can be CO's," Dorothy says. And she tells how, in the Second World War, "We had lots of visits form the FBI at Mott St., and they were most interested in our discussions, and seemed most tolerant of our point of view." And the Vatican has sent the *Catholic Worker* a very full and special blessing, to all on the staff, and all connected with the paper."

At thirty-eight, Dorothy wished she were married, living the ordinary happy life, and that she had not come under

Peter Mauren's influence. But she overcame her discontent, reasoning with herself that she had had the love of a man, had had a child and must admit that: I am a mother, and the mother of a very large family at that." Why she and Peter never married she has never explained; her daughter's father would not marry her because he did not believe in bourgeois ties. But when he was dying, he came back to Dorothy, and she nursed him tenderly to the end. She now has seven grandchildren, and still is as concerned as ever about the problem of evil: why did God permit the burning alive of babies in Vietnam?

Fiercely decentralist, she wants factories to be part-owned by the workers, and set in green fields. Every worker also should have his own home, his garden and ideally his three acres and a cow.

"I don't want people just to want more things, but to want to make more things. I want people to grow more of their own food, and make more of their own clothes. When there's a war, we're all told to grow more and more food. As soon as it's over, we're told that we shouldn't grow any food, that it's uneconomical. That doesn't make sense," Dorothy says scornfully.

And she is indignant because it is only in prisons and in asylums that people are taught to make things. "Almost the only place flax is grown in America," she says, "is in prison yards and the grounds of institutions. In fact, when I meet anyone with a skill or a craft, I'm pretty sure he's done time." Everyone realizes the value of making things. Why, she asks, wait until people are naughty or nuts?

Begun in the depression, flourishing through hot war and cold war, Dorothy and her movement go on, declaring that the only cure for humanity is a Christian revolution.

Dorothy says:

It's the only revolution that's never been tried. Its motto for the employer is, "Quit exploiting"; for the state, "Quit expanding"; and for us all, "Quit evil."
"When I became a Catholic forty years ago, I felt

with joy that my faith brought me what scripture calls 'a rule of life and instruction.' So I recommend the Gospels which are so potent, so grace-bearing, that the priest says when he has finished reading the Gospel 'By the words of the Gospel may my sin be blotted out.' "[4]

And in 1965 she wrote: ". . . it is hard to keep clean. It is hard to forget the body, this cumbrous instrument of the mind and soul. When the senses are all at peace, satisfied and content, the exercises of the mind and soul seem to be going smoothly. I have thought a good deal along these lines in connection with poverty and destitution, and the attitudes of those who suffer from affronts in a prosperous land. I have thought of them when people talk of the demands of labor for higher wages and for shorter hours. There have been occasional critical comments about the *Catholic Worker* why do we emphasize the material things? . . . We emphasize the material because we are working to make that kind of society in which it is easier for men to be good."[5]

NOTES CHAPTER 19

1   Dorothy Day, *The Long Loneliness* (New York: Doubleday, Image Books, 1950), pp. 73–74.

2   *Ibid.*, pp. 98–102.

3   *Ibid.*, p. 153.

4   Dorothy Day, *On Pilgrimage: The Sixties* (New York: Curtis Books, 1972), p. 160.

5   *Ibid.*, p. 204.

20

SIMONE WEIL
(February 3, 1909–August 24, 1943)

Simone Weil was born in Paris, at 19 Boulevard de Strasbourg. The house has since been pulled down. Her father, Dr. Bernard Weil, and her mother had one older child, Simone's brother André, a mathematical prodigy. They were devoted to their children, and a visitor once remarked, pointing to the two children, "That one (André) is genius itself, the other is beauty"—a remark which annoyed the small girl and which she never forgot. In 1912 the family moved to 37 Boulevard St. Michel, where they remained until the outbreak of World War I, when Dr. Weil was immediately called up. His family moved with him, to the Vosges, to Mentone, to Mayennes for two years, then to Chartres and Laval.

Simone as a very small child astonished her doctors and nurses, when she was having her appendix removed, by her vocabulary. Before she was five she would wash in cold water, repeating, as she shivered, Turenne's remark on the battlefield, "You tremble, old carcass." André and Simone used to learn Racine by heart, and the one who flubbed got slapped by the other.

Simone refused to eat sugar, as the soldiers at the front had none, and once, before she was five, sat down in the snow and refused to budge when the family was moving, because her father had given André the heaviest luggage to carry.

André had taught himself to read, and decided as a birthday present for his father, to teach Simone, who was not yet six, working with her under the tablecloth for as much as eight hours a day so as to be unobserved. On New Year's Day, 1915, André told Simone to read the newspaper aloud to her father—which she did.

She did not begin her schooling until she was eight years old, when she entered the Lycée at Laval. At this time she was very pretty, with delicate features, fine black almond-shaped eyes and black, curly hair which suggested Byzantine frescoes. She disliked physical contact from an early age and when a friend of her mother's kissed her tiny hand, she ran away in tears crying: "Water! Water! I want to wash."

At war's end, the Weils went to a seaside resort in Brittany, and Simone would watch the sunset for hours. Asked if she did not want to play, she declared she much preferred to look.

At the end of 1910 she entered the Lycée Fénélon, on the Left Bank, a girls' public high school. Her literature teacher objected because she made the other students learn the whole of Racine's *Athalie* by heart. She was hopeless at drawing and wore herself out drawing maps, until offered a consolation prize if she came in last, as she did.

She was horrified by the Treaty of Versailles. "I was ten years old at the time of Versailles, and up to then I had been patriotically thrilled as children are in wartime," she wrote to George Bernanos in 1938. "But the will to humiliate the defeated enemy which revealed itself so loathesomely everywhere at that time was enough to cure me once for all of that naive sort of patriotism."

With puberty, came searing headaches. At fourteen, she later wrote to Father Perrin,[1] she had "seriously thought of dying because of the mediocrity of my natural faculties. I fell into one of those fits of bottomless despair that come with adolescence. The exceptional gifts of my brother, who had a childhood and youth comparable to those of Pascal, brought my own inferiority home to me. I did not mind having no visible successes, but what did grieve me was the idea of being excluded from that transcendent kingdom to which only the truly great have access and wherein truth abides. I preferred to die rather than live without that truth."[2] But after months "of inward darkness" she suddenly had "the everlasting conviction" that any human being can penetrate that kingdom "if only he longs for truth and perpetually concentrates all his attention upon its attainment."

Simone's parents were complete agnostics, and did not even advise her of the distinction between Jews and Gentiles. Leslie Fiedler wrote of her that "she appears to have had no sense of alienation from the general community connected with her Jewishness, but grew up with a feeling of belonging quite firmly to a world whose values were simply 'French,' that is to say, a combination of Greek and secularized Christian elements."[3] As soon as she reached adolescence, she writes, "I saw the problem of God as a problem the data of which could not be obtained here below, and I decided that the only way of being sure not to reach a wrong solution, which seemed to me the greatest possible evil, was to leave it alone."[4]

Though she declared that never "at any moment in my life have I 'sought for God,' " yet she "never hesitated in my choice of an attitude; I always adopted the Christian attitude as the only possible one. I may say that I was born, I grew up, and I always remained within the Christian inspiration."[5]

At fifteen, on June 22, 1924, she passed her *baccalauréat* Latin-Langues. She got 19/20 for her oral test. She hesitated whether to take mathematics or philosophy for the second part of her *bachot*. She decided on philosophy, some say by tossing a coin. She chose the Lycée Victor Duruy for her year of philosophy. On June 27, 1925 she passed the *bachot* in philosophy.

In October, 1925 she entered the Lycée Henri Quatre, where she became a pupil of Alain (Émile Chartier), who admired her but told her she ought to try to write more legibly. She also despised history, and her Latin was mediocre. "She tries too hard to achieve originality and becomes eccentric," wrote one of her teachers. When she took her test at the end of the first year she failed miserably, but the year 1927–1928 was better. She was already attracted to trade unionism, and was giving courses of instruction to young syndicalist railwaymen.

In 1928 she sat for the entrance examination for the École Normale Supérieure, where she came in first. (Simone de Beauvoir came in second. These two were at the top of a list of thirty men.) There had been three women (for the first time) the year before: they were dubbed "the gleaners." Simone Weil continued to attend Alain's course in philosophy at the Henri Quatre and he published her first writing in his periodical, *Libres Propos*. Her first essay was on work, her second, on time. Her parents, meanwhile, had bought a duplex, on the seventh and eighth floors of a new building facing the Luxembourg Gardens, where they remained until 1940. They also had a small country house at Chevreuse, for the summers, to which their children accompanied them.

Some friends of Simone's had founded a kind of workingmen's college at 3 rue Falguère. It was to help railway workers to graduate from manual labor to white-collar work. Simone devoted herself wholeheartedly to this, and also signed in *Libres Propos* in July, 1931 a pacifist manifesto co-signed by Romain Rolland, J.P. Satre and others.

In July, 1931 Simone passed her *agrégation*, seventh *ex equo* of only 11 passes out of 107 candidates. "A brilliant candidate, who appears to be well informed not only about philosophy, but about literature and contemporary art," wrote one of her examiners. Now she had a right to a State teaching job. The Director of the École Normale, Bouglé, was once lecturing on patriotism when Simone got up and read "without commentary a speech from the Official Gazette of 1912," in which Raymond Poincaré seemed to recommend an invasion of Belgium. Bouglé took out his watch and remarked "It's time for lunch," which became a catchword, to his detriment. When Simon's name came up for a job, Bouglé said, "We'll give her a job as far away as possible. Then at last we'll hear no more of her." So she was nominated to Le Puy, to the girls' lycée there, which did not please her, as she had wanted "a port or an industrial town in the north or centre."

But she found in Thévenon, assistant secretary of the Loire branch of the Federated Syndicalist workers, the entrance she sought to working-class studies in St. Etienne, and bought books for it with her own money. The miners regarded "the Red Virgin," as they called her, as some sort of a mascot. A small mine-owner even allowed her to go down a mine and use an automatic drill. It only made her headache worse.

Le Puy, some seventy miles south-west of Lyons, is a picturesque town of some 15,000 inhabitants, with a splendid Romanesque cathedral. Simone taught there only fourteen students her first year, wearing a beret, and speaking in a monotonous voice. Her pupil's notebooks were later to be searched to prove she had taught shocking material, but what were found were edifying maxims such as: "God is, in a sense, the only way of eliminating God; Labor is the only thing that makes us grasp the idea of necessity; The world is a web of necessity." Seven of her students presented themselves for the *bachot* at the end of the year; only two passed. Yet none of her students held their lack of success against her, and all even came to an optional extra lecture she gave Thursdays on the history of science.

There was severe unemployment at Le Puy, and Simone accompanied a delegation of unemployed to ask the mayor for unemployment pay. The mayor asked where she worked, and Simone said she taught at the girls' lycée. At a meeting of the town council to discuss the promise the mayor was supposed to have made to give the unemployed twenty-four francs a day, a group of workers, led by Simone Weil, "entered and ranged themselves at the back of the hall." The mayor ordered the hall cleared; the unemployed went to the Labor Exchange; Simone went to a café. The mayor ordered her watched, and the school inspector at Le Puy was given a police report about the girl. He summoned her on December 19, and she admitted all the charges, and, moreover, agreed to go again to the mayor with two of the unemployed, to give him an agenda. Her dismissal was requested, and on January 12 at five p.m. she was arrested and taken to the police station. Here she was threatened with detention, but released at once.

Now she was asked to resign, or to ask for a transfer. She refused. The local papers were full of "the red virgin of the tribe of Levi." but the unemployed got their unemployment benefits—sixteen francs a day simply for signing on. There was a great deal of *fracas*, but the parents of Simone's own pupils wrote to the Ministry of Education and asked that she *not* be transferred. "She has been a most valuable influence on all the girls she has had in her charge." However, finally she signed an application to be transferred to Auxerre, saying as she did so, "I have always regarded dismissal as the natural culmination of my career."

Meanwhile, she had spent her holidays digging potatoes or cleaning windows, and had even learned how to unbolt a rail. When the school year ended she went to Germany. During the summer of 1932, she was tremendously impressed by the "magnificent working-class youth with their sports, camping, singing, and reading," but she disliked the Communists there as much as she had disliked them at home. She emphasized "at every opportunity the points of resemblance between Hitler's national socialism and orthodox communism."

In the fall of 1932, Simone took up teaching in Auxerre. Once again, her pupils doted on her—they even "typed out the tracts she composed for the railway workers." But her relations with the administration were appalling. She would not stand up when the headmistress came into the room, as the students did, and at faculty meetings would hide behind a Russian newspaper and smoke. She avoided her colleagues, disappeared after her classes, and invited the poor in from the streets: "Mlle. Weil told me to come and eat here," one beggar told the headmistress. Her students were the best the lycée had in years, yet only four of her twelve students passed. The lycée abolished the chair of philosophy after the exam just in order to get rid of Simone.

In *L'Effort* on July 22, 1933, Simone wrote a most prophetic article. The USSR had closed its frontiers to German Communist refugees, and she was certain that the collaboration between Nazi Germany and Soviet Russia would end in a non-aggression pact. Trotsky himself wrote a reply, "The Fourth International and the USSR," which appeared in October, 1933. That fall Simone distributed leaflets put out by a splinter Communist group, the Democratic Communist Circle, written by her friend Boris Souvarine. She had a job teaching at Roanne, but spent most of her time commuting between Roanne and St. Etienne, a distance of some 655 miles. Her relations with her colleagues at Roanne were not better than they had been at her previous posts: she was only briefly visible, usually reading *Das Kapital* or some other such heavy tome. On December 3, 1933, Simone took part in a "march of the miners." More than 3,000 of these carrying flags, led by Simone carrying the big red flag of the St. Etienne labor exchange, marched there. On the following first of May she skipped class and marched again with the workers, singing the Internationale.

She now asked for a year's leave for personal reasons, and got a job through a friend who knew August Detoeuf, managing director of Alsthom. There she worked for four months, racked by headaches, her eyes smarting while the monotony and ugliness oppressed her. Then, on April 11, she acquired a job (it only lasted until May 7) at the Forges de Basse-Indre in Boulogne Billancourt. "You've no idea how filthy this is," she wrote. Yet she packed 400 pieces an hour the first day. She was told by the foreman, "If you don't do 800 I won't keep you. Some of them do 1,400."

Dismissed after less than a month, she next got a job at the Renault works "as a specialized worker, at the cut price of 1.25 francs an hour." She felt herself a slave: "a few weeks of this existence had almost sufficed to transform me into a docile beast of burden." She became terribly rundown, and her devoted parents carried her off to Portugal. "While I was there I left them to go alone to a little village. I was, as it were, in pieces body and soul. The contact with affliction had killed my youth. I received forever the mark of a slave . . . Since then I have always regarded myself as a slave. In this state of mind then, and in a wretched condition physically, I entered the little Portuguese village, which, alas, was very wretched too, on the very day of the festival of its patron saint . . . The conviction was suddenly borne in on me that Christianity is pre-eminently the religion of slaves, that slaves cannot help belonging to it, and I among others."[6]

That fall of 1935 she started to teach at Bourges. She spent a relatively quiet year, unmarked by any major rows with her superiors, though the inspector complained of her monotonous voice and her "lack of grooming." The year round, she wore the same skirt, with a red or green pullover, no gloves and an old, battered overcoat. On her days off she went to Paris to see Boris Souvarine, who said he had not met anyone so intelligent since the death of Rosa Luxemburg.

Next she wished to learn about life on a farm, so she got friends to arrange a meeting with relatives of one of her pupils, who invited her to share their life. She did not stay with them, but when she had free time went and helped—dug up beets, piled up manure, drew water for the troughs, and tried to milk the cows. After a month the farmer's wife went very embarrassedly to see the person who had put Simone in contact with them to ask if Miss Weil would please not come any more, as she never washed her hands before milking, she never changed her clothes, she talked endlessly about the future martyrdom of the Jews and when offered a fine cream-cheese, she pushed it aside, saying the little Indo-Chinese children were hungry.

Simone was in Paris when the Spanish Civil war broke out. She was torn between her pacifism and her anarchist duty to support her comrades. She wrote: "I do not like war . . . When I realized that in spite of myself I had to take part morally in this war—that is to say, I could not help wishing, every day, and at all hours, for the victory of one side and defeat of the other—I said to myself, Paris was the rear."

She got a certificate from a Paris trade union saying she was a journalist, and went to see Julian Gorkine, member of the revolutionary committee in Barcelona. She suggested to him she should cross into Franco territory and look for a trade-union leader who had disappeared. Gorkine wasn't having any. He told her that with her face she would give herself away instantly. So she joined the anarchist-syndicalists some nine miles from Saragossa and was given a gun. She was hopelessly clumsy and more of a danger to friend than foe. Left behind to do the cooking, she poured boiling oil over her leg and was sent back to base by her thankful captain, glad to be rid of her. She returned in half an hour, bandaged, but next day had a fever and was in hospital for some time, before her family got her back on a crutch after less than two months. She had realized that the Civil War had had nothing to do with the starving peasants, but was a sheer power play between Russia, Germany and Italy. Her health grew worse and worse: she had anemia, and could not teach, and in 1937 –38, she applied again for sick leave.

She had been disgusted by factory work and disillusioned by the Civil War. But her admirers still admired. Though she wrote: "Revolution is not possible, because the revolutionary leaders are incapable. It is not to be wished for, because they are traitors." *Feuilles Libres de la Quinzaine* commented: "So that is what S. Weil thinks. It's sad. But why isn't it hateful? Because she is Simone Weil, and she has a right to this view, she, the saint, who gives all. The heroine of tomorrow, of anytime."

In the spring of 1937 Simone visited Italy, as a tourist, and wrote in her *Spiritual Autobiography*:[7]

"In 1937 I had two marvelous days at Assisi. There . . . something stronger than I was compelled me for the first time in my life to go down on my knees." She went back to teaching in October, 1937, at St. Quentin, some 60 miles north of Paris. She only taught till January, 1938, when her headaches became so terrible she was granted sick leave till June. Dr. Vernet in 1939 discovered that her headaches were due to sinus, and was able to some extent to alleviate them.

From Palm Sunday, 1938 to Easter Tuesday, Simone went to Solesmes, attending the Benedictine services for eight hours a day. "I was suffering from splitting headaches, each sound of the Gregorian chant hurt me like a blow . . . This experience enables me by analogy to get a better understanding of the possibility of loving divine love in the midst of affliction. It goes without saying that in the courses of those services the thought of the Passion of Christ entered into my being once and for all."[8]

Here she met a young English Catholic who introduced her to the seventeenth century English metaphysical poets:

George Herbert, John Donne, Richard Crashaw. George Herbert's *Love* she learned by heart, and "it was during one of those recitations that . . . Christ himself came down and took possession of me . . . I had never foreseen the possibility of that, of a real contact, person to person, here below, between a human being and God . . . in this sudden possession of me by Christ, neither my sense nor my imagination had any part: I only felt in the midst of my suffering the presence of a love."[9]

Yet she still half refused "not my love but my intelligence. For Christ "likes us to prefer the truth to him because, before being Christ, he is truth. If one turns aside from him to God toward the truth, one will not go far before falling into his arms."

She described, as best she could what happened next. "Space seemed to be torn open. Leaving the wretched body abandoned in a corner, the spirit was lifted to a point outside space, which was not a point of view, from which there was no perspective, and from which this visible world was seen as real, without perspective." She further wrote: "He came into my room and said: 'Come with me and I shall teach you things of which you know nothing . . . He led me out again, and took me to an attic from which, through the open window, the whole town could be seen . . . He made me sit down.

"We were alone. He spoke. Occasionally someone entered and joined in the conversation, then left again . . .

"At times he would fall silent, take some bread from a cupboard, which we shared between us. This bread really tasted like bread. I have never again found that taste.

"He poured out for me and for himself, wine which tasted of the sun and the soil upon which this city was built.

"He had promised to teach me, yet he taught me nothing. We spoke of all sorts of things without plan and without order, as old friends do.

"It was no longer winter, yet nor was it spring, the branches of the trees lay bare, in a cold air full of sunlight.

"At times we would stretch out on the floor of the attic, and I was overcome with the sweetness of sleep. Then I awoke and drank in the light of the sun.

"One day he said, 'Now go.' I fell down before him, I

clasped his knees, begging him not to drive me away. But he put me out on the stairs. I went down knowing nothing, my heart broken. I wandered about the streets. Then I discovered I had no idea where that house was . . .

"I know well that he does not love me. How could he love me. And yet something deep within me, some part of me, cannot help thinking, with fear and trembling, that perhaps in spite of everything, he loves me.

"I understand now that he had been mistaken for coming for me. My place is not in that attic. It is anywhere, in a prison cell, in one of those middle-class rooms filled with curios and red plush, in a station waiting room. Anywhere, but not in that attic."[10]

Simone's health was still too bad to allow her to go back to teaching, and in July, 1939, she applied for a year's further sick leave. She saw the Prado exhibition in Geneva with her parents, then, on the outbreak of World War II returned to Paris with them. She was now reading the Bhagavad-Gita, and started to study Sanskrit. She also wrote a long three-part essay on the origins of Hitlerism, tracing "the Great Beast" to Rome, which she declared demonstrated a combination of the most horrible cruelty combined with an equal amount of perfidy. And she stated flatly: "The analogies between Hitler and Rome cannot be conjured away by the plea that morality changes. There is no ground for believing that morality has ever changed. There is every ground for believing that men in the most remote ages conceived the good, when they conceived it at all, with the same purity and perfection as we ourselves, in spite of the fact that they practiced evil, and praised it when it was victorious, exactly as we do."

Evil for Simone was above all the social: "Idolatry is a vital necessity in the cave." The collective-state, nation, church-usurp in the human soul the place of God. Rome did this, for five centuries—"but thank God there were the barbarians;" Israel did it, the Church did, and does it—which is the reason, reiterated over and over, why Simone refused, in spite of her complete certainly that Christ was God, to be baptized. In her "Letter to a priest" written to Father Couturier in New York in 1942[11] she notes: "Israel and Rome set their mark on Christianity, Israel by causing the Old Testament to be accepted by it as a sacred book, Rome by turning it into the official religion of the Roman Empire." (p. 44) "The cruelties bound up with the cult of Jehovah, the exterminations commanded by him, are defilements . . ." She called the Church "a big totalitarian animal," and as for Israel, "Everything is soiled and atrocious, as though on purpose, from Abraham inclusive (except for a few prophets), as if to indicate clearly: Attention! That is *the* evil. A people elected for blindness, elected to be Christ's executioners." But it was Christianity which "fabricated the poison of the notion of progress . . . Christianity wanted to find harmony in history. That is the germ of Hegel and of Marx. The idea of history as directed continuity is Christian. It seems to me there are few ideas so totally false. To look for harmony in what is to come is the contrary of eternity."

Simone Weil suggested to a Senator who, she hoped, would push it through, that a corps of nurses, "a Front-Line Nursing Squad," be formed, to work with the army since "many soldiers' lives could be saved if there were immediate care available in cases of shock, exposure, or hemorrhage." Nothing came of her idea, and after Paris was declared an open city she followed the retreating from the Nevers, then walked from Nevers into unoccupied France, and stayed with her parents at Vichy for two months. In October she left Vichy with her parents and went to live in Marseilles. There, the first thing she wrote was *The Iliad, or the poem of Force*, published in the *Cahiers du Sud*, and later, beautifully translated into English by Mary McCarthy, by Dwight MacDonald in *Politics, in New York*.

In an essay on *The Love of God and Affliction*, written at this time, Simone expresses her belief that, in creating, God separated Himself from us. "This universe where we are living, and of which we form a tiny particle, is the distance put by Love between God and God . . . Here are all the scales of distance between the creature and God. One distance where the love of God is impossible: matter, plants, animals. Evil is there so complete that it destroys itself: there is no more evil: only a mirror of the divine innocence. We are at the point where love is just possible." And of herself, she wrote: "All created things refuse to be ends for me. That is God's supreme mercy toward me. And that itself is evil. For evil is the form God's mercy takes in this world." The central law of this world, from which God has withdrawn by his act of creation, is the law of gravity, which is found, analogically, at every level of existence. How can we escape from what, in us, resembles gravity? Only by grace . . . Since gravity is the law of creation, the work of grace in us consists in 'de-creating' us. Thus the ego, this shadow projected by error and sin, which prevents God's light reaching us and which we take for a reality must be abolished. This ego must bs killed from within by love. But it can also be killed from without by extreme suffering and abjection. The hero wears armor, the saint is naked. And armor, while it preserves the body from blows, prevents any contact with reality. This process of 'decreation' is the work of grace, and not of the human will. As Hermes Trismetistus noted: the saint has no choice, he seeks the good as the bee the flower. Instead of trying to fill the distance between ourselves and God with vain imaginings (God the ersatz Father, progress, science) one should accept the two contradictions, of good and evil, of yes and no, and let oneself be torn apart by them. For it is in this rending asunder, which is in man a kind of echo of God's creative act that separates God from Himself, that the primeaval identity of the good and the necessary can be found. Because this world is empty of God, it is God Himself. Necessity, in so far as it is the opposite of Good, *is* the good." And she adds, "The extreme greatness of Christianity lies in that it does not seek a supernatural remedy for suffering, but a supernatural use of suffering." She admits she would have found Christianity much easier to accept without the Resurrection: what proved to her the divinity of Christianity was Christ's cry "My God, my God, why hast thou forsaken me?"

Man can only save himself by renouncing past and future, and living in the naked instant. And God "silent in his love" effaces himself out of love. In order to bring his creature to absolute purity he allows her to travel, alone and abandoned, the whole extent of suffering and of darkness. "Yet

God's love is impersonal: he loves as an emerald is green: he is *I Love*."

In June, 1941, Simone met an almost blind Dominican priest, the Rev. Père Jean-Marie Perrin. He encouraged Simone in her Sanskrit studies, and asked her to write on *The primary condition of non-servile labor*, in which she declared that, in so far as revolution was against social injustice, it was good; in so far as it was a revolt against servitude and suffering, it was a lie, for no revolution can abolish labor, or the servitude and suffering inherent in labor. This aspect of revolution is as surely the "opiate of the people" as religion. Only by a labor which is a "consent to the order of the universe" (one is reminded of Thoreau's comment on a lady's statement that she "accepted the universe—she better had") can labor escape servitude and suffering. And this Simone Weil wrote out of her own experience.

Simone was still anxious to find work on a farm, and Father Perrin wrote to a friend of his, Gustave Thibon, to ask him if he would receive Simone in his home. Gustave Thibon hesitated. Without any overt anti-Semitism, he was yet quite aware that neither the qualities nor the defects of the Jewish temperament were particularly suitable to the "exigencies of life in common." He also was leery of philosophers, especially those who were female intellectuals seeking a return to the soil. But he felt obliged, in view of the persecution of the Jews just beginning, to overcome his initial reaction, and a few days later Simone Weil arrived. She talked his head off, in an inflexible, monotonous voice, and he was at first worn out by these discussions. But he found she "gained immensely by being in an intimate atmosphere." She soon found Thibon's house too comfortable and moved to a half-ruined old farm belonging to his parents-in-law. She came to work each day, and occasionally accepted meals, though generally she would just eat berries she picked. Each month she sent half her ration tickets to the political prisoners.

She began teaching Thibon Greek, and started with the text of the *Pater Noster*. They promised each other to learn it by heart. He did not; she did, and took to reciting it at every moment. Until that time, she wrote Father Perrin, "I had

245

never once prayed in all my life, at least not in the literal sense of the word. I had never said any words to God, either out loud or mentally. I have never pronounced a liturgical prayer." But the effect of saying the *Pater* in Greek "with pure attention is extraordinary and surprises me every time, for, although I experience it every day, it exceeds my expectation with each repetition. At times the very first words tear my thoughts from my body and transport it to a place outside space where there is neither perspective nor point of view. The infinity of the ordinary expanses of perception is replaced by an infinity to the second or sometimes the third degree. At the same time, filling every part of this infinity of infinity, there is a silence, a silence which is not an absence of sound but which is the object of a positive sensation, more positive than that of sound . . . Sometimes, also, during this recitation or at other moments, Christ is present with me in person but his presence is infinitely more real, more moving, more clear than on that first occasion when he took possession of me."

Finding she was treated too kindly by the Thibons, she went off after a few weeks to work in the vineyards where, unknown, she could share the work of real agricultural laborers. She stood it for a month, then joined her parents in Marseilles, where Gustave Thibon visited her several times. He saw her for the last time in May, 1942. She gave him a satchel of papers, and when he said, as his farewell, "Au revoir, in this world or the next," she replied with the utmost gravity, "In the other, one does not see each other again."

Simone Weil and her parents had applied for, and after some delay had obtained, visas for the U.S. Before embarking, Simone Weil and her parents were sent to Morocco, on May 17, 1942. There they were placed in the camp of Ain Seba in Casablanca. Jacques Cabaud described the conditions:[12] "There 900 refugees, most of them Jews, slept on the ground in blankets. The food was poor and meagre, and unhappily for the orthodox Jews, was cooked entirely in pork fat." Simone "kept busy writing, monopolizing all day long one of the eighteen chairs available . . . Whenever she left her chair for a moment, her parents sat on it for fear that someone else might take it."

After seventeen days they embarked on the *Serpo Pinto*, a Portuguese ship for New York. The crossing took a month. They arrived on July 8, 1942. Simone stayed in her room in New York on Riverside Drive eating nothing, going Sundays to a Baptist church in Harlem, and every day to Mass at Corpus Christi on 121st Street, where Mass was said in English, which she preferred. She met Father Couturier, whom she liked and who liked her, and Father (now Monsignor) Oesterreicher, to whom she seemed "a soul in torment."

On November 9, 1942, she left for England on the Swedish boat Valaaren, which took sixteen days to reach Liverpool. She remained in a local detention camp until December 14, when Maurice Schumann, a fellow *Normalien*, had her released. At first she lodged in the barracks of the Free French Women Volunteers, but in January, 1943 she moved to 31, Portland Road, Holland Park, where she had taken rooms with a Mrs. Francis. She got a job at the Ministry of the Interior, working for the Comissariat of Action for France. André Philip, one of de Gaulle's cabinet, "gave her the job of writing on all documents of a political nature which came from France." She had hoped to see her idea of a front-line nursing squad implemented, but de Gaulle rejected it out of hand. Her other idea, that a Supreme Council of the Revolt be created "so that the impetus to liberation" might come from within Europe, appealed to de Gaulle, and he nominated George Bidault, a resistant, to head it. No one wanted Simone in France: the free French in London were urged on no account to send her over, as she was "too obviously Semitic, and too clumsy, to be anything but a liability."[11]

She wrote *The Need for Roots* while working for André Philip, and a magnificent essay, *This War is a War of Religions*, and another on the colonial question, in which she equated the French treatment of their colonies with Hitler's treatment of the French. She also foresaw that "the Americanization of Europe" would lead to the Americanization of the whole world. "If we are only saved by American money and machines we shall fall back, one way or another, into a new servitude like the one which we now suffer."[12] And she feared that "there is perhaps no way in which Europe can avoid being desintegrated by the American influence except through a renewed contact with the East on a really profound level . . . to sum up, it seems that Europe periodically requires genuine contacts with the East in order to remain spiritually alive . . . We need an injection of the Oriental spirit."

In mid-April, she was found incapacitated on the floor of her room, and sent to Middlesex Hospital by Dr. Izad Bennett. She was put into a private room over her objections. She asked to see a priest, and saw Father de Naurois three or four times. She wrote: "I believe in God, in the Trinity, in the Incarnation, in the Redemption, in the teachings of the Gospel. Up to now I have never made a formal request for baptism to any priest. I do not make it now." On August 17 Madame de Closen, of the Free French, took her by car to Ashford Sanatorium in Kent. She was a stretcher case on admission, and refused all nourishment. She seemed to sleep all the time, and on August 24 she died at 10:30 p.m. Her death certificate read: "Cardiac failure due to myocardial degeneration of the heart muscle due to starvation and pulmonary tuberculosis. The deceased did kill and slay herself by refusing to eat while the balance of her mind was disturbed."[13]

Leslie Fiedler wrote of Simone Weil: "eight scant years after her death this young Frenchwoman has come to seem more and more a special exemplar of sanctity for our time, the Outsider as Saint in an age of alienation . . . Catholic and Protestant, Christian and Jew, agnostic and devout, we have all turned to her with the profound conviction that . . . she is really ours."[14] As she wrote to Father Couturier:[15] "Personally, I would never give even as much as a sixpence towards any missionary enterprise. I think that for any man a change of religion is as dangerous a thing as a change of language is for a writer." And so, in her *Spiritual Autobiography*, she tells Father Perrin that she has always remained[16] "at this exact point, the threshold of the Church, without moving, quite still, only now my heart has been transported forever, I hope, into the Blessed Sacrament exposed on the altar." And she concludes that "Every time I think of the crucifixion of Christ I commit the sin of envy."

Simone Weil cannot be understood except at the level she reached. But we all can learn from her that "Only God is worth concern."

NOTES CHAPTER 20

1 Simone Weil, *Selected Essays 1934-43* (OUP, 1962), p. 175.

2 Simone Weil, *Waiting for God* (New York: Capricorn Bros.), p. 64.

3 *Ibid.*, p. 13.

4 *Ibid.*, p. 62.

5 *Ibid.*, p. 62.

6 Weil, *Spiritual Autobiography, Waiting for God*, pp. 66–67.

7 Weil, *Waiting for God*, p. 67.

8 *Ibid.*, p. 68.

9 *Ibid.*, p. 69.

10 E.W.F. Tomlin, *Simone Weil* (Yale University Press, 1954), pp. 28–29.

11 Jacques Cabaud, *Simone Weil* (New York: Channel Press, 1964), p. 274.

12 Weil, *Selected Essays, 1934-43*, p. 217.

13 Cabaud, *Simone Weil*, p. 348.

14 Weil, *Waiting for God* (G.P. Putnam's Sons, 1951), p. 3.

15 Simone Weil, *Letter to a priest* (G.P. Putnam's Sons, 1954), p. 33.

16 Weil, *Waiting for God*, p. 76.

MOTHER TERESA
(1910 –   )

Since Jesus Christ told His followers that whatever they did to anyone they did it to Him, one of the most popular ways to God for Christian men and women has been by attending to the poor who, Jesus Christ announced, "you have always with you." For after 1977 years of Christianity, there are more people hungry, more people who are illiterate, and more who are marginal to society, today than ever before.

One of the most remarkable single persons doing something about this sad fact is Mother Teresa. Born Agnes Gonxha Bojaxhius, in Skopje, Yugoslavia on August 27, 1910, her parents were of Albanian origin, and her father, like St. Francis of Assisi's father, was a cloth merchant. After he died, his widow carried on his business.

Agnes while at school joined a Catholic association called the Sodality of Mary. At the Sodality meetings letters were read aloud from Yugoslav priests working in Bengal, India. Agnes decided to become a nun in order to work in Bengal. She entered the Sisters of Loreto at Loreto Abbey, Rathfarnham, Dublin, Ireland, and was sent for her novitiate training to Darjeeling, India. Taking her first vows in 1931, and her final vows in 1937, she became a teaching sister, teaching geography at St. Mary's High School in Calcutta. Later she became Principal of the school.

At the time of partition, in August, 1946, life in Calcutta was brought to a standstill by communal violence. No food supplies reached her school, so Mother Teresa, as she was now called, walked through the city trying to buy necessities. A month later she received what she termed "a call within a call." This was to remain a nun, but to work outside convent walls.

On August 1, 1948, she received permission from her church authorities to lay aside her habit as a Sister of Loreto, and to put on a sari like that worn by poor Bengali women, made of cheap white cotton with a blue border. She then went to Patna, in Bihar, where the American Medical Mission Sisters gave her a short, intensive nursing course.

In December, 1948, she returned to Calcutta. She was completely alone. She started a free school in the Motihijl slum, gathering the children round her, using the earth for a blackboard, marking out the letters with a stick. In February, 1949, she was given the attic in the home of a family called Gomes. Here her first volunteer joined her, and soon others followed. By October 7, 1950, the new community, called Missionaries of Charity, was recognized by the Catholic Church. Members take the usual vows of poverty, chastity and obedience, and a fourth vow of "whole-hearted free service to the poorest of the poor." The community moved to Lower Circular Road, and opened schools in several of the worst slum areas of Calcutta. The Sisters also opened clinics for mothers and children, and began to pick up the dying. These were taken by a wheelbarrow or taxi (if money was available) to the nearest hospital, but Mother Teresa and her patients were often turned away as the hospitals were full. So she rented one room, and then another, where the destitute dying could die in relative peace and comfort, and above all, in dignity. Now she has a whole Home for the Dying, which was once the pilgrim's hostel attached to the temple of Kali (Ananadamayi Ma's goddess). It is dimly lit by small windows high up in the walls, and is named Immaculate Heart.

Young women flocked to the Missionaries of Charity. Soon teams of Sisters spread out into fifty Indian cities, opening free clinincs, anti-leprosy clinics, free schools, and vocational training centers. Invitations came to the Missionaries to do similar work in other countries, and today there are Sisters teams working in Australia, Ethopia, Israel, Jordan, Maruitius, Papua, Peru, Tanzania and Venezuela. Also in cities—London, Naples, New York, Palermo and Rome.

On Lady Day (March 25), 1963, the Missionary Brothers of Charity were formed, headed by a Jesuit priest who calls himself Brother Andrew. The Brothers work in Calcutta, sheltering homeless boys and squatters in the large railroad stations there, and have also sent teams to work among the refugees in Cambodia and Vietnam. In 1965 the Missionaries of Charity, male and female, were recognized by the Holy See as a pontifical congregation.

What the poor want most, Mother Teresa feels, is to be wanted. They need the joy that only comes from being loved. Her Sisters and Brothers identify totally with the poor among whom they live. "They eat the same food, wear the same clothes, possess as little, are not permitted to have a fan . . . even at their prayers, the clamour and discordancies of the street outside intrude, lest they should forget for a single second why they are there."[1] The day begins for the Sisters with prayer and meditation at 4.30 a.m., followed by Mass. After Mass, chores, breakfast, and then they go to their outside duties as, for example, to the Home for the Dying. Over 23,000 of these have been picked up from the streets, of whom 50% died, the others recovered, needing only rest and a little food. Other Sisters go to the schools and dispensaries, some to the lepers, some to take care of the unwanted babies. "The babies come from midwives, or, as sometimes happens, are picked out of dustbins. Middle-class Indian girls and youths . . . are beginning to be promiscuous, and not having yet advanced to the point in civilization when birth-control appliances and abortions are easily available, are liable to produce unwanted children, some of them quite extraordinarly minute because their birth has been prematurely induced. These, in the Sisters' charge, soon become hearty infants."[2]

In spite of the fact that most religious orders are short of vocations, the Missionaries of Charity are beseiged with volunteers clamouring to join them.

At the time of the partition of the sub-continent, Mother Teresa became a citizen of India. In 1969, she was given the Nehru Award by the then President of India, President Giri, who stated: "Mother Teresa is among those emancipated souls who have transcended all barriers of race, religion, creed and nation. In the troubled world of today, embittered by numerous conflicts and hatred, the life and work of people like Mother Teresa bring new hope for the future of mankind."

In 1962, the Magsaysay Foundation gave Mother Teresa its award and grant of $20,000 which was used for a children's home.

In 1971, the Pope John XXIII Peace Prize was given to Mother Teresa by Pope Paul VI. In the same year, she received the Kennedy International Humanitarian Award, the funds from which were used to initiate the Kennedy Center for Handicapped Children in Dum Dum, near Calcutta.

In 1973, Mother Teresa was chosen from among 2,000 nominees to receive the Templeton Prize for Progress in Religion. $85,000 was made available to the poor through her. The judges came from among the world's leading spiritual traditions, including Hinduism, Buddhism, Judaism and Christianity.

In 1975, Mother Teresa was nominated for the Nobel Peace Prize by the Hon. Shirley Williams, a member of the British Government, Lady Jackson, better known as Barbara Ward for her writings on development and international problems, and Maurice Strong, the Executive Director of the United Nations Environment Program.

Mother Teresa was a member of the Vatican delegation to the United Nations Woman's Year Conference in Mexico City in June, 1975. She participated in the anti-birth-control vote cast by the Vatican delegation.

Mother Teresa has appeared most successfully on television, in both England and the United States. The response to her appeals is fantastic; her first television appearance in England resulted in donations of more than twenty thousand pounds; English schoolchildren provide daily bags of bread for the lepers and the dying of Calcutta; in New York, a single appearance on CBS resulted in many offerings and also in many vocations.

Mother Teresa has spoken of her "way of love." About holiness, she writes "Our progress in holiness depends on God and ourselves—on God's grace and our will to be holy. We must have a real living determination to reach holiness. 'I will be a saint' means I will despoil myself of all that is not God; I will strip my heart of all created things; I will live in poverty and detachment; I will renounce my will, my inclinations, my whims and fancies, and make myself a willing slave to the will of God."[3] Of suffering she writes: "Without our suffering, our work would just be social work, very good and helpful, but it would not be the work of Jesus Christ, not part of the redemption. Jesus wanted to help by sharing our life, our loneliness, our agony, our death. Only by being one with us has he redeemed us. We are allowed to do the same: all the desolation of the poor people, not only their material poverty, but their spiritual destitution, must be redeemed, for only by being one with them can we redeem them, that is, by bringing God into their lives, and bringing them to God."[4]

NOTES CHAPTER 21

1   Malcolm Muggeridge, *Something Beautiful for God* (New York: Ballantine Books, 1971), p. 24.

2   *Ibid.*, p. 48.

3   *Ibid.*, p. 66.

4   *Ibid.*, p. 67.

CONCLUSION

From Eve and Antigone to Anandanmayi Ma and Mother Teresa, through more than twenty-five centuries, women like men have been seeking and finding their various ways to God. Women like men, and perhaps to an even greater extent. How so? In the last analysis, the human response to God's love must be the female one. That union of creature with Creator which is man's highest aim and final objective, can only be achieved by the total surrender of the creature to the Creator. That surrender, which is adumbrated in the surrender of the female, biologically, to the male, is at the spiritual level, the one essential act, for male as for female. As Father Martin D'Arcy, S.J. pointed out: "The primary activity of the creature is not to possess God but to belong to Him."* Through the ages, that activity has been harder for men, since total surrender is, for a man, not prefigured in his physical make-up: biology can offer no model for it. So perhaps Goethe was right when he wrote, in *Faust*, Part II, that *"Das ewig Weibliche ziehet uns hinan,"* the eternal feminine draws us upward.

Yet the saints go marching on, male and female, showing us ordinary men and women, what we could become, if only. . . .

If only we wanted to.

*Martin D'Arcy, S.J. *The Mind And Heart of Love* (New York: Henry Holt & CO, 1947) p. 325.